TREASURES FROM PAUL

Galatians

KEN CHANT

Treasures From Paul

Galatians

Ken Chant

ISBN 978-1-61529-168-7

Vision Publishing
1115 D Street
Ramona, CA 92065
www.booksbyvision.com

Copyright © 2015 by Ken Chant

All rights reserved worldwide.

No part of this book may be reproduced in any manner without the written consent of the author, except in brief quotations embodied in critical articles of review.

A NOTE ON GENDER

It is unfortunate that the English language does not contain an adequate generic pronoun (especially in the singular number) that includes without bias both male and female. So, "he, him, his, man, mankind," with their plurals, must do the work for both sexes. Accordingly, in the following pages, wherever it is appropriate, please include the feminine gender in the masculine, and vice versa.

FOOTNOTES

A work once fully referenced will thereafter be noted either by "ibid" or "op. cit."

TRANSLATIONS

Unless otherwise noted, all scripture translations are my own.

TABLE OF CONTENTS

AN ANGRY MONK 7
PREFACE 11
Chapter One RESURRECTION 15
Chapter Two EDEN 26
Chapter Three CHURCH 37
Chapter Four GRACE 51
Chapter Five OXYMORONS 61
Chapter Six FELLOWSHIP 67
Chapter Seven JUSTIFIED 80
Chapter Eight LIFE 92
Chapter Nine WHIPPING 100
Chapter Ten MIRACLES 109
Chapter Eleven DYNAMITE 116
Chapter Twelve LAW 122
Chapter Thirteen GOSPEL 130
Chapter Fourteen FAITH 153
Chapter Fifteen REDEMPTION 163
Chapter Sixteen HEIRS 170
Chapter Seventeen TIME 177
Chapter Eighteen "ABBA!" 188
Chapter Nineteen ANGELS 198
Chapter Twenty FREEDOM 210
Chapter Twenty-One RIGHTEOUSNESS 229
Chapter Twenty-Two RIGHTEOUSNESS – 2 235
Chapter Twenty-Three BUTTERFLIES 246
Chapter Twenty-Four LOVE 252

Chapter Twenty-Five CALLED 258
Chapter Twenty-Six WALKING 268
Chapter Twenty-Seven BROTHER 276
Chapter Twenty-Eight GIVING 286
Chapter Twenty-Nine GOLDEN 299
Chapter Thirty CALVARY 306

ABBREVIATIONS

Abbreviations commonly used for the books of the Bible are

Genesis	Ge	Habakkuk	Hb
Exodus	Ex	Zephaniah	Zp
Leviticus	Le	Haggai	Hg
Numbers	Nu	Zechariah	Zc
Deuteronomy	De	Malachi	Mal
Joshua	Js		
Judges	Jg		
Ruth	Ru	Matthew	Mt
1 Samuel	1 Sa	Mark	Mk
2 Samuel	2 Sa	Luke	Lu
1 Kings	1 Kg	John	Jn
2 Kings	2 Kg	Acts	Ac
1 Chronicles	1 Ch	Romans	Ro
2 Chronicles	2 Ch	1 Corinthians	1 Co
Ezra	Ezr	2 Corinthians	2 Co
Nehemiah	Ne	Galatians	Ga
Esther	Es	Ephesians	Ep
Job	Jb	Philippians	Ph
Psalm	Ps	Colossians	Cl
Proverbs	Pr	1 Thessalonians	1 Th
Ecclesiastes	Ec	2 Thessalonians	2 Th
Song of Songs	Ca *	1 Timothy	1 Ti
Isaiah	Is	2 Timothy	2 Ti
Jeremiah	Je	Titus	Tit
Lamentations	La	Philemon	Phm
Ezekiel	Ez	Hebrews	He
Daniel	Da	James	Ja
Hosea	Ho	1 Peter	1 Pe
Joel	Jl	2 Peter	2 Pe
Amos	Am	1 John	1 Jn
Obadiah	Ob	2 John	2 Jn
Jonah	Jo	3 John	3 Jn
Micah	Mi	Jude	Ju
Nahum	Na	Revelation	Re

* *Ca* is an abbreviation of *Canticles*, a derivative of the Latin name of the *Song of Solomon*, which is sometimes also called the *Song of Songs*.

AN ANGRY MONK

> There's a great text in Galatians,
> Once you trip on it, entails
> Twenty-nine distinct damnations,
> One sure, if another fails. (1)

Thus spoke a disgruntled monk in an anonymous monastery in Spain. He was hoping to curse a saintly fellow monk, whose godly life mightily annoyed the worldly speaker.

Casting around for some way to destroy the pious monk, the angry monk "trips on" a verse in *Galatians*, which, says he, presents 29 distinct pathways to damnation. Delighted by his discovery, the backslidden monk begins to plot ways by which he can entice the other to step onto one of the forbidden pathways just before he dies. The speaker, despite his own carnal state, believes that anyone who dies before confessing every sin to a priest will surely be condemned to hell. So the carnal monk, hating his "perfect" brother, strikes a bargain with Satan to entice the godly man to sin and then at once to slay him.

Of course, no such verse exists in *Galatians*. Further, anyone who understands the gospel will know that even if Paul *had* outlined 29 ways to damnation, and even if a man had pursued every one of them, and then died, still he would be safe if at the end he truly trusted in Jesus! For, as Paul so boldly asserted, *"we are justified by faith alone, apart from any work of ours"* (even the work of audible confession!) (Ga 2:16-17).

That was a discovery I did not truly make until, many years ago, I was asked to present a series of lectures in a Bible School on the doctrine of *"Justification"*. I glibly agreed, and set to work preparing the twelve lectures. After a week or two, I gave up in despair, telling the principal of the college that I couldn't do it. I had the ideas in my head clearly enough; but in my soul they had no life, no drama, no sparkle! I asked him to postpone the lectures until the last term of the year. He agreed, and I set to again. Then a

---

(1)   Robert Browning, Soliloquy of the Spanish Cloister (1842); lines 49-52.

miracle happened! After some weeks of pouring through scripture, ingesting many a massive tome, thinking, and praying – suddenly – *I knew*! I knew what it means to be *justified by faith alone, apart from any works of my own*. I knew it vividly. I knew it deeply. It became an explosive force in my soul. I jumped up from the desk, hastened down to the kitchen, swooped Alison away from what she was doing, and danced her around the table, shouting, *"I know what justification means!"*

MARTIN LUTHER

Perhaps ten years after that, and after teaching on "justification" many times in many places, I came across Martin Luther's 16th century commentary on *Galatians*. I devoured all 600 pages of it. What a book! Luther's passion, fire, wit, his tough language and sharp insights, carried me along with delight from the first page to the last. Not that I agreed with all that I read. Some paragraphs had me steaming with indignation! But mostly, the book was a revelation, and my life was changed again.

However, the experience did have one unhappy consequence. I have ever after been chary of writing anything of my own on *Galatians*. Luther did the job so well that anything more seems superfluous, and must be inferior. Still, having embarked on this series, *Treasures from Paul*, it would be irresponsible not to include *Galatians*. So here it is. I cannot pretend to anything like Luther's erudition, genius, or to the sheer power of his writing. After all, he changed the face of Western Civilisation and altered the course of human history! So much, that our modern world is still deeply influenced by the doctrines that Luther propounded, notably his writings and sermons on *justification by faith*. [2] I cannot aspire to such universal impact.

Nor will I make any attempt, in emulation of Luther, to present a verse by verse commentary on Paul's letter. I will be content to

---

(2) This became one of the five catch-cries of the 16th century Reformation – we are saved *Sola Gratia* – by grace alone; *Sola Fide* – by faith alone; *Solus Christus* – by the work of Christ alone; *Sola Scriptura* – by scripture alone; *Soli Deo Gloria* – for the glory of God alone.

follow the pattern of the other books in this series, and simply discover "treasures" in *Galatians* that I hope and pray will enrich your life. Nor will I write 600 pages! A smaller, more modest, volume will suffice.

The following *Preface* contains a brief Introduction to *Galatians*. If you are interested in more information about the historical background of the letter, of how and why Paul wrote it, the circumstances in which it was born, and many other questions and issues the letter raises, simply turn to the internet. Countless excellent articles and studies exist on-line. My intention here is only to pluck a number of pearls from its pages and expound them for you to the best of my ability. And if you happen to come to the end of the book shouting, as I did while I was waltzing my wife around a table, "Now I *know!*" – I shall be satisfied indeed.

You could also do yourself a wonderful favour by purchasing and reading a copy of Luther's *Commentary on Galatians*.

And a final word. There is inevitably an overlap between some of the ideas in this book and other books that I have written, notably *Great Words of the Gospel*. I hope the differences will be sufficient to compensate for the similarities. The reason, of course, is that I found it impossible to exclude those ideas when *Galatians* itself is full of them. But even if you have read the earlier book and recognise some sentences akin to it in this one, I still pray that you will find as much pleasure and benefit from reading this book as I gained from its writing.

PREFACE

Galatians was written by the apostle Paul, not to one specific church, but to the group of churches in the Galatian part of Asia Minor. The genuineness of this letter is doubted by few if any major scholars, and its' Pauline origin is universally acknowledged.

WHY IT WAS WRITTEN

The churches in Galatia were founded by Paul himself (Ac 16:6; Ga 1:8 4:13, 19). They were composed mainly of converts from heathenism (Ga 4:8), but included also Jewish converts, who (probably under the influence of Jewish teachers) sought to incorporate the rites of Judaism into Christianity. By their active zeal these Judaisers had succeeded in persuading the majority of the churches to adopt their views (Ga 1:6-3:1). They taught that to be saved, one had to become a Jewish proselyte and keep the laws of Moses. Paul passionately reasserted Christian liberty, insisting that we are justified solely by faith. The letter shows that believers are no longer under the law but must be saved by faith alone. In addition, Paul wanted to recall the Galatians to the simplicity of the gospel, and to vindicate his assertion (against the false teachers) that he was a divinely-commissioned apostle.

As an American might say, this book could be called a *Declaration of Independence* – not independence from God, but independence from legalistic church control. It is a book that encourages us to enjoy full Christian freedom, yet without violating the rule of love.

WHEN AND WHERE?

The letter was probably written soon after Paul's second visit to Galatia (Ac 18:23). Various references in the letter appear to agree with this conclusion. The visit to Jerusalem (mentioned in Ga 2:1-10) is identical with that described in *Acts 15:1-4,* and it is spoken of as a thing of the past; hence this letter was written subsequent to the council of Jerusalem. The similarity between *Galatians* and the letter to the *Romans* has led to the conclusion that they were both written at the same time, namely, in the winter of A.D. 57, during Paul's stay in Corinth (Ac 20:2,3). This letter to the *Galatians* was written with a sense of urgency, tidings having reached Paul of the sad state of the church; but the letter to the *Romans* shows a more deliberate and systematic style, although it expounds the same great doctrines of the gospel, expressed within a forensic framework.

WHAT IT CONTAINS

In *Galatians* you'll see the contrast between law and grace, faith and works, the flesh and the fruit of Holy Spirit, and between the world and the cross –

THE CONTRAST BETWEEN LAW AND GRACE

- Law shows us our need; Grace shows God's provision for meeting that need.
- Law is of works, saying "do"; Grace is a free gift, saying "done".

THE CONTRAST BETWEEN FAITH AND WORKS

- Faith receives Salvation by simply believing.
- Works receives Salvation by striving to earn it.

THE CONTRAST BETWEEN THE WORKS OF THE FLESH AND THE FRUIT OF THE SPIRIT

- The flesh, left alone, naturally produces carnal works.
- The fruit of the Spirit must be cultivated and allowed to flourish.

THE CONTRAST BETWEEN THE WORLD AND THE CROSS

- The worldly system is based upon selfishness.
- The Cross-system is based upon sacrifice.

Here too, depicted by Paul, is the beauty of the cross-life being activated in one's own life. When we recognise and identify with the cross of Christ, and allow the cross to be the focal point of our own lives, the Holy Spirit begins to transform us into the very image of Christ. We recognise that the liberty Christ has brought to us does not give us permission to sin, but frees us rather to live a life that is pleasing to God.

The great question Paul was confronting was this: is the Jewish law binding on Christians? The letter is designed to prove against the Jews that people are justified by faith in Jesus alone, without adding obedience to the laws of Moses. Accordingly, after an introductory address (Ga 1:1-10) the apostle at once raises the subjects that had occasioned the letter –

- He defends his apostolic authority (Ga 1:11-19-2:1-14).
- He shows the evil influence of the Judaisers in destroying the very essence of the gospel (Ga 3:1-4:31).
- He exhorts the Galatian believers to stand fast in the faith as it is in Jesus, to abound in the fruit of the Spirit, and in a right use of their Christian freedom (Ga 5:1-6:10).
- He concludes with a summary of the topics discussed, and with the benediction (Ga 6:11-18).

The letter to the *Galatians* and that to the *Romans* taken together "form a complete proof that justification is not to be obtained meritoriously either by works of morality or by rites and ceremonies, though of divine appointment; but that it is a free gift, proceeding entirely from the mercy of God, to those who receive it by faith in Jesus our Lord."

In the conclusion of the letter (Ga 6:11) Paul says, *"You can see with what large letters I am writing to you with my own hand!"* This differed from his ordinary practice, which was to write only the concluding salutation with his own hand; for the rest, he dictated his letters to an *amanuensis* (a kind of secretary; see Ro 16:22; 1 Co 16:21; etc). Regarding this conclusion, Lightfoot, in his *Commentary* on the letter, says–

At this point the apostle takes the pen from his amanuensis, and the concluding paragraph (vs. 11-18) is written with his own hand. From the time when letters began to be forged in his name (2 Th 2:2; 3:17) it seems to have been his practice to close with a few words in his own handwriting, as a precaution against such forgeries. In the present case he writes a whole paragraph, summing up the main lessons of the letter in terse, eager, disjointed sentences. He writes it, too, in large, bold characters

(Gr. *pelikois grammasin*), that his hand-writing may reflect the energy and determination of his soul.

Other commentators read it differently – *"You can see what a large letter I have written with my own hand!"* – which suggests that Paul dispensed with an amanuensis altogether, and wrote out the entire letter himself. In either case the lesson is the same: Paul is pressing upon the Galatians the vast importance of what he is teaching, and urging them never to compromise the gospel by mixing it with the stagnation of law. (3)

---

(3) This introduction was adapted from <u>Easton's Bible Dictionary</u>, and from <u>New Testament Survey</u>, by Stan DeKoven (Vision Publishing, Ramona, CA.).

Chapter One

RESURRECTION

> Christ is risen from the dead,
> Trampling down death by death,
> And upon those in the tombs,
> Bestowing life!

That simple quatrain is known as the *Paschal Troparion*, [4] and it is sung at Easter by people who belong to the Eastern Orthodox churches. No one knows who wrote it, but it is deeply woven into the paschal liturgies of the Orthodox churches. It is associated too with the *Paschal Greeting*, where, on Easter Sunday, instead of a normal greeting, people address each other with the cry, "Christ is risen!" To which they all offer a joyful response, "He is risen indeed!" Many denominations and churches around the world have adopted this *Paschal Greeting* as part of their Easter practice.

The greeting echoes the story found in *Luke*, where the angels said, *"The Lord has risen!"* (24:6), and later the disciples declared, *The Lord has risen indeed!"* (vs. 34). And according to legend, it was taken up by Mary Magdalene (out of whom the Master had cast seven demons, Mk 16:9), when she went to Rome to preach the gospel. She was called before the Emperor Tiberius, and at once said to him, "Christ is risen!" She also gave him an egg painted red, which the emperor received, because an egg was commonly given by poor people in those days as a sign of respect to a benefactor. But on asking why it was red, Mary explained that the colour symbolised the death of Christ on the cross, and the egg

---

(4) "Troparion" simply means a short hymn, usually having only one stanza, similar to the "choruses" that are often sung in evangelical and Pentecostal churches.

was a sign of his resurrection from the dead and of the new life we receive from him. (5)

I am commencing this book with the resurrection of Christ because that is where Paul begins his passionate letter to the several churches in Galatia –

This letter comes to you from an apostle, Paul, who was not chosen or ordained by any human agency, but rather by Jesus Christ and by God the Father, **who raised him from the dead** (Ga 1:1-2).

We have heard the words so often that they often leave us unmoved. Yet their impact upon the Greek and Roman world must have been stunning. God has raised a man from the dead! Nor was that dead man merely resuscitated, only to die again. No! He was *raised – never* to die again!

Here was an entirely new concept – a corporeal resurrection to a new kind of eternal fusion of flesh and spirit. Other people had been known to rise from the dead – think of Lazarus (Jn 11:1-44) – or had been transported to heaven – think of Enoch (Ge 5:24), or Elijah (2 Kg 2:11-12); but the resurrection of Jesus was majestically different. He died. He rose from the dead. He ascended to heaven. He came back again. He returned to the Father in heaven, but with a promise to come again at the end of the age.

Christ showed himself not only to be tangible (he was no ghost, Jn 20:27; Lu 2:39), but also sublimely spiritual (he could appear and disappear at will, Lu 24:36-37; Jn 20:19-20). His marvellous resurrection made him *"The firstborn of many brothers and sisters"* (Ro 8:29), and *"the firstborn from among the dead"* (Cl 1:18) – that is, the beginning of the New Creation of God. And now, in him, we too are called the *"firstborn"*, members of the congregation of God, enrolled in heaven (He 12:23), sharing his new kind of indestructible resurrection life.

---

(5) There are many variations in the legend about Mary and Tiberius. It is, of course, highly unlikely to be true; but it does show that giving and receiving eggs at Easter has a very long tradition behind it.

AN INTERESTING QUESTION

Galatians is probably the earliest surviving letter written by Paul (around 49 A.D.), so it is striking that the first great idea it contains is a bold affirmation that Christ died, but was then raised from the dead by the Father. Many commentators have wondered why Paul introduces the resurrection so sharply in the first line of the letter, especially since this is the only place in the letter where that stunning event is specifically mentioned. Many suggestions have been made, among them –

- The resurrection of Christ is the foundation of the gospel, for without it, Jesus would have been merely another martyr. But his resurrection showed him to be the Son of God with Power, fitted to be the Saviour of the world (Ro 1:4).
- Paul knew that he was about to expound the full glory of the gospel, and of our justification by faith alone, and he desired to set down at once the basic proposition upon which everything else would depend – *"God raised Jesus Christ from the dead!"*
- Paul wanted to assert and confirm his apostolic authority against some enemies, who were saying that he was unfit to be an apostle. They argued that, unlike the other apostles, Paul had never been with Jesus as a disciple. But Paul insisted that he was fully qualified, because he had seen and been spoken to by the risen Christ, and that the same God who raised Jesus from the dead was the one who had called him to his ministry (Ga 1:1).
- Paul had felt *"the power of the resurrection"* (Ph 3:10), and he was full of that power as he began to write. He placed the resurrection of Christ at the head of his letter both to assert its importance in his own Christian life, its effect upon his apostolic ministry, its importance to all that would follow, and to glorify both Christ and God, who had raised Christ from the dead and who had sent Paul to preach the good news to the world.

But can we believe it? What proof do we have for such an astonishing event? Is it reasonable, against all normal experience, to accept the truth of a miracle so transcendent above any other that has ever been claimed?

Luke answers with a strong affirmative. He said that Jesus *"showed himself alive after his passion by **many infallible proofs**, being seen of them forty days, and speaking of the things pertaining to the kingdom of God"* (Ac 1:3, KJV).

Can we have a similar boldness? Are there strong proofs we too can call upon, to establish beyond reasonable doubt that Jesus truly is alive, and able to save to the uttermost everyone who believes in him? (He 7:25)

TOO FEW WITNESSES

A common argument against the resurrection is that too few people claim to have seen Jesus alive after he had been crucified and buried. Sceptics ask, "Why didn't God cause multitudes of people, especially those of high rank, trustworthy witnesses, to see the risen Christ? But instead, we have only the word of a handful of people, mostly insignificant, whose testimony is too weak to be trusted."

We answer – there *were* enough witnesses! Further, they were people who had no vested interest in proving that Christ had conquered death; rather, they placed their very lives in jeopardy by their witness! Elsewhere, Paul gives a list (1 Co 15:3-8) –

> *Christ died to take away our sins as the Scriptures predicted. He was placed in a tomb. He was brought back to life on the third day as the Scriptures predicted. He appeared to **Cephas**. Next he appeared to the **twelve** apostles. Then he appeared to more than **500 believers** at one time. (Most of these people are still living, but some have died.) Next he appeared to **James**. Then he appeared to **all the other apostles**. Last of all, he also appeared to me (**Paul**). I'm like an aborted fetus who was given another chance to live.*

So there were at least 513 people who claimed that Jesus had appeared to them, that they had seen him with their own eyes. If that is insufficient proof, how many does the critic require? Five thousand? Five million?

The point is, if the people to whom Jesus chose to show himself before he ascended back into heaven, are an insufficient witness, then no greater number will be adequate. Critics will still find an excuse for unbelief, calling up such weary arguments as "mass delusion" ... "resurrection is impossible" ... "the body was stolen and hidden" ... "Jesus merely recovered consciousness in the grave, and walked out, only to die again later"—and so on.

Those arguments and many others like them, have been adequately dowsed countless times over the centuries. No one today is going to come up with an objection to which the church will be unable to respond sensibly. Hence, all efforts nowadays are put into trying to discredit the story itself, to show that the gospels are a fake, no more to be believed than any other ancient fable.

But then the critics have to explain where the story came from, and why people would endure hideous torture and death rather than deny it, and how the church arose and straddled the earth, preaching that Christ is alive! In the end, it is easier to believe that the gospels are simply true. God did indeed *"raise Christ from the dead!"* [6]

What nobody can deny is that Paul based his apostolic authority upon the fact that he was one of the few who had seen the risen Christ. And those few, as Peter said, were chosen by God to bear witness of the resurrection, and were deemed by God to be sufficient (Act 10:41) –

---

[6] For more extensive discussions on the resurrection of Christ, and its proofs, see my books *The Cross and the Crown;* and *Treasures from Paul – Corinthians: The First Letter.*

> *They killed Jesus by hanging him on a tree, but God raised him up on the third day and arranged that he should be seen – not by everyone, but rather by us, because he had already chosen us to be his witnesses. We even ate and drank with him after he rose from the dead. And he commanded us to preach to the people and to warn them that he is the one appointed by God to be the Judge of everyone who has ever lived.*

Until some reason can be shown why those apostles and the other 500 who saw Jesus on the mountain top must be treated as liars, fools, or deluded simpletons, their testimony should be taken as reliable. They saw Jesus die. They buried him. Some days later, they saw him alive again – and not just restored to physical life, but *"raised"* into a new kind of existence, with a *"spiritual body"* – that is, *intangible* and *tangible* at the same time – freed from the normal limitations of time and space.

Paul does not again specifically mention the resurrection of Christ in *Galatians*, but that stunning miracle was certainly a major part of his theology. Indeed, in his various letters, he shows that because of the resurrection everyone who believes now possesses indestructible life in Christ, along with some other splendid benefits –

RIGHTEOUSNESS

> *Righteousness will be credited to us who believe in God, who raised from the dead Jesus our Lord (Ro 4:24).*

What a strong word that is – "righteousness"! It has a certain toughness. It is redolent of the Almighty, whose very name is *Holy in Righteousness*! (Is 5:16) It can inspire both delight and terror (Pr 21:21; 15:9). It is the name of the New Jerusalem, the *City of Righteousness* (Is 1:26). Without righteousness there will be no peace, nor any security; but where righteousness prevails, *"the effect of righteousness will be peace, and the result of righteousness, will be quietness and trust forever"* (Is 32:17).

Indeed, the idea of righteousness is mentioned more than 300 times in the Bible, so great is its importance. Yet Paul says that abundant righteousness has become ours simply because we believe the good news we have received in Christ!

Therefore, I call myself "righteous", not because I have ever done any righteous thing, but solely because I do believe in God, and I believe that he raised Jesus from the dead. You may ask, "How can you say that you have never done any righteous thing? Surely you have prayed, preached, helped people, cared for your wife and children, served the church, and performed countless other good works?" Yes, I have. But so long as I am in this corruptible and mortal frame (1 Co 15:53-54), everything I think, or do, or strive to achieve, is dyed scarlet by sin. Not "sins" that I may commit; but "sin" – that is, an inner principle of sin that is ever at work even in the most saintly of saints. Hence the prophet wept that even his most righteous deeds were putrid, like discarded menstrual rags (Is 64:6). And Paul insisted that *"because I have once sinned and fallen short of the glory of God, now I keep on causing myself to sin again and again"* (Ro 3:23). (7)

So while I strive to live as righteously as I can, in the end I must place all my confidence in the righteousness God has wrought for me in Christ, a righteousness that was sealed by his resurrection from the dead.

Paul does the same. In a remarkable passage in which he commends himself to the church as a true apostle of Christ – his sufferings, privations, beatings, imprisonments, and so on – he suddenly inserts a statement that seems unconnected with all that goes before and after it –

> *holding weapons of righteousness in my right hand and in my left!* (2 Co 6:7; see vs. 4-10 for the context.)

He means that while he may commend himself to the church as a worthy apostle, deserving their honour because of his ministry, he would never do so in the presence of God. When he presents himself to the Lord, he empties his hands, both of them, of

---

(7) That translation echoes what Paul actually wrote. He uses two archery terms – one describes an arrow that is widely astray of the target; the other, an on-target arrow that falls short of the mark. He means, because, in the past, we have shot wide and missed the target, now, even when we are on-target, we can't reach it. The phrase *"keep on causing myself"* reflects the middle voice used by Paul, which means something one does to oneself.

everything, except the righteousness that is God's gift to him in Christ. That is his only boast before the Lord, his sole claim to be accepted into the holiest, his sole right to approach the heavenly throne.

The same idea was expressed by the poet –

> Nothing in my hand I bring,
> Simply to thy cross I cling!

Like Paul, we should always be busy in the work of the church and of the Kingdom of God; but in the end, when we stand before the King, let your trust be fully and only in the righteousness of Christ, held firmly in both hands, with room for nothing else! And let us always be singing the haunting and deeply evocative oracle of Amos –

Let justice roll down like waters, and righteousness like an ever-flowing stream (5:24, ESV).

JUSTIFICATION

Christ was delivered up to death because of our sins, and he was raised for our justification (Ro 4:25).

If my justification required the death and resurrection of the Saviour, then it is plain that no action of mine can either enhance or diminish that great work. I have only one recourse — receive the gift of God with joyful and hearty faith. Of course, if I truly do that, then inevitably I will yearn to demonstrate the reality of my joy and faith by striving to live Christian-ly. I will be committed to reflecting the heart of the Master, who loves righteousness and hates iniquity! (He 1:9) Nonetheless, I remain ever justified solely by the merits of Christ, without any reference to any work of mine, whether good or bad.

I do not mean that continuance in wilful sin cannot have any deleterious effect on my salvation, for it certainly can. What effect? Simply, if a person deliberately chooses a lifestyle of iniquity instead of righteousness, then faith will eventually become so eroded that the person will lose connection with Christ and will fall again into a state of darkness, bereft of any hope of eternal life. It may even become impossible for him or her to stir up faith again, or find any place to believe the gospel, or to renew any prospect of salvation (He 6:4-6; 10:26-29; 12:15-17).

NEWNESS

> *By baptism, we were buried with Christ into death, so that, just as Christ was raised from the dead by the glory of the Father, we too might walk in newness of life* (Ro 6:4).

While I personally prefer baptism by full immersion in the water, for believers only, the promise can be appropriated by any baptised person, no matter when or how the baptism was done. The action is important, but faith is more necessary. Faith is the key that unlocks the benefit of baptism. Merely being plunged into a river, the sea, a bath, a baptistery, or having water sprinkled on your head or body, will change nothing. To suppose that the water has any divine properties or powers is superstition. Faith in the promise of God *must* be present, followed by a commitment to *"walk in newness of life"*. Lack of faith or of any commitment to rise up with new life and obey God invalidates any baptism of anyone by anyone anywhere.

But if you have been baptised, whether long ago or recently, or by whatever method, then the promise is yours to appropriate — that is, to reckon yourself by faith to have been buried with Christ, and then risen with him by the glory of the Father, so that you can walk each day in his resurrection life.

Thus Paul declares —

> *Likewise, my brothers, you too have died to the law through the body of Christ. Now you belong to another, I mean to Christ, who has been raised from the dead. And all this is so that we may bear fruit for God* (Ro 7:4).

And again —

> *If the Spirit of him who raised Jesus from the dead dwells in you, then God, who raised Christ Jesus from the dead, will also pour life into your mortal bodies through his Spirit who dwells in you.* (Ro 8:11) ... *God, who raised the Lord from the dead, will also raise us up by his power.* (1 Co 6:14)

> *... He who raised the Lord Jesus will raise us also with Jesus and bring us with you into his presence* (2 Co 4:14).

So the message is clear. The resurrection of Jesus from the dead is not merely a dogma — rather, it is a way of life; it is the power of God to overcome death; it is the enabling force that fits us to do the will of God day by day; it is the surging glory of God that compels us to know that we cannot truly die, because everlasting life is already at work in us. No wonder Paul cried that he would gladly cast the entire world and everything it contained onto a dung hill, if that were the price of *knowing* Christ and of experiencing the power of his resurrection! (Ph 3:8-10)

Chapter Two

EDEN

> *Christ gave himself for our sins to deliver us from the present evil age* (Ga 1:4).

It is not at all obvious why we need salvation. There are many good people outside the church whose lives outshine those of many Christians. Indeed, most people think of themselves as tolerably good, not wicked, and that whatever faults they may have, ought to be easily forgiven.

Why then is scripture so adamant? Why does it insist that every person has an absolute need to find salvation in Christ? Why was it necessary for the Son of God to submit himself to a hideous death in order to *"deliver us from the present evil age"*? It is because of –

THE FALLEN CONDITION OF MANKIND

See **Genesis 3:1-20.** Sin, we are told, produced certain consequences that still torment people –

THE NAKED CONSEQUENCE OF SIN

> *The eyes of Adam and Eve were opened, and they knew that they were naked* (Ge 3:7).

Sin, any sin, all sin, from the slightest to the blackest, causes a fearful sense of nakedness; that is, of exposure, deprivation, and vulnerability. Hence the first act of Adam and Eve, when their consciences were awakened, was to try to cover their nakedness. In itself, being *unclothed* is not a crime against either God or man; but *nakedness* saps confidence and erodes strength.

That is why the Caesars kept their palace slaves, male and female, young and old, naked, refusing them any right to be clothed. Across the centuries of Rome's empire, not once did those demoralised, naked palace slaves ever rebel.

Likewise the Nazis, in their concentration camps, herded their naked and unresisting prisoners into the gas ovens. There are no doubt many terrible and complex reasons why so many went so passively to an awful death, but nakedness is one of them. When men and women are compelled to mingle together naked, much of the fight drains out of them. You may be objecting, "But what about primitive races who go largely or fully unclothed; or what about nudist colonies?" I'll come to that situation in a moment, but here let me just say that there is a difference between nakedness and nudity. My focus here is on the former.

So, to continue, the Assyrians, the Babylonians, the Persians, and other conquerors in the past all recognised the vulnerability of nakedness. They stripped their prisoners naked and drove them off to slavery, sometimes stringing them together with hooks in their noses (cp. Is 37:29).

Sin has the effect of making people feel naked. To combat this, they have vainly trusted two solutions –

THE CAMOUFLAGE OF "FIG LEAVES" [8]

God has used fallen humanity's dislike of nakedness to drive the growth of civilisation. We yearn to clothe everything; we are repelled by nakedness. Thus we are driven to garb our naked bodies with as much beauty as we can create. We do the same for a naked wall in our homes, adorning it with lovely art. We feel compelled to put a footprint on a pristine beach or upon a patch of pure white snow. Indeed, all the creative effort that humans put into art, architecture, and music, are at least in part an expression of this urge to clothe the naked, to fill the empty, to mark the blank, from empty spaces to empty canvas, from walls to land, and naked bodies.

---

(8) The story of Adam and Eve resorting to fig leaves is told in *Genesis 3:1-7*.

In all this there is a sense of divine mystery, which Thomas Carlyle captures in his satire on clothing, *Sartor Resartus*. [9] In one place, a mythical and slightly dotty philosopher, Professor Teufelsdrockh, after giving many examples of the mystical and spiritual value of clothes, continues –

> Why multiply instances? It is written, the heavens and the earth shall fade away like a Vesture; which indeed they are – the Time-vesture of the eternal. Whatsoever sensibly exists, whatsoever represents Spirit to spirit, is properly a Clothing, a suit of Raiment, put on for a season, and to be laid off. Thus in this one pregnant subject of CLOTHES, rightly understood, is included all that men have thought, dreamed, done, and been: the whole eternal Universe and what it holds is but Clothing; and the essence of all Science lies in the *Philosophy of Clothes*. [10]

So the use of "fig leaves" is a step in the right direction; but in the end even the best of them prove inadequate to camouflage our nakedness. Thus Adam and Eve found, and the professor also admitted -

> The horse I ride has his own whole fell: strip him of the girths and flaps and extraneous tags I have fastened around him, and the noble creature is his own sempster and weaver and spinner; nay, his own bootmaker, jeweller, and man-milliner; he bounds free through the valleys, with a perennial rain-proof court-suit on his body; wherein warmth and easiness of fit have reached perfection; nay, the graces also have been considered, and frills and fringes, with gay variety of colour, featly

---

(9) Written in 1833-34; the title means <u>The Tailor Patched</u>. It is a satire based around a fictitious "Philosophy of Clothes", which can be summarised – "Visible things are but the manifestations, emblems, or clothings of spirit. The material universe itself is only the vesture or symbol of God ... (In) everything that man creates for himself he merely attempts to give body or expression to thought." (From the "Introduction" by W. H. Hudson to a 1908 edition of the book, by J. M. Dent & Sons Ltd, London; pg. xiii.

(10) Ibid. Bk I, ch. 11.

appended, and ever in the right place, are not wanting. While I — good Heaven! — have thatched myself over with the dead fleeces of sheep, the bark of vegetables, the entrails of worms, the hides of oxen or seals, the felt of furred beasts; and walk abroad a moving Rag-screen, overheaped with shreds and tatters raked from the Charnel-house of Nature, where they would have rotted, to rot on me more slowly. Day after day I must thatch myself anew; day after day, this despicable thatch must lose some film of its thickness; some film of it, frayed away by wear and tear, must be brushed off into the Ashpit, into the Laystall; till by degrees the whole has been brushed thither, and I, the dust-making, patent Rag-grinder, get new material to grind down. [11]

So, since our "fig leaves" ultimately fail to solve the "nakedness" problem, people have turned to a second solution —

A QUEST FOR "INNOCENCE"

BY PHYSICAL NAKEDNESS

The modern practice of nudity began in Germany with Paul Zimmerman and his family, who from 1902-1909 lived and worked naked on their farm. He was an ascetic vegetarian, a disciple of Nietzsche, who gave up his job as a teacher to "go back to nature". Friends began to share his beliefs and to join him and his family, until eventually the property had to be expanded into a large naturalist park. Their philosophy was summed up by Maurice Parmelee –

> Mankind has become largely cut off from nature, and life is too artificial, much to the detriment of its health and happiness. This is strikingly exemplified in the concealment of the body, which gives rise to unhealthy mental complexes.

---

(11)   Ibid. Bk. I, ch. 8.

The underlying idea in nudist practice is this: by nakedness to express innocence, sincerity, and frankness, unencumbered by the taboos of clothed society. (12)

However, despite noble intentions, the practice of nakedness founders on two rocky shoals, either –

- a probably inescapable tendency to decay into fornication; or,
- the creation of a new set of "fig leaves".

In the latter, "nakedness" is transformed into "nudity". I mean that modern nudists become like the ancient Egyptians, or some primitive native tribes. They may appear to be naked, but actually their unclothed state is governed by many rules about how to walk, sit, kneel, bend, and the like. Many postures are forbidden, others are frowned upon as being in bad taste. In the end, they are as much restrained in their nudity as other people are in their clothing.

BY SPIRITUAL NAKEDNESS

In what Derek Kidner calls "the cult of frankness", some Christians try to hide their sin by exposing it. They engage in open and public confession of sin, often to the acute embarrassment and sometimes disgrace of family, friends, or anyone involved in the confessor's wrongdoing. Carnality, pride, prurience, and other sinful motives can be displayed whenever sin is confessed aloud to a congregation.

Someone may object, "Surely we should be totally honest with each other? Isn't confession good for the soul? And shouldn't we *'walk in the light as God is in the light'?"* Indeed we should. But confession that brings pain to others while it eases the penitent is nothing but self-indulgence – so there are times when by far the best policy is to keep your counsel to yourself; or at least to share your secret only with someone who cannot be harmed by it, and who can be trusted not to make harmful use of it.

---

(12) The above information on nudism came from an article "Naked and Unashamed" by David Gunston, in International History Magazine #33, September 1975; pg. 86ff.

BY GOD'S WORD

God's answer to all these "naked" problems is to re-clothe us with his eternal **"word"**– *"They heard the 'voice' of the Lord walking in the Garden"* (Ge 3:8). That is what the Hebrew text says. It is so strange, though, to talk about a "voice" walking, that many translators modify it to something like, "They heard the Lord walking in the Garden." But indeed, it was the "*voice*" of the Lord walking and talking to Adam and Eve. It is the first example in scripture of God sending his all-powerful word to bring pardon, salvation, and life to his people. The same idea starts the gospel of John, *"In the beginning was the Word, and the Word was with God, and the Word was God!"*

Always the voice of the Lord is waiting to speak to us, to re-clothe us, to bring us into his eternal Paradise.

THE LONELY CONSEQUENCE OF SIN

Adam and Eve hid themselves from the presence of the Lord God among the trees of the garden. But the Lord God called to them, "Where are you?" (Ge 3:8-9)

Sin always brings separation: from God; from ourselves; and from each other. Philosophers have realised this alone-ness, and they have expressed it in a rather eccentric theory called solipsism. [13] But God is always seeking in Christ to bring us back: to himself; to ourselves; and to each other. This is one of the great distinctives of the Bible, for there is nothing like *Genesis 3:9* in any other sacred writing. Everywhere else, religion is a search by man for God; it is man crying, "Where are you God?" But in the Bible it is always God crying, "Where are you Adam?" Religion is man's search for God. The gospel is God's search for *you*!

---

(13) "Solipsism" is a belief that the only thing somebody can be sure of is that he or she exists, and that true knowledge of anything else is impossible. Edgar Alan Poe described it thus –"All that we see or seem is but a dream within a dream."

THE ANXIOUS CONSEQUENCE OF SIN

Adam said, "I heard the sound of you in the garden, and because I was naked I was afraid, so I hid myself." (Ge 3:10)

When sin entered, fear came with it; indeed, our fears prove that we are sinners. By contrast, think about Jesus. He was without sin, therefore he did not have the courage of ignorance that knows no better; nor of braggadocio driven by a hunger for praise; nor of pride that refuses to admit fear; nor of fear driven by a horror of scorn; nor any fear at all, except the fear of God. His bravery, his freedom from fear, were pure, natural, and an innate part of a life without sin.

But we are *sinners* and therefore *afraid*. And that fear is probably your chief enemy. Hence Jesus, before he could tell a man to *"believe only"*, had to tell him, *"fear not!"* (Lu 8:50). And the antidote to fear is love, for *"there is no fear in love, for perfect love casts out all fear"* (1 Jn 4:18, KJV).

THE TOILSOME CONSEQUENCE OF SIN

By the sweat of your brow you will get your food, till you return to the ground. You began as dust; you are dust; and to dust you will return (Ge 3:19).

We cannot entirely escape this curse until after the resurrection (Ro 8:19-23), but the right use of our restored authority in Christ changes the character of our toil, and brings to it a supernatural dimension. Thus, for us who believe, even the most mundane tasks become acts of worship, gaining redemptive power, transformed into steps up to Paradise —

> Another day of toil and strife,
> Another page so white,
> Within that fateful Log of Life
> That I and all must write;
> Another page without a stain
> To make of as I may,
> Which done I shall not see again
> Until the Judgment Day.

...

> O Record grave, God guide my hand
> And make me worthy be,
> Since what I write today shall stand
> To all eternity;
> Aye, teach me, Lord of Life, I pray,
> As I salute the sun,
> To bear myself that every day
> May be a Golden One. (14)

THE BRUISING CONSEQUENCE OF SIN

Christ will crush your head, Satan, and you will bruise his heel (Ge 3:15).

"SATAN WILL BRUISE HIS HEEL!"

Here is the source of all our misery — the serpent's fang; his poison is at work, spreading around the world disease, poverty, blasphemy, and every manner of vice and cruelty. If not Satan, whom shall we blame? Ourselves alone? But what an appalling race of beasts that makes mankind! Then shall we blame God? How can that be, if he is indeed Good and is rightly called Love? The fact is this — if the biblical account of the Fall is not accepted, then only three other sources can be blamed for the state of things: (a) mindless atoms; (b) an irredeemably foul human race; or (c) a blemished deity.

If the universe is self-existent (not made by God), then it is without mind or purpose, utterly amoral, so that wickedness and goodness become solely human values, which anyone can accept, reject, or change at will. Or if God did create all things, and is also the author of all things vile, then he too must lose all my respect and love. Thus Omar Khayyam wrote in his 12th century *Ruba'iyat* –

> Since the Upholder embellishes the material of things,
> For what reason does he cast it into diminution and decay?

---

(14) Robert Service; *Golden Days*; from Ballads of a Bohemian – Spring; T. Fisher Unwin, London, 1921; pg. 50.

> If it turned out good, why break it?
> If it turned out bad, whose fault was it? (15)

The Bible answer to this dilemma, of course, is that both God and his creation are wholly good, but Satan and sin have corrupted the earth. Satan has *"bruised the heel"* of mankind. But the Lord has a remedy –

"YOU WILL BRUISE HIS HEAD!"

Mark the contrast here between a superficial wound (a bite on the heel) and a mortal blow (crushing his head). It was a prophecy of how little harm the serpent could do to Christ (despite the cross), and how great harm Christ has done to the serpent by the cross! And what is said of Christ is also said of us —

> *I have given you authority to stomp on snakes and scorpions and to defeat all the enemy's power. Nothing will truly hurt you!* (Lu 10:19)

Early in one summer, many years ago, I was driving a horse and cart down a country road when a magnificent sight caught my eye. On the other side of the fence lay a paddock with many flat-top rocks. On them a variety of snakes, each wearing a sparkling new skin, was basking in the warm sun. The array of colours was dazzling. I was entranced! Without thinking I stopped the horse, jumped over the fence, and began walking among rocks admiring the bright colours and subtle beauty of each animal. Suddenly, after advancing some way into the field I realised there were deadly snakes behind me and I had no idea what they were doing! (16) I remembered, too, that I was wearing ordinary shoes,

---

(15) Translated by Peter Avery & John Heath-Stubbs; Penguin Classics, 1983; Quatrain # 11.

(16) According to *Australian Geographic* (July 25, 2012) there are 140 varieties of land snakes in Australia, some of them equipped with venom more toxic than any other snake in the world. The two most deadly are the tiger snake and the inland taipan. The inland taipan is the more dangerous because it is bigger and strikes more effectively, but the tiger snake venom is probably the most toxic in the world (it is about 100 times more deadly than the American rattle snake). There is enough venom in one tiger snake strike to kill 100 full grown adults, or 23000 mice, or 20 horses! Fortunately for its victims, the tiger snake seldom strikes cleanly or delivers its full load of venom.

not boots, and I had no weapon in my hand to prevent any snake from reaching me. [17]

With the most amazing care I tip-toed out of that place, hoping fervently not to disturb any of the poisonous creatures. Breathing heartfelt relief when I reached the fence, I jumped to safety, loosed the horse, and proceeded again down the road, regretting only that I had no camera to record the spectacle!

I was fortunate to escape unbitten, and I doubt that *Mark 16:18* would have protected me from such lack of prudence.

But in the case of that greater Serpent, the Devil, known as Satan, we can indeed defeat him! Because of the work of that true *"seed of the woman"*, Christ, we have vast authority over Satan and all his demonic minions. So the challenge is ever before us to take our stand in Christ, to arm ourselves with the weapons of our warfare, and to strike the enemy down!

So there we have the *fallen condition* of the human race, and the reason why even the very best of people stand in need of a Saviour. That is why *"Christ gave himself for our sins to deliver us from the present evil age."* (Ga 1:4)

Which brings me to –

THE RESTORED CONDITION OF MAN

Christ came to destroy the works of Satan and to restore us to our proper dominion; therefore our resolve should be the same as his: to win at all costs; to be loosed from all the consequences of sin; and to live daily as victorious children of God. As the great General Douglas MacArthur once said: "In war there is no substitute for victory [18] . . . It is fatal to enter any war without the will to win it!" [19] But how can we lose? Are we not **"more than**

---

(17) Usually, when we went onto the farm, or into the country, we wore calf-high boots, and carried a long length of heavy-grade fencing wire. The wire would now be forbidden, for all snakes in Australia are protected by law, and there is a heavy penalty for killing one.

(18) From a letter written to Representative Joseph W. Martin Jr., (20 March 1951).

(19) From a speech at the Republican National Convention in July 1952.

conquerors" through Christ, who loved us and gave himself for us? Are we not the beneficiaries of the glorious triumph over Sin and Satan that he gained when he walked out of the tomb on that first Easter morning? Christ surrendered his life into the hands of wicked men, he allowed the devil to bruise his heel; but then *"God raised him from the dead"* (Ga 1:1). Satan's head was crushed, and liberty was wrought for everyone who believes and proclaims Christ as Lord.

Chapter Three

CHURCH

> To the **churches** of Galatia ... you have heard of my former life in Judaism, how I persecuted the **church** of God violently and tried to destroy it. ... And I was still unknown in person to the **churches** of Judea that are in Christ (Ga 1:2, 13, 22, ESV).

Paul mentions the church only three times in *Galatians*, and all in his first chapter. But his many references in his other letters display his passionate love for the church and his fierce zeal for its welfare. All his heart is echoed in one victorious cry: *"To God be glory in the church and in Christ Jesus throughout all generations, forever and ever. Amen!"* (Ep 3:21, ESV)

But what sort of church did Paul have in mind? What would he think of the modern church?

In the *Book of Acts,* church growth is spontaneous, not the result of a vast output of organisational effort. No doubt, as we set out to plant churches across the land, there is room for a measure of planning, promoting, and programming. But too much focus on such human efforts can lead more to the erection of a religious organisation than to the creation of a true church. We need to have a clear view of biblical principles, so that we build churches that are living parts of Christ, moving irresistibly in the power of the Holy Spirit, giving birth to true disciples.

What are the identifying marks of such churches? What comprises a true *"pentecostal"* (that is, an *"apostolic"* or *"New Testament"*) church? Let me suggest the following – [20]

---

[20] I have described some of these "marks" in more detail than others, which is not so much an indication of their relative importance as it is of my personal inclination when I wrote this study.

UNIQUE – NOT EXCLUSIVE

There is a kind of Christianity that is dully legalistic and scant in lively revelation, while demanding stifling conformity to a rigid pattern of doctrine and behaviour. This is often accompanied by a narrow exclusivism, which insists that *"my church alone is right – all others are wrong!"*

Sometimes that *"correctness"* is expressed through an insistence that *"we alone possess true doctrine"*. At other times it is expressed through an assumption that *"our way of doing things is the only right way"* – such as when liturgical and non-liturgical congregations accuse each other of deficient worship; or when strictly separated saints accuse the more liberated of *"worldliness"*, who in turn charge their accusers with *"fanaticism"*, or scornfully call them *"narrow-minded"* and *"puritans"*..

I hope you understand that no church has a monopoly upon truth either in doctrine or in practice. At best none of us can do more than *"know in part"*; we are all *"peering through a dark glass"* (1 Co 13:9,12) – which remains true even when some do manage occasionally, in some areas, to see a little more clearly than others. It would indeed be good if some of our more dogmatic brethren could remember that their glass is as dark as anyone else's!

Surely any kind of arrogant, self-satisfied exclusivism must be as unpleasant to God as it is to other beholders. Yet, while avoiding any nonsensical claim to be exclusively correct, there is a great need for local churches to strive to be dynamically unique. Each local church should find self-assurance, confidence, strength of outreach, in the knowledge that it has found the distinct identity and task appointed for it by God. This is discovered by raising up churches that in the freedom of Christ –

- **Become dynamically different from each other as they express the special genius built into them by God.**

Could anything be more stifling than the grey uniformity that characterises so many pentecostal [21] churches across the nation. They sing the same songs, follow the same liturgy, pursue the same goals, use the same methods, ape the same life-style, set up the same programmes, and the like.

Surely the God who declines to make two identical snowflakes must desire more difference among our churches? Surely he would delight in diverse approaches and emphases, different outreaches and aims? I am persuaded that one of the reasons the pentecostal movement is not prospering as it should is this: few pastors are willing to seek God for instructions about just how the Holy Spirit would like to shape each local church. Most of us are conformists at heart, fearful of being different, afraid to embark upon an idea that no one else has ever tried! [22]

- ***Permit liberty of spiritual development and diversity of lifestyle among their members***

Have you ever observed how you need only look at some people, or talk with them for a few minutes, to know at once what denomination they belong to? There is something ill-shaped about a church that turns all its people into replicas of each other, using the same clichés, dressing in the same manner, enjoying the same entertainments, locked into the same taboos and mores. Surely the purpose of Christ is to set men and women free to be fully themselves, to express richly, joyfully, uniquely, everything he has called each one of us to be and to do as diverse members of his *"body"* on earth?

Christian life should be liltingly dynamic, not suffocatingly conformist, for *"where the Spirit of the Lord is there is liberty to advance from glory to glory to glory!"* (2 Co 3:17-18).

---

(21) Forgive me for talking here about churches of my own connection – that is, pentecostal. The remarks, however, do apply, at least in some measure, to all local churches everywhere.

(22) This idea is explored more fully in my study on "The Tower of Babel", found in my book Building the Church God Wants.

SUPERNATURAL – NOT MECHANICAL

Any church eager to follow the NT model must be committed to a ministry attended by signs, wonders, and miracles (Mk 16:20; Ac 2:43; 5:12-16; Ro 15:18-19; 1 Co 2:4-5; 1 Th 1:4-5; He 2:4). The kingdom of darkness is a supernatural kingdom and nothing less than a supernatural church can hope to overthrow it. A church that depends primarily upon advertising, activities, associations, and administrations for its life and growth may achieve great statistical success, but it will pose little real threat to the devil.

Jesus did not say, "Go into all the world and gather a crowd!" (which the world can do better than we can anyway), but *"Go into all the world and make disciples!"*

No doubt we should use every tool and resource available to help us fulfil the task of the evangel; but they must all be subsidiary always to *"a demonstration of the power of the Spirit"* (1 Co 2:4).

In this connection, let me offer a warning against some perils that are currently besetting the pentecostal movement –

- *Once separated from the world, now eager to reflect its lifestyle and to chase after its material goals;* but we are called to pursue, not happiness, but holiness (He 12:14).
- *Once scorned the yoke of legalism, now devising new sets of rules and regulations about going, doing, eating, wearing, and behaving;* but the kingdom of God does not consist of such rules, but of righteousness, peace, and joy in the Holy Spirit (Ro 14:17; Cl 2:16-23).
- *Once opposed to fixed creeds, now busy setting up and defending their own dogmas;* but while the church must be committed to sound doctrine, let us avoid the conceit of claiming that our group alone possesses truth.
- *Once embraced miracles as the sign of a new era, now use them as crowd-catching gimmicks;* but "falling under the power", "holy laughter", convulsions, and the like, were not the kind of miracles the apostles

used to turn their world upside-down, but rather true healings, deliverances, and genuine acts of divine power.
- ***Once rejoiced in personal liberty and church autonomy,*** but now building ever-bigger bureaucracies.
- ***Once majored on sound doctrine,*** but now focussed on the pursuit of personal happiness; yet we dare not tolerate intolerable deviations from truth just to catch a crowd.
- ***Once saw worship as a sacrifice to offer,*** but now a sensation to be experienced.
- ***Once focussed externally on evangelism,*** but now internally on structure and conformity, and on buildings, programmes, and organisation.
- ***Once content with Holy Spirit baptism,*** but now restlessly craving some new stimulant. However, if people were truly baptised in the Spirit, and learning how to live and walk in the Spirit, they would not be yearning for some new "key" to victorious life in Christ.
- ***Once built around prayer and revival,*** but now depending on programmes and entertainment.

Consequently there is a general push toward pastors who are friendly, sympathetic, faulty, and ambivalent – one of *us*, rather than self-controlled, courageous, imaginative, assured, strong, and holy men of God. Indeed, many congregations prefer a shepherd who maintains the status quo, rather than a leader who forces them, under the absolute lordship of Christ, to break into new dimensions of faith, growth, discipleship, and the genuinely supernatural.

Our goal should be that the faith of the people *"might not rest upon human wisdom, but upon the power of God"* (1 Co 2:5); instead it is often now the very people of God who insist that their pastor (against the teaching of Paul, 1 Co 2:1-4) should dangle in front of them *"eloquent"* sermons, and *"clever"* programmes, and an enticing *"vision"* in place of the Cross of Christ. They are not attracted to a crucified life; they do not really want the power of God, but prefer exciting programmes and mere sensation.

PROPHETIC – NOT DOGMATIC

The glory of the early church and the source of its remarkable evangelistic success arose from its identity as a **prophetic community** (Ac 2:17-18; 1 Co 14:24-25; and cp. Pr 29:18, *"Where there is no prophetic revelation the people will become lawless."*)

Israel was marked by its possession of the law; but the church is identified by the spirit of prophecy (Ro 9:4; Re 19:10). Satan vigorously opposes this (cp. 1 Co 2:9-14); therefore we must the more earnestly maintain this prophetic character. It is expressed through –

PROPHETIC CHARISMATA

See 1 Co 14:1, 5 ,24-25, 29, 39; 1 Th 5;19-20. However, here I want to focus more upon

PROPHETIC PREACHING

We must be committed to a bold proclamation of the word of God in the power of the Holy Spirit, never doubting: that our first mandate is to *preach* (Mk 16:15); that preaching is the highest office in the church; and that the power of God flows out of our preaching (Ac 10:42; Ro 1:15-16; 10:8-17; 1 Co 9:16; 2 Ti 4:2; etc). See also 1 Co 1:17-25, and notice again how Paul scorns the addition to the gospel of secular wisdom and methodologies. Obedience to this preaching mandate requires the preacher to declare three things –

THE "ESCHATA"

That is, the *"last things"*; the coming end of the age, the return of Christ, the resurrection of the dead; the future judgments of God; the realities of hell and heaven.

THE "KRIMATA"

That is, the present and continuing judgments of God, beginning with the proclamation of the evangel, and continuing with the gospel demand that we subdue the flesh and live righteously before God, knowing that judgment begins at the church (1 Co 11:27-32; 1 Pe 4:17).

THE "CHARISMATA"

That is, the splendour of what God has done for us in Christ; the message of grace and faith; the marvel of our enthronement with Christ in the heavenlies; the richness of the blessing we have received (Ep 1:3); along with all the other glories that are ours in Christ and by the power of the Spirit. [23]

But let the preacher preach with confidence, never doubting that if all else is taken away from us, so long as we can *preach* the gospel, the church will grow. Truly, nothing should be allowed to be more central in the church than the pulpit – not the eucharist, not worship, not fellowship, not charitable works, and certainly not mere entertainment, programmes, activities, and the like. Indeed, a church that is not built upon the Word of God is in the end no church, for the preached *logos* is simply an incarnation of the eternal *Logos*, upon whom alone the church can stand.

Consider 1 Co 3:10-11; and note that the dread warning in vs. 12-15 refers primarily to false teachers, builders of false doctrine, and to those who try to underlay the church with anything other than the preaching of Christ; and then compare again 1 Co 2:2-4.

INVOLVED – NOT ISOLATED

Against the isolationism that has been practised by many evangelicals and pentecostals (who have carried the idea of "*separation from the world*" to the extreme of *isolation* from it) the NT calls us to a life of involvement with the world around us. But there are many who try to do the very thing that Paul said was not only impossible but wrong, that is, to escape temptation by hiding in some sort of Christian ghetto (1 Co 5:9-10).

We may not be *of* the world, but we are certainly still *in* it, and have a duty to be *"the salt of the earth"*, and to shine brightly like *"a city set on a hill"*, and to be like *"the leaven in a loaf"* (Mt 5:13-16; 13:33; etc).

---

(23) For more on this, see below, under "Christian – Not Religious".

Christians should be encouraged to become involved in the life of the larger community in as many ways as possible; but many churches keep their people so busy going to church meetings that they never have any opportunity to shine as a light outside the church. Instead, we need Christians to be active in all three levels of government; in a wide range of social and community organisations; in political parties; and the like – so that they mingle with the ungodly and bear a fragrant witness for Christ.

But a word of caution: Christians who go into politics should do so, not for the dishonest purpose of using political office as a cloak for pulpiteering, nor to push some sectarian agenda, but to be the best *politician* possible, albeit one whose moral character, philosophy, and commitments, are shaped by his or her relationship with Christ.

MISSIONARY – NOT PAROCHIAL

I see this as entailing two things –

THE CHURCH MUST BE EVANGELICAL

That is, committed to the inspiration and authority of the Bible and to the supreme importance of fulfilling the Great Commission (see Mt 28:18-20; Mk 16:15-20; Ac 1:6-8). Note that the command is not to stay at home and pray, but to *go out*, plant churches, and make disciples (Ac 11:19-21). Despite the stories of countless "saints", of contemplative monasteries and nunneries, and the like, there is a notable lack of mysticism in the Bible, which is an immensely practical book. Think about *Proverbs*, or about the complete absence of any mystical elements from such Jewish writings as *Sirach* and the *Wisdom of Solomon*. The Bible message is always go out and do, not come here and hide. I do not doubt the need for everyone to *"come apart"* for a time, to take time out to rest and pray; but I find it impossible to accept that abandoning society for a lifetime is the best way to serve the Lord.

THE CHURCH MUST BE REPRODUCTIVE

Each local church has a duty to reproduce itself, which is the real pattern of *"revival"*: lively local churches established in strategic locations, and then those churches sending ministry teams into nearby communities to establish more churches. No church is a sufficient end in itself; it dare not be locked into a self-centred parochial concern; it must have a missionary vision – local, national, international.

However, remember that statistical increase is not part of God's guarantee to any congregation, for we are in the end called, not to be *"successful"*, but to be *faithful*.

At a pastors' seminar in New Zealand I was once asked to address the question: *"What is God's strategy today for successful world evangelisation?"* I had to say that God does not have such a strategy; rather he has a purpose, not to win the world for Christ, but to *"call out of the nations a people for his name"* (cp. Ac 15:14).

Scripture says that this world *"is under the control of the wicked one"* (1 Jn 5:19), nor did Jesus dispute the devil's claim that *"the kingdoms of this world and all their glory"* belong to him (Mt 4:9-10), and that he (Satan) can *"give them to anyone he chooses"* (Lu 4:6). Our task therefore is not to claim the world for Christ, nor a nation, nor a city, nor even a suburb, but simply to go out, plant churches, make disciples, and get as many people as we can thoroughly out of hell and thoroughly into heaven.

Success is guaranteed to the church in general (Mt 16:18), but not in particular (Lu 10:10-11).

PRAYERFUL – NOT NATURALISTIC

The local church should be committed to the proposition that collective and individual prayer is the key to unleashing spiritual life in the church. Whatever is done in the church, or happens there, apart from answered prayer, is straw that will be consumed on the Day of Judgment. And in the local church, perhaps the most powerful prayer is pulpit prayer, offered as part of the common assembly of the saints. Yet in our time powerful pulpit prayer seems to have become a lost art.

I often preach in churches where there has been at best a brief and largely ineffective prayer, and sometimes no prayer at all, before I am invited to the pulpit. Here then is one of the most powerful resources of the church being allowed to go untapped; yet see what extraordinary influence Paul gives to corporate prayer, sufficient to influence *"kings"*! (1 Ti 2:1-4)

When was bold, believing prayer last raised up for (or against) the government across the pulpit of your church?

It is said that people always get the government they deserve, and that certainly seems to be true of us Christians; we have no confidence that our prayers could influence government policy, so we do not pray for those who rule over us, and then we complain because they pursue a godless agenda!

WORSHIPFUL – NOT CEREMONIAL

Some of the best witnessing work of the church can be done when it assembles together as a worshipping community, under the lordship of Christ, and carrying a prophetic unction (Ac 4:23-31; 1 Co 14:24-25).

But let worship be worship indeed, not just a shallow romp, nor merely a solemn ceremony. We want neither a crass emotionalism nor a dead formalism, but a proper combination of sparkling life with grace and beauty. We should strive for a godly blend of charm and dignity, with winsomeness and sobriety (cp. 1 Co 14:40).

No one could doubt the vibrancy of the Spirit-enriched worship of the early church; but neither was it shallow and superficial, a mere noisy celebration. The high level of theology, the literary beauty, contained in the few snatches of hymns and poetry that are scattered through the NT, display the seriousness and strength that must have been characteristic of the worship of the first Christians (see 1 Ti 1:17; 6:15-16; Ph 2:5-11; Ep 1:3-14; Ro 8:31-39; 1 Co 13:4-7).

Remember, too, that for the first four decades Christians had the majestic liturgy and gorgeous ceremonial of the temple in Jerusalem standing before them as an example. The temple was destroyed by the Roman army, but its standard of *"glory and beauty"* continued to guide the churches (Ex 28:2; Ps 50:2).

Worship is the one thing we can do that the world cannot even begin to emulate, it is the one supreme joy that is uniquely ours. If the world is not ready to hear our words they can perhaps still be won when they see our worship.

True worship, says Paul, creates a tangible sense of the presence of God, which causes unbelievers and outsiders to *"fall down and worship God, crying out, 'God really is in this place!'"* (1 Co 14:25b). By contrast, bad worship practices will drive the same unbeliever right out of the church (vs. 23).

ESCHATALOGICAL – NOT TEMPORAL

I have already made some comment on this above, but here I am thinking more about the need for Christians to live with a vision of the invisible, to be people of heaven more than of earth, of eternity more than of time, of spiritual things more than material (Mt 6:19-21; Cl 3:1-4). And we are to do this while we are still living ordinary daily life, *"in the world, but not of it"*

Unhappily, there are many in the church today, as there were already in Paul's time, *"whose god is their stomach, whose glory is in their shame, whose destiny will be destruction, because their minds are fixed on earthly things"* (Ph 3:18-19, KJV).

Can there be any more wretched spectacle than a materialistic, earthbound, money-clutching, carnal Christian? We should be of a different temper, with a loftier goal (vs. 20-21). And here is a test: if your heart is fixed in the right place, then you will be like those Christians of whom the apostle joyfully boasted, who *"cheerfully accepted the confiscation of all their goods, because they knew that they had much better and lasting possessions in heaven"* (He 10:34).

CHRISTIAN – NOT RELIGIOUS

Religion is built around sensations, but the *gospel* is based upon assent to the truth (1 Jn 5:10-12; Ro 10:9; Jn 20:31). *Religion* depends upon feelings, but the *gospel* stands upon faith alone (2 Co 5:7). *Religion* wants to buy God's favour by good works, but the *gospel* rests entirely upon the merits of Christ (Cl 2:13-14). Indeed, the expression "the Christian religion" may be seen as an oxymoron – if it is good religion then it is probably bad gospel; if it is true gospel, then it will abjure false religion.

Therefore, although we do revel in a rich and varied experience of the presence, power, and grace of God, nonetheless our emphasis must not be upon personal experience but rather upon divine revelation. We do not preach the human *situation* but rather our heavenly *position*; indeed, the couplet at the head of this section could have been *"Positional – Not Laborious"*, for our attention should be focussed, not on the believer's *state* on earth, but on our *standing* in heaven; we do not look at what we are in ourselves, but at what we are in Christ.

Therefore we do not talk about our poverty on earth but about our blessings in the heavenlies; our message is one of faith not sight; of prosperity not poverty; of authority not weakness; of life not death; of liberty not legalism; it is positive not passive; affirmative not negative.

Above all, it is based upon *revelation* knowledge, not upon *sense* knowledge (see Ep 1:3,15-23; 3:14-20; Cl 1:9-14; 3;1-10; etc).

This walk of faith is difficult to maintain, because it runs so counter to our natural senses; but, against all sense and feeling, we must continue to speak the truth as it is in Christ (Ro 3:4). Indeed, before he attacks anything else in Christian life, the devil is likely to attack this, trying to drive the believer away from a place of bold assurance (He 10:19-23). But those who fall away from firm confession of the position God has given them in the heavenlies in Christ, and who lapse back into speaking only about their situation on earth, will soon find themselves locked in bondage; faith-walk will then become sense-walk, liberty will decay into legalism, and they will be robbed of the joy of the Lord.

We dare not allow our thinking nor our confession to become dominated by our actual state on earth. Rather, we must set ourselves to affirm day and night the position, the legal standing, God has given us in the heavenlies in Christ. A daily affirmation of that standing will cause it to be transferred from the heavenlies into dynamic reality in daily life.

PROCLAIMING – NOT APOLOGISING

At a pastors' conference I was once asked this question: *"What issues should be our priority, so that we can be relevant in today's society?"* I was offended by the word *"relevant"*. We don't have to be *"relevant"*, only faithful!

Indeed, if the church is behaving as it should, it will never be relevant in the sight of this world (Mt 10:16-18; Ph 2:15); in fact, if we ever did become relevant, so that all start speaking well of us, then we ought at once be deeply alarmed! (Lu 6:26)

We don't have to justify our presence in the community; we are here whether they want us or not, in obedience to the mandate of Christ. So do not yield to the pressure the secular world tries to place on the church, saying it must justify its existence by doing some good work, or performing some useful community service. We are, of course, free to run hospitals, refuges, orphan homes, schools, welfare programmes, and the like; nonetheless, we should never apologise, even if we never do anything more than the most useful service we can render any community, which is to preach the gospel and make disciples. We have no higher task than that, and whether the world loves us or hates us, wants us to preach or not, grants us permission or tries to deny it, still we will obey God rather than man, and continue to fulfil the divine mandate.

Yet no church should take on sundry external programmes without a clear word from God to do so. On the whole, most of them will be better run if they are owned and managed, not by the local church, but by groups of committed lay-people, independent of ecclesiastical control.

The church is the most wonderful institution on earth, and the only one that is ultimately indestructible. To belong to it is an inexpressible privilege. Let us echo Paul's shout of triumph, and do all that we can to make it true: *"Unto God be glory in the church by Christ Jesus throughout all ages, world without end. Amen"* (Ep 3:21).

50

Chapter Four

GRACE

Grace *to you and peace from God our Father and from the Lord Jesus Christ* (Ga 1:3) ... *I am astonished that you are so quickly falling away from him who called you in the **grace** of Christ and are turning to a different gospel* (vs. 6) ...*But (God) set me apart before I was born, and called me by his **grace*** ... (vs. 15) ... *When James and Cephas and John, who seemed to be pillars, perceived the **grace** that was given to me, they gave the right hand of fellowship to Barnabas and me* (2:9) ... *I do not nullify the **grace** of God, for if righteousness were through the law, then Christ died for no purpose* (vs. 21) ... *You are severed from Christ, you who would be justified by the law; you have fallen away from **grace***. (5:4) ... *The **grace** of our Lord Jesus Christ be with your spirit* (6:18).

Seven times (the number of perfection) "grace" is mentioned in the *Letter to the Galatians*. It is one of the most glorious themes in the letter. Let me explore it with you, beginning with a strange practice known as

HESYCHASM

Hesychasm is the idea that one can gain an experiential knowledge of God by retreating into a form of inner quietness, or stillness, in which all sensation other than of the holy ceases. The word admittedly has been used in different ways over the centuries, but I am confining it here to the concepts also known as Illuminism, Quietism, or Passivism. They all embrace the same basic notion, that God cannot be reached aside from some heroic achievement of inner stillness, which banishes all awareness of the outside world, leaving space only for a beatific vision of God. There are diverse methods followed by quietists to achieve this hesychastic state, but they are all compressed within the word "stillness" – that is, of achieving an absolute quietness of mind, body, spirit, and emotion, without which (it is said) the soul cannot hope to discover God or to see his divine light.

I wonder if such passivists have ever truly even read, let alone properly understood *Ephesians* and *Colossians,* and related passages. I find it hard to believe that anyone could deeply grasp the meaning of Paul's teaching about our position in the heavenlies in Christ (Ep 2:4-6), which belongs to every believer, yet go on some mystical quest to discover God.

It seems to me that, say, *Ephesians 3:12* and *Hebrews 10:19-23* are richly sufficient to put an end to all uncertainty about the believer's welcome in Christ. In both places, and others in the NT, we are told that in Christ we have been given bold access to the very throne of God; that we can enter the holiest by faith and by the blood of Christ alone; and that there we can speak confidently to God and expect a powerful response to prayer. Those scriptures seem to me so far removed from the sentiments expressed in hesychastic writings that I cannot comprehend how the two concepts can exist in the same church.

Of course, in reality they don't co-exist. Anyone who is addicted to quietism could never heartily embrace the Pauline revelation that every Christian is *already* enthroned in the heavenlies, with Christ, at the Father's right hand, far above all dark principalities and powers. Likewise, anyone who *knows* that in Christ he or she has *already* been granted full, free, and open access to the very footstool of the Lord, could never find any reason to abase themselves with breast-beating misery in order to advance a little closer to God.

Surely the awful sufferings imposed upon themselves by the hermits, eremites, stylites, both in the past and now, in a futile attempt to get closer to God, are sufficient to show that any such quest is vain. We either enter the holy of holies by faith in Christ, by the blood alone (apart from *any* work of ours), which means by grace alone, or we don't get there at all. Could Paul today react in any other way to such ideas than he did to the Galatians? –

> *I am astonished that you are so quickly falling away from him who called you in the **grace** of Christ and are turning to a different gospel (1:6).*

For indeed, any teaching must be called *"a different gospel"*, if it says there is any other way to draw near to God than the way of grace channelled through faith. Hesychasm and its ilk should be spurned by all who claim the name of Christ.

"But," says someone, "what about Paul's claim that he *'beat himself black and blue'* (1 Co 9:27, Wuest)?" Yes, he did say that, using very vigorous language. But he is not talking about his right to approach the throne of God freely. Rather, he is describing how serious he is about his ministry, and his desire ever to remain fit to serve Christ well and to well fulfil his apostolic calling (see the context in vs. 16-27).

MYSTICISM

I said in the previous chapter that the Bible is not a mystical book, which is simply true. The Bible does not contain mystical ideas. Mysticism can be found in scripture only by forcing meaning into words that they do not naturally have – such as, for example, when the simple words of Jesus in *Matthew 6:6* are turned into a complex edifice of deeply mystical and illuminist practices, about which the Saviour himself might well have been horrified. Or, I try to imagine Paul engaging in such practices, and inspiration fails me. He didn't have time for them!

The Christian mandate is not focussed on making oneself perfect, nor on gaining some perfect revelation of God, nor on achieving some mythical quality of sainthood, nor on getting a vision of the divine light. Nor is reaching some sort of ethereal mystical state the highest human achievement. Rather, the Christian mandate consists of spreading the gospel, planting churches, and making disciples. It is down to earth. It is practical. It requires ordinary people living ordinary lives to be out there in the world, not looking for the divine light but rather *themselves* shining as lights in the darkness. And in the meantime, we are already made perfect in Christ, we already have an open door into the holiest, we are already fully saints! We are required only to *believe* it, and then to live it out.

If the quest is to become more righteous, then that search too is vain, for by divine grace we have already been made the very righteousness of God in Christ (2 Co 5:17-21). And until we do heartily embrace our God-given righteousness we are no better than those whom Paul castigates for going about trying to establish some righteousness of their own (Ro 10:3-4). Ask the question: who can behave righteously? *Answer:* only the righteous can behave righteously; and indeed, they can hardly do otherwise. Righteous people do righteously. But the ungodly do ungodly, and even when they seem to do good it is still ungodly, for it is inevitably poisoned by sin. So, if you want people to do righteously, then make them righteous and they will do it naturally. But there is only one way we *can* be made righteous, and that, as scripture bluntly declares, is by the grace of God alone in response to a believer's simple faith in Christ. (24)

I certainly don't deny the right of any man or woman to sequester themselves, either alone or with others, if that is what they wish to do, and if that is how they think they can better serve God. But I have little interest in emulating them. They seem to me, not to be obeying the call of God, but disobeying it (Mt 28:19-20; Mk 16:15-20).

All true knowledge of God must come from scripture not from any sort of illuministic experience. Also, a hesychastic approach to life, as well as lacking any substantive biblical foundation, is impossible for an average person. Few there are who can usefully devote countless hours to prayer and meditation. Seldom can ordinary people focus on a search for some mystical dimension in which they hope to see the shining face of God. The demands of daily life, for most people, make any such retreat from the world irresponsible. Are they then never to meet God personally? How absurd! They need only murmur the name of Jesus, and they are

---

(24) I do not mean that those made righteous by God are at once free from all sin. We remain in mortal and corruptible bodies, which will not be entirely free of darkness until after the resurrection (1 Co 15:53-56). But I do mean that we are *reckoned* fully, absolutely, utterly righteous by God the moment we truly believe in Jesus, which righteousness we should also reckon of ourselves (Ro 6:11).

at once in the holiest, at the throne of God, as close to the Lord as anyone will ever be, even in eternity! (He 10:19-23).

Yet never forget that we are called to walk by faith, not by sight (2 Co 5:7). This is highlighted by a remarkable passage from the apocryphal work, *2 Esdras* –

> I will give your houses to a people that will come, who <u>without having heard me will believe</u>. Those to whom <u>I have shown no signs</u> will do what I have commanded. They have <u>seen no prophets</u>, yet will recall their former state. I call to witness the gratitude of the people that is to come, whose children rejoice with gladness; <u>though they do not see me with bodily eyes</u>, yet with the spirit <u>they will believe the things</u> I have said. (1:35-37; NRSV; italics and underlining are mine).

We are that people; we are those who have not seen the Lord with their eyes, nor heard his voice speak aloud, nor met an ancient prophet, nor witnessed any extraordinary signs, but who still believe the things he has said. This we do despite any contrary evidence our senses may produce. We may lack outward evidence of the truth of scripture affirmations – indeed our senses may be shrieking the opposite – but we do not walk by sight, *we walk by faith!*

So then whether or not I *feel* that I am in the presence of God, and even when I lack any evidence apart from scripture that I am standing in the holiest before the blood-sprinkled golden lid of the Ark of the Covenant, still I choose to *believe* what the Bible tells me. And what does it say? Simply that I may at any time come boldly and with full assurance into the throne room, in the name of Jesus, where I will be welcomed by the Father! (He 10:19-23; Ep 3:12). No hesychastic diversion will ever deter me from grasping that promise and acting on it.

PIETISTIC FOLLY

In my opinion, the quest of some pietists to rid themselves of all passion, and/or of all natural human desires, is not only against human nature, and civic responsibility, but also against scripture and is in opposition to the creative fiat of God himself.

The quarrels of the Fathers about degrees of pietistic isolation, and about diverse mystical states, seem bizarre and foolish to me. How absurd to excommunicate one another on a difference of opinion about something so arcane as hesychastic ideas and practices (which has happened in the past). At best, such theologians were poor examples of their craft, trying to devise dogma with scant biblical backing, and to promulgate practices that are meaningful only to a few people who possess the right sort of temperament. They would have done better for themselves and their churches to have pondered what Paul actually did teach in his letters, and what the gospel really does require of those who profess to believe it.

Probably because they never did grasp the real meaning of Paul's letters, the pietists became side-tracked (as did many eremites, hermits, and others) into esoteric ideas and dead-end practices that could not possibly bring any true fulfilment. Nor could any genuine revelation of Christ or of his purpose for them be gained by becoming a recluse and striving to know God outside of scripture. I think that anchorites, and the like, with their illuminist, hesychastic ideas, fail dismally as theologians.

For myself, amid a busy life of ministry and service, when I need to enter the presence of God quickly, I heed the counsel of Paul –

> *God had an eternal purpose that he has now accomplished in Christ Jesus our Lord, in whom we have* **bold** *and* **confident access** *to God through our* ***faith*** *in Christ!* (Ep 3:12)

Mark what the apostle affirms –

- The work of God in Christ Jesus our Lord is now fully ***accomplished***.
- Therefore, we need nothing more than ***faith*** to draw near to God – weeping, pleading, sacrifice, suffering, fasting, intercession, cannot advance us toward the throne by so much as a single step. They may all be vastly useful in other ways, but not when I seek to draw near to God. Paul is adamant: we have access to God solely by faith. Nothing more is needed. Anything more will undermine the simplicity and purity of faith.

- This we should do **boldly**, never doubting that the door to the throne room of the Father is and will always remain wide open. One trustful murmur of the name of Jesus and I am instantly in the holiest, closer to God than even the archangel dares to approach.
- And we should draw near to God with **confidence**, expecting that he will surely hear and answer prayer, knowing that if we ask according to his will we already have the petitions we desired of him (1 Jn 5:14).
- We cannot be denied **access** to the throne of God, because the blood of the everlasting covenant has sealed our right to walk in by *faith*, with **boldness** and **confidence!**
- So once again, let the Holy Spirit burn this stunning revelation deeply into your spirit, so that you will never to be able to resile from it: *"We have __bold__ and __confident__ __access__ to God through our __faith__ in Christ"* – and only through faith.

Where in that passage of scripture is there even the least room for any sort of hesychastic idea? It demolishes *every* notion that only by some heroic piety can we open the door to the throne room of heaven. We enter by faith, and by faith alone.

And all this has come to us by

THE GRACE OF GOD

In Paul's thinking there is no way to reconcile the Law with Grace, and we must choose to live by one or the other –

> *I do not nullify the __grace__ of God, for if righteousness were through the law, then Christ died for no purpose* (Ga 2:21)
> *... You are severed from Christ, you who would be justified by the law; you have fallen away from __grace__* (5:4).

Paul has in mind Jewish teachers who insisted, in addition to trusting in the work of Christ on the cross, that Christians must also observe some aspects of the laws of Moses. Any such action, says he, would *"nullify"* what Christ has done. That is, if you do place any dependence upon law-keeping then you will invalidate the grace of God, and make it ineffective.

If salvation, or justification, or sanctification, or righteousness depend in any respect upon some work of ours, or some rule we think we must keep, then Jesus *"died for no purpose"*, his death was in vain.

Will you render the cross futile? Will you spurn the grace of God? Will you insist upon trying to earn your salvation by good works, or by law observance? But reconciliation, and justification, and righteousness, and sanctification cannot be *earned*; they can only be *received*, as a free gift of God in Christ, by faith, through grace alone (1 Co 6:11).

How many there are who try to persuade God that they deserve to be saved because of the good they have done! But if salvation can be earned, then it does not come by grace; yet scripture is adamant that by grace and grace alone are we saved –

> *By grace you have been saved through faith. Nor can this be gained by some work of your own. It is the gift of God. It is never a result of human working. God leaves no one any room to boast* (Ep 2:8-9).

Why did Christ die if some effort of ours can justify us? The very fact that he did die is sufficient to show that no work of a fallen sinner can ever bring an escape from sin and its dread penalty of death. It is enough that he died for our sin and rose again for our justification. I need no more. There is no more.

Why, too, would I risk being *"severed from Christ"* by cancelling grace through the folly of trying to be *"justified by the law"*? (Ga 5:4) I can have grace, or I can have law; I cannot have both. For if I try to merit salvation, or earn the right to approach the throne of God, by any sort of good work or law-keeping, I will gain nothing except the awful penalty of being *"severed from Christ"*. But it is only in him that I have any hope! So away with the law and all its rules about eating, drinking, going, doing, being; I *will* have Christ, and Christ alone as my sole Redeemer, my one and altogether sufficient Saviour.

People who think they can score points in heaven by a set of good works, even deep sacrifices, are simply calling God a liar, and declaring that the Cross is inadequate, and Christ insufficient.

If my own merit is enough to save me, why would I need the merit of another? "But," argues someone, "I need the merits of Christ to make up what I lack." How foolish! All our righteousness is like a bloodied rag (Is 64:6), fit only to be cast into a rubbish bin.

We have no merits, nor can we earn any, that are worth preserving. We ourselves are utterly condemned along with all our works, both good and bad. Either we flee to the cross and take refuge under the merits of Christ, or we are doomed for ever. It finally comes down to this: if Christ, and Christ alone, is not fully my Saviour, then he is no Saviour at all. He does not offer a part-salvation that I have to bring to fruition by some personal good work. No! He offers an entire salvation which I must either accept in full, or reject in full. No other choice is available.

GOOD WORKS ARE VALUABLE

None of this means, of course, that good works, personal sacrifice, patient suffering, hard toil for the gospel, and so on, have no value. In fact, they all have immense value! Do they not serve God, benefit the church, enhance human happiness, and promote a good reputation? But if they are being done in order to win human plaudits and to purchase righteousness in the sight of God, then, while they may still benefit others, they will bring no spiritual profit to the doer –

> *If I give away everything I own to feed others, and if I am burned to death as a martyr, but do it without love, I am profited nothing* (1 Co 13:3).

Or, to put it differently, if I am doing good *because* I know that apart from any work of mine I am saved by grace, then every work will be transformed on the Day of Judgment into *"gold, silver, and precious stones"*. But if I do such things hoping to *become* justified, then they will turn on that day into *"wood, hay, and stubble"* (1 Co 3:12-15).

We should be doing righteously because we know that in Christ we already possess full righteousness, not because we hope that doing good things will make us good. No one can turn a thorn bush into an orange tree by hanging oranges on it. But turn the bush into an orange tree and it will naturally produce a rich harvest!

Christ has caused me to become his very own righteousness, hence I joyously behave righteously (which is not the same as *perfectly*) (2 Co 5:21). I strive to be godly, not to *become* godly, but because in Christ I already *am* godly, and I wish now only to work out what is already in me.

There is a vast difference between striving to *activate* what you already *are* and striving to *become* what you are manifestly not. I am not on earth trying to live in heaven; rather, I am in the heavenlies working out on earth all the spiritual blessings Christ has bestowed on his church (Ep 1:3).

And all this is by the grace of God – that is, by his marvellous free and unmerited kindness to me in Christ. My life, like the letter to the *Galatians*, begins and ends with grace –

> **Grace** to you and peace from God our Father and from the Lord Jesus Christ (Ga 1:3) ... The **grace** of our Lord Jesus Christ be with your spirit (6:18).

Chapter Five

OXYMORONS

> *There will always be people who will try to upset you; people who distort the gospel of Christ. But if we ourselves, or even an angel from heaven, should preach any gospel contrary to the one we have preached to you, let him be accursed in hell! As we have said before, and I will say again – if anyone is preaching to you any gospel contrary to what you received, let him be accursed in hell!* (Ga 1:8-9)

What is this one true gospel that pronounces a curse upon any other gospel, even were it preached by an angel from heaven? It is the gospel that stands apart from what is commonly called "religion". Indeed, as I suggested briefly some pages back, the phrase "Christian religion" could be called an oxymoron.

You have no doubt heard about oxymorons, which comes from two Greek words: *oxys = sharp, pointed;* and *moron =* dull-witted. It describes two opposite or incongruous ideas when they are joined together. My dictionary defines it as *"a smart saying, which on second thought seems foolish ... a contradiction in terms"* – such as: "there was a *thundering silence*" – "her departure brought *sorrowing joy*" – "he was an *honourable thief*." Some other not so polite examples are: *military intelligence; civil service; teenage music; amateur sportsman; business ethics; honest broker.*

Those examples are amusing; but **"*Christian religion*"** is tragic. Why is that phrase an *oxymoron*? Simply because if it is truly **Christian** it cannot be *religion*; [25] and if it is *religion*, it cannot be truly **Christian**! Why? Because the very essence of *religion* is

---

(25) I am plainly using the word "religion" here in a restricted sense, meaning the things that commonly pass as "religious" in popular thinking, and especially when religion is seen as a way for people to reach God by their own efforts. In a broader sense, the phrase "Christian religion" is acceptable. Rather like "civil war" is an oxymoron only if "civil" is restricted to meaning "polite" or "courteous".

to build *barriers* between God and people, saying *"stop here, you can go no further!"* But the very essence of the *gospel* is to *tear down* those barriers and to open a door to the throne of God!

Therefore the message of the gospel can be summed up in the saying: **"*The way into the holiest is now made open by the blood of Jesus to everyone who believes!*"** (See *Hebrews 4:16; 10:19-23; Revelation 22:17; John 3:14-17; Ephesians 3:12;* etc.)

Let us then look at the barriers that religion builds and the doors that the gospel opens.

THE BARRIER RELIGION BUILDS

You have probably thought that religion exists to bring people to God. But no; religion has always existed for one purpose: *to place as many barriers as possible between heaven and earth*. That was true even of Israel's God-given religion. For example, note the limitations imposed by the laws of Moses upon worship at the Tabernacle, which continued in the Jerusalem temple until it was destroyed by the Roman army in 70 A.D. Here is a simplified version of the floor plan of Herod's Temple. Notice the succession of walls, from the outer court of the Gentiles, to the Sacred Precinct, followed by the Court of the women, then the Court of Israel (men only), then the Court of the Priests, then the Holy Place, and, finally, the Holy of Holies, which contained the gold-covered Ark of the Covenant. There the *shekinah* – *the glory of God* – was said to dwell, between the wings of the overshadowing cherubim. At each main gate there was a warning of death (execution by a temple guard) if anyone unqualified tried to pass through. So never imagine that this temple was a place where people could come to meet the living God, Yahweh of Israel. Between the humble worshipper and the Almighty a cluster of impassable barriers prevented any possible access to his presence.

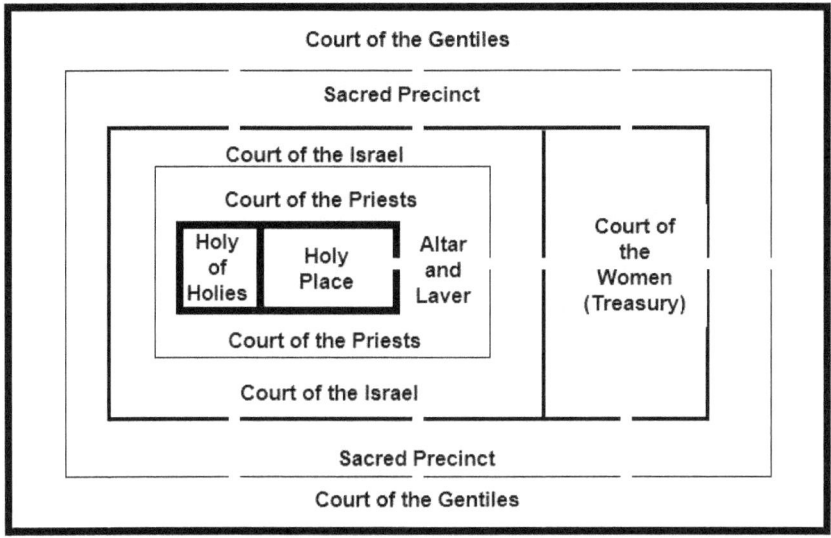

Those many barriers were comprised of a –

RESTRICTION OF <u>PERSON</u>

In general, only true Israelis were allowed to pass from the outer Court of the Gentiles to the Sacred Precinct, the one exception being those few gentile male converts who had undergone circumcision. But even among Israelis, only the ceremonially clean were allowed past the outer court, and no woman, Jewess or Gentile, clean or unclean, was ever permitted to go beyond the Women's Court into the Court of Israel. Indeed, any female who attempted to pass through that gate would be confronted by a sign warning her that the penalty for her incursion would be instant death by spear or sword. The same warning applied to ceremonially unclean males, Jew or Gentile.

Even penitent sinners who wished to bring a lamb or goat for sacrifice were not allowed to go beyond the gate to the Court of the Priests. Only ceremonially clean priests who were rostered for duty on that day were permitted to enter that court. Others could look through the gate and watch the sacrifices being slaughtered, but they were not permitted to cross the portal and approach the altar – see *Leviticus 1:2-3*. To do so meant certain death.

Likewise, only ceremoniously clean and rostered priests were allowed entrance to the Holy Place in the temple proper, where stood the seven-branched candlestick, the altar of incense, and the table for the special bread. And into the Holy of Holies, the innermost part of the sanctuary, only the high priest could go, and even he only once a year, on the great Day of Atonement.

Thus many barriers prevented ordinary people from ever drawing near to Yahweh.

RESTRICTION OF PROVISION

No sacrifices or offerings were allowed except those prescribed by the Mosaic rules. All others were banned, and some might even attract a severe penalty if they were deemed blasphemous or singularly crass. Even an offering of prayer was forbidden if the worshipper was deemed "unclean" in some way.

Israelis could pray anywhere, but prayer offered within the precincts of the temple, or even facing the temple from far away, was deemed especially efficacious. (1 Kg 8:33-49). Even then, it was presumed that prayer would be ignored if anyone other than a ceremonially clean, law-abiding Israeli citizen offered it (Pr 15:8; 28:9; Jn 9:31).

RESTRICTION OF PLACE

Jerusalem was the sole city designated to house the temple. To it people had to come from all over the world. In no other building could an authentic altar be located. Nowhere else would the *shekinah* manifest itself. Blood sacrifices made anywhere else were not legitimate. This and this alone was *Bethel – The House of God*. And the only priests recognised by the Lord were those who officiated lawfully in that temple.

Those barriers were all present in the temple that stood in Jerusalem when Jesus walked its streets and worshipped there. Nor could even he get closer to Yahweh than the Court of Israel. Between him and the Holy of Holies stood massive barriers – the wall that sequestered the Court of the Priests, the door to the Holy

Place, and the heavy veil that hid the Holy of Holies and the Ark of the Covenant.

How impossible it was for ordinary men and women ever to gain close access to the Presence, to experience the *shekinah*, or to discover the glory of God who dwelt in thick darkness between the wings of the cherubim!

But now in Christ the Tabernacle and Temple, with their walls, gates, doors, and veils are no more. The blood of Jesus is sprinkled on the *mercy seat* in heaven, and all who believe anywhere in the world have open access to the Holy of Holies and the very **_Throne of God_**!

Which brings us to –

THE DOOR THE GOSPEL OPENS

Anything that tries to place a wall between you and your rightful free access to the throne of God should at once be cast aside as mere empty "religion", an enemy of the gospel. Jesus came to open doors, not close them. He came to give us free access to the Father, so that we can bravely enter the heavenly sanctuary by his blood alone through faith alone. He tore down the veil, made himself our great high priest, and calls us to draw near to him trustfully, with full assurance that nothing bars our way or can rob us of our right! (He 10:19-22). Behold! The door is *open*, no one can close it, and we should walk in easily and confidently.

Let me share with you three aspects of that open door. It is –

THE DOORWAY TO DIVINE AUTHORITY

God does not expect to do for us what he has made us able to do for ourselves! So rise up in the name of Jesus and take authority over all the works of the Evil One. Enforce the victory that is rightfully yours in Christ! (See *Luke 10:18-19; Romans 16:20*). You have a right to lay hands on the sick and heal them; to loose and to bind (Mt 16:19; 18:18); to turn aside the fiery darts of the evil one (Ep 6:16); and to resist Satan, certain that he will flee from you! (Ja 4:7) The only restraint is that everything must be done in harmony with the purpose of God and for his eternal glory.

THE DOORWAY TO DIVINE LIFE

We are a people destined to live for ever! **Our future is guaranteed by the unassailable fact of the resurrection of Christ.** So let nothing drive you to despair, for how can **anything** in this present life stand against the splendour that awaits everyone who trusts in Jesus? (See *2 Corinthians 4:16-18*).

Who else has such a hope? Let us then cast off the shackles of "religion", and rejoice in the glorious liberty of those who have become the free-born children of God through the sweet message of the gospel!

THE DOORWAY TO DIVINE HELP

See *Hebrews 4:16*. The word translated *"help"* is an ancient nautical term, whose English equivalent is "frap" = to wrap a strong rope around the planking of a sailing ship, to prevent it from sinking in a storm. It is found in one other place in the NT –

> *Then the sailors <u>wrapped ropes around the ship</u> to hold it together* (Ac 27:17).

When you are falling apart at the seams, God's help is there, and this help is always "timely"!

The text that began this chapter bluntly declares that there is only one gospel, which opens the way to God through Christ, by faith alone, through the blood alone, wrought by Christ alone. Everything else is "religion" and is accursed, even if preached by a dazzling angel (Ga 1:8-9) Make sure, then, to be aware of and avoid the pitfalls of the oxymoronic "Christian Religion"! If it puts a barrier between you and God, it is "religion". If it tells you the way is open by the blood of the everlasting covenant, and whoever believes in Christ may walk in boldly, it is the gospel.

Hold fast to the freedom and authority God has given you in Christ; rejoice in his royal victory day by day; and cling firmly to the gospel, the true gospel, rich in grace, full of mercy, mighty in God to save everyone who believes!

Chapter Six

FELLOWSHIP

> *When James, Cephas, and John, who were the leaders of the church in Jerusalem, recognised the grace that had been given to me, they gave to Barnabas and me the right hand of **fellowship** (Ga 2:9).*

People often ask me, "What is God doing around the world today?" My reply: "In *general*, just what he has always done, as described in scripture. In *particular*, no one knows, and anyone who says he does know is ridiculous." The mind of God is not accessible by mortals, and his actions (as Jesus said) are like the wind – we don't know whence it comes; we don't know where it is going. As for me, I am content to heed the rebuke of Christ (Jn 21:21-22), and so leave the other fellow to get on with his task, unhindered by me, while I focus on taking up my own cross daily, following Christ wherever he may choose to lead me.

I do share the concern of many people, which is a desire for another Reformation. But whether or not that will happen, who can say? Jan Hus was burned at the stake. Martin Luther died peacefully in his bed. Who can tell, except in general terms, what lies ahead for any of us or what God has planned for his church? Perhaps an explosion of revival? Perhaps a tornado of persecution? Perhaps both, around the world, or at different times in different places? Or perhaps the worst of all scenarios, a lapse into universal indifference, where faith will scarcely survive anywhere (Lu 18:8; 1 Th 5:2-6).

But then, perhaps Christ will come soon and put an end to all our debates!

In the meantime, Paul says that a characteristic of the church is *"the right hand of fellowship"*. This raises the question of whether the church should be

A THEOCRACY, A MONARCHY, OR A DEMOCRACY?

My discussion here will have a

PURPOSE

To present <u>some</u> of the theoretical bases for arguing in favour of local church autonomy, in contrast with the easy trend of virtually all denominations toward an ever-burgeoning bureaucracy, which too often turns the church from a movement into a monument.

METHOD

To show that the biblical bias is toward a "family" concept of the local church, with the group of churches functioning as a "theocracy". Therefore we should resist the constant pressure to turn the church into a copy of a secular organisation.

ARGUMENT

How should we view the local church, and also the company of churches? There are two major alternatives –

A SODALITY

Those who embrace a *sodality* model of the church, see it primarily as a fellowship, a brotherhood, or a family; that is, a group of people who are united on the basis of personal relationship, not by membership in an organisation.

This stands in contrast with the bureaucratic nature of

A MODALITY

When a church (or group of churches) embraces a *modality* model, it begins to behave more like a secular organisation than a Christian family. Structure then becomes more important than relationship; brotherhood is turned into membership; and the church becomes increasingly dependent upon secular techniques of management. A *modal* church expects its growth to come, not so much from natural generation (as in a family), but from entrepreneurial methods, promotions, strategies, and the like.

Can the two mix? Imagine a well-run, happy, and flourishing family. We know that it must have *some* structure; yet surely, any attempt to impose a predominantly modal structure upon that family would dramatically change its character, or even destroy it. Can membership in a family be reduced to adherence to a set of rules? Can a family survive the rigidity of corporate structures, the heavy hand of bureaucracy? Could such a company of people still be called, in any meaningful sense, a *"family"*?

Therefore, I argue that the local church should cling to the following principles –

LIBERTY

Since the very beginning, ecclesiastical leaders have been scandalised by the quality of freedom that is inherent in the gospel, and have sought, if not to eradicate, at least to restrain it. Paul fought furiously against this trend. Although he recognised the potential for abuse that always resides in liberty (*"shall we sin more, so that grace may abound?"* Ro 6:1)), still he refused to surrender one iota of it (*"stand fast in the freedom for which Christ has made you free"* (Ga 5:1)).

In the main, however, church leaders do not trust, and never have trusted, the people of God; nor do denominations trust their pastors. Hence the authorities feel impelled to set their dogmas in concrete, and to regulate firmly the lives and choices of both the sheep and their shepherds, making ever more rules to cover every imaginable contingency and every possible abuse. The end result is a stifling conformity, far removed from the sometimes chaotic but always sparkling life that marks God's creation worldwide.

GOD ACCEPTS RISK

The gospel shows how much risk the Lord is willing to take of his grace being abused. He refuses to tie a ball and chain of regulation around the souls of his children. He trusts us, in the end, to get it right, so long as we remain in fellowship with him, and are led by the Spirit. And if we fail to do so? Then the Father tolerates our follies, seldom intervenes, and calmly continues to ensure that his ultimate purpose is done - if not by me, then by another. If God is not afraid of freedom, being willing to accept its pains for the sake of its benefits, why do we fear it so?

It is difficult for me to see on what *biblical* or *spiritual* grounds I should yield authority over my ministry (and even less over my life) to an *elected* or even *appointed* executive. At least some members of most church councils hold office by default, simply because no one else wants the job. Seldom does the membership of various ruling bodies embrace only the most biblically informed, the most mature, the most spiritually capable, the wisest, or the best choices from among the adherents of the church.

Further, why should anyone put themselves without scruple under the authority of an executive whose membership (say) three years hence, may be quite unknown to them? How can they say *today* that an anonymous group *tomorrow* will hold the right to judge their morals, their doctrines, their ethics, their ministry practice? I think that we should yield to an *elected* body no more *spiritual* authority than it reasonably and/or biblically deserves.

Plainly, the leaders of a local church do have a measure of spiritual authority over its members. Paul too expected the churches he founded would respect his rule (Ac 20:28; Ph 2:12; 1 Ti 5:17; He 13:17; etc). Nonetheless, no one in the church can rightfully claim absolute rule over anyone, for we are each members of God's royal priesthood and must finally answer only to our own consciences (1 Jn 2:27). Then, too, Titus was given authority over a group of churches (Tit 1:5), and we should still respect such regional authorities. But again, their rule is not, and cannot be absolute. No one has any right to coerce any believer into actions or beliefs that he or she finds unacceptable, unbiblical, or contrary to a reasonable sense of the will of God.

CORPORALITY

The church should be *corporeal* not *institutional*. Therefore we should resist the pressures toward institutional conformity that come both from within the local church, and from denominational authorities. Those pressures can lead to two errors, which are often observed -

- the leaders of the church become *maintainers of the institution* instead of *proclaimers of the faith;* and

- the scramble for statistical success undermines the importance of sound doctrine and godly character.

Doctrinal *diversity* should be respected; but of course doctrinal *heresy* cannot be allowed, nor ungodly conduct. Both faults must be disciplined, whatever that might cost in empty chairs. [26]

So we need a strong proclamation of Christ, matched by a humble recognition that our knowledge of the gospel is less than perfect; *therefore we also need <u>organisational openness</u>*, so that we may learn from others more of the beauty of Christ. But institutions are often innately blind; they have too much privilege and status to defend to allow any admission of error; they prefer organisational tightness rather than dynamic freedom and openness.

AUTONOMY

Here we come to a matter upon which sincere people have diverse opinions: should the local church be autonomous, and if so, how far does that autonomy extend?

Some argue that each local church is a complete unit and should function with complete autonomy, even to the point of ordaining its own pastors, and that no authority outside the local church has any right to interfere with it. Others argue that each local church must be in communion with other churches of like mind, and that the company of churches must be under the authority of a "bishop" or some organisational equivalent to a bishop.

Another way to express the argument, is to ask whether each congregation possesses complete authority within itself, or should there be other levels of authority, at regional, state, and even national levels. That is, how much central control should there be over the group of churches within a particular fellowship or denomination?

Still another way to approach the matter is to ask, "Which model should the church follow: one that is *bureaucratic* or *theocratic*?"

---

(26) Except that in the case of heresy, be wary of denouncing as heretical something that the Bible leaves open to diverse interpretations, or something that is merely a matter of opinion, where one person's notion may be as valid as another's.

This study is not the place to open up a wide-ranging discussion of the issue; instead, I want to express the problem in a special way, as something to think about, using Israel as an example.

Under the judges, culminating in Samuel, Israel functioned as a theocracy, that is, a people whose ruler was Yahweh. Samuel represents a **theocratic, de-centralised**, and **minimalist** approach to authority. For more than 20 years the nation flourished under Samuel's guidance (1 Sa 7), enjoying a great spiritual renewal, and prospering politically and commercially; it was a fine demonstration of how well the theocracy could work.

However, the people became discontented, and they began to demand a king (1 Sa 8:1-5). The ostensible reason was the failure of Samuel's sons to follow their father's example, but the real reason was their desire *"to be like all the other nations"* – which was a pathway to inevitable ruin (Ex 23:23-24; Le 18:1-4; De 4:5-8; 18:9-14; etc).

After being instructed by God to do so, Samuel yielded to their demands, but warned that they were changing one set of problems for another far worse (1 Sa 8:10-18; and cp. De 17:14-20). For his part, the Lord agreed to delegate his authority to a king and to work through that monarch. This partnership with God enabled some of the kings to achieve such great things that they became worthy types of the King of kings (e.g. David).

But the earthly monarchy still remained less than God's ideal, which was always toward a true theocracy in which he himself was the sole monarch.

From that time on there remained a tension in Israel between *(a)* a prophetic, vocational leadership, and *(b)* a civil authority linked with a dynastic monarchy. That tension was never resolved. The question was asked but never finally answered: which is better, a pure theocracy expressed through a prophetic voice; or a modified theocracy expressed through a king? Both had their *perils* (note the last verse of *Judges*, but also note the corrupt lives of many of the kings); both had their *benefits*. Hence one of the main dangers that has beset all human authority across the centuries, is the corrupting influence of power, which leads the ruler(s) to usurp the governance of God, so that the people of God are no longer free to obey him, even if his voice can still be heard.

THEOCRACY OR BUREAUCRACY?

There was never any doubt that the *divine* preference lay with a full theocracy; but at the national level there remained a constant ambivalence, which sometimes descended into fierce conflict between prophetic and dynastic authority. Thus even the story of Samuel veers between disapproval and approval of the monarchy: *disapproval* (1 Sa 8); *approval* (1 Sa 9; 10:1-16); *disapproval* (1 Sa 10:17-27); and so on.

Even the story of the ideal theocratic king, David, displays the gradual abandonment of a minimalist, prophetic quality in the monarchy. Increasingly David's reign took on the character of a sedentary bureaucracy (with its sorry aftermath in the seduction of Bathsheba and the murder of her husband, 2 Sa 12:10). Significantly, it was the **prophet** Nathan who was sent by God to expose the king's sin and to pronounce judgment upon him. Note, too, Joab's protest against the census (2 Sa 24:3), which was a sign of the growing complexity of the civil administration and its lessening reliance on the rulership of Yahweh.

That ongoing tension between the prophet and the prince is exemplified in the writings of the prophets, who often rebuked the prince along with his allies in the priesthood. The oracles of the prophets kept before the people the divine ideal of an absolute theocracy, where God himself is the sole King. Think, for example, about Isaiah's denunciations of the temple rituals and sabbaths (Is 1:10-15), which would hardly have endeared him to the priests! This conflict is subtly shown by the differences between *Kings* and *Chronicles*, where the former mostly reflects the prophetic viewpoint, while the latter echoes more the voice of the temple, speaking for the priesthood and the royal family.

The point of this discussion is that the experience of the church parallels that of Israel: we face the same choice they did, between a *theocracy* or a *bureaucracy*. The crossover from one to the other occurred early in church history, for by the middle of the second century rule by apostles and prophets was being replaced by a monarchical episcopacy. And the process continues in our time:

movements that begin in revival, headed by charismatic leaders, within a few decades seem always to move toward an ever more centralised bureaucratic control. They do so mostly for the same reason that motivated ancient Israel and later the church Fathers: they feel unsafe under the rule of an invisible Sovereign, and wish for the apparent safety of a visible governor.

Is that a wrong choice? Note the following –

FREEDOM OR REGULATION?

In its introduction to the book of *Numbers* the NRSV says: "These narratives do not idealise the wilderness period. Again and again the people complained, sensing the contrast between the relative security of slavery in Egypt and the precarious insecurity of freedom in the wilderness." The same tension occurs (as I have already mentioned) in the writings of Paul (notably *Romans* and *Galatians*), where the apostle insists that we should *"stand fast in the liberty for which Christ has made us free"*, while the people always preferred to lapse back into the "bondage" of legalism – that is, a life based upon rules and upon established authority structures.

Sadly, the stunning freedom offered in the gospel has always been scandalous, and as frightening, to the leaders of the churches as it has been to the people themselves; so from the very beginning both pulpit and pew have preferred to establish comfortable norms to protect themselves from all risk of aberrant behaviour. There is always the feeling that God cannot really be trusted to care for his church, and that we ourselves must provide adequate safeguards, which we do by erecting an ever more complex hierarchy of bureaucrats, rules, regulations, standards, levels of ordination, canon law, and the like.

Hence across the centuries there has been a continuous quarrel between those who argue

- that loyalty to the gospel principle of liberty demands the full autonomy of the local church, and as little restriction as possible upon the freedom of choice enjoyed by each Christian; and those who argue

- that the leaders of the churches have both a divine mandate and an inescapable responsibility to maintain the safety and well-being not only of each local church but also of the collection of churches.

Which then is the correct view: that which tends toward a full theocracy; or that which tends toward a full monarchy?

There seems to be the same ambivalence in the NT as in the OT; that is, no clear guidance is provided as to who should have final authority in a local church, or among the company of churches, whether it should be the apostle/prophet, or the bishop. The quarrel between the two styles began in the early 2nd century, when church leadership was snatched out of the hands of apostles and prophets and grabbed by the bishops. The letters of Ignatius strongly exemplify this change, which was probably the most radical shift in the nature of the church that has ever happened. The dynamic and flexible sodalist style of the apostles and prophets changed into the static and rule-infested style of the bureaucratic episcopacy. Canon law overwhelmed *koinonia* (fellowship), and the church has never recovered from the blow.

In their formative years, new denominations tend to re-capture that early sodality, but in every case (so far in church history) they eventually move toward modality. Law begins to replace life; structure crushes spirit; dynamism becomes bureaucracy; freedom vanishes under a morass of form.

God seems to be willing to accommodate himself to this change, just as he was willing to accept Israel's demand for a king; and he is willing to work powerfully through the new leadership, just as he worked through Israel's better kings. What great things were wrought by many of Israel's kings, beginning with Saul himself! (1 Sa 14:47; 2 Sa 1:19,23-24) Indeed, it could be argued that such triumphs could not have been achieved without a monarch's leadership. Nonetheless the price paid by the nation was appalling, for their kings, who had led them to splendour, also carried them down into ruin, which always seems to be the eventual outcome of an abandonment of the theocratic principle, whether in the nation or in the church.

In the case of the church, then, it seems that we can say three things –

- God has provided (or is willing to provide) the church with enough charismatic leadership to enable it to function as Israel did during Samuel's prime; that is, to flourish under a theocratic, decentralised, minimalist authority.
- Such a regime can be sustained successfully only in an environment of genuine spiritual renewal, strong faith in God, and unwavering trust in the efficacy of the divine government.
- Because the people of God are frequently unable to maintain such a high level of spiritual maturity they begin to demand a modified theocracy, in which the invisible rule of God from heaven is represented by a visible ruler on earth. The end result is certain: authority becomes increasingly located in some central council or bureaucracy. Scripture seems to accept, with reluctance, that this change may be, if not desirable, at least inevitable.

I once addressed our denominational executive (in vain, I might add) on this matter, and told them the fable of the *Arab and the Camel's Nose* –

> One very cold night a Camel looked into the tent where his master was lying and said: "Kind master, will you not let me put my head inside the door? For the wind blows very chill tonight."
>
> "Well, I suppose you may," said the Arab. "There is plenty of room."
>
> So the Camel moved forward and stretched his head into the tent. "Ah!" he said, "this is what I call comfort."
>
> In a little while he called to his master again. "Now if I could only warm my neck also."
>
> "Then put your neck inside," said his master, kindly. "You will not be in my way."
>
> The Camel did so, and for a time was very well contented. Then, looking around, he said: "If I could only put my

forelegs inside I would feel a great deal better and be able to run better tomorrow."

His master moved a little and said: "You may put your forelegs and shoulders inside, for I know that the wind blows cold to-night."

The Camel had hardly planted his forefeet within the tent when he spoke again: "Master," he said, "I keep the tent open by standing here. I think I ought to go wholly within, otherwise I will freeze and be of no use to you tomorrow."

"Yes, come in," said the Man. "There is hardly room for us both, but I do not want to keep you out in the cold, for perhaps you will then not be able to carry your load in the morning."

So the Camel crowded into the tent. But he was no sooner inside than he said: "You were right when you said there was hardly room for us both. I think it would be better for you to stand outside and so give me a chance to turn round and lie down."

Then, without more ado, he rudely pushed the Man out at the door, and took the whole tent for himself.

Once let the nose of bureaucracy into your tent, and in time the whole camel will occupy every space, all in the name of efficiency and productivity. Yet I don't know what the alternative may be, except to abandon corporate perfection and be content to remain more or less chaotic – rather like a family, in fact, instead of a business. But then we would have to abandon accreditation, respectability, and organisational competence.

Yet one cannot help wistfully yearning that God alone might be King!

KOINONIA

Let us now come back to the word Paul used in our text (Ga 2:9), when he said that he had been extended the *right hand of fellowship"* (Greek: *koinonia*). The early church was both renowned and reviled for the loving fellowship that so much separated them from their ungodly neighbours –

> It is mainly because of our godly and loving deeds that so many put a brand upon us. "See," they say, "how much these Christians love one another," for they themselves are animated by mutual hatred. And they say, "How these Christians are ready even to die for one another," for they themselves will sooner put others to death. And they are angry with us, too, because we call each other *'brethren'*; for no other reason, as I think, than because among themselves names of consanguinity are assumed in mere pretence of affection." (27)

Thus, in the third century, Tertullian described the scornful mockery heaped upon the church by people who despised Christians for the love they showed toward each other. The pagans saw it as a sign of effeminacy and weakness. Yet in the end, that same love conquered the empire, so that before another century had passed, the emperor himself (Constantine the Great) had embraced the gospel!

Nowhere is this quality of love more strongly shown than in the 6 injunctions to *"greet each other with a holy and loving kiss!"* –

> *Greet each other with a holy kiss* (Ro 16:16; 1 Co 16:20; 2 Co 13:12) ... *Greet every saint in Christ Jesus with a kiss* (Ph 4:21) ... *Greet all the brethren with a holy kiss* (1 Th 5:26) ... *Greet all the believers with the kiss of love* (1 Pe 5:14).

The early church quickly embraced this command and commonly shared the kiss immediately after the eucharist. The kiss demonstrated their genuine fondness and care for each other, their *koinonia*. It marked their triumph over pagan passions. It reflected the beauty of Jesus within each believer.

An example of this early sodality can be seen in Acts 2:44-46a, and 4:34-35. But make sure to note that the verbs are in the imperfect

---

(27) Tertullian was a Christian apologist and lawyer (c. 155-c. 240 AD), in his *Apology 39*.

tense: *"they used to sell ... they used to divide ..."* In other words, this community sharing was a temporary, not a permanent practice in the early church. Today the action may be changed, but not the principle; we do not have to follow their example of selling, but we do have to follow their practice of fellowship. If we are truly Christian then we will have a genuine concern for each other, being aware of each other's needs, and willing to offer whatever assistance we can, even to the point of personal sacrifice.

Chapter Seven

JUSTIFIED

> *We know that a person is not **justified** by works of the law but through faith in Jesus Christ, so we also have believed in Christ Jesus, in order to be **justified** by faith in Christ and not by works of the law, because by works of the law no one will be **justified**. ... (We are) **justified** in Christ ... Now it is evident that no one is **justified** before God by the law, for "The righteous shall live by faith" ... Christ came so that we might be **justified** by faith ... If you seek to be **justified** by the law, you have fallen away from grace!"* [28] (Ga 2:16, 17; 3:11, 24; 5:4)

Here is another word – *"justified"* – that occurs seven times in this letter, marking the perfection of the ideas Paul shares here. *"Justification"* is a legal term. It is used in the NT (especially by Paul) to offer what is called a *forensic* explanation of the salvation God has given us in Christ. This is in contrast, say, to the *sacerdotal* (priestly) explanation given in the letter to the Hebrews; or to the *regenerative* explanation given in the writings of John. In other words, the writer of Hebrews explains salvation as something achieved by a *priestly sacrifice* at God's altar; John explains it in terms of a *new birth*; but Paul (when he uses the expression *justification*) thinks of salvation as an act of *acquittal* in a court of law, an acquittal that comes to us solely in response to faith – see *Romans 1:17; 3:28; 5:1; Galatians 2:16; 3:11, 24; Hebrews 10:38*.

---

(28) Some of the paragraphs in this chapter closely resemble parts of the more extensive discussion on *Justification* found in my book Great Words of the Gospel (Vision Publishing, Ramona CA). Mostly, though, this chapter differs from that.

AN ACT OF ACQUITTAL

In all three languages (Hebrew, Greek, and English) a "justified" man is one who has stood in the dock for sentencing, but has been pronounced innocent, and therefore released from the charges that were laid against him.

Notice something very important: *a legal sentence is not an act of power, but simply a verbal declaration*; hence it has four vital limitations –

ACQUITTAL REQUIRES ONLY LEGAL INNOCENCE

You must have noticed how our law courts sometimes condemn innocent people and acquit guilty ones. That is because, in practice, the law does not deal with the *factual* guilt or innocence of an accused person, but rather seeks only to discover whether his innocence or guilt can be *judicially* established. It is, of course, hoped that the *judicial* decision will match, not just the law, but the actual truth of the case. But in the, end, whatever the true facts may be, the legal judgment (which may be based upon false evidence, or a failure to grasp the truth) will prevail.

Thus acquittal in a court of law does not really depend upon the actual innocence of a person who is on trial, but rather upon the failure of the prosecutor to prove any case against that person. Consequently, the accused is pronounced *legally* innocent, and is discharged from the court free, and without penalty. He may in fact be guilty. His crime may be hideous. The judge, the lawyers, the jury, the spectators, may all *know* that his hands are crimson with the blood of his victim. But if his guilt cannot be established by lawful means the judge has no choice except to declare him innocent and to dismiss the case.

In the same way, God knows (and you know) that you are guilty of offending heaven's law, and the Lord makes no attempt to change that. Instead, he has found a way in Christ to declare you *legally innocent*. You are a sinner; nonetheless God justifies you in Christ, and you may walk away from his court free of any charge.

So remember: your justification in no way depends upon you establishing in the sight of God any kind of past, present, or future innocence. In Christ you are reckoned acquitted of all sin, and free of all penalty. The sentence of full and free dismissal has been passed in your favour in the court of heaven.

That leads on to the second vital limitation: your justification is

NOT DEPENDENT UPON MORAL CHANGE

A sentence spoken by a judge has no power to effect any change in a person's *character;* it changes only his *legal standing* within the community. No *moral* work is done in him or her. The relationship of the accused to the law simply changes from a state of suspicion to one of acquittal. Whereas the person once stood accused, now he is reckoned innocent; but morally he is still the same person.

Likewise, our justification is an act of *declaration*, not an act of *power*. It is a work of God external to the sinner, not something accomplished within his or her nature. It has to do with a change in God's attitude toward us and a change in our relationship to his law. Whereas we once lay under the wrath of God, now, being justified, we are admitted to his favour, cleared of all the charges that were previously laid against us.

Therefore we must reject any demand that a moral change must occur solely because we are fully justified in Christ. There are some who do endeavour to attach a moral sense to justification; that is, they view it as arising from, or at least incorporating, an act of divine power within the believer's own life. They associate a transforming work of grace with justification that makes the believer holy. This is a sad error even though in a little while I will be stating vigorously that true justification should lead on to a sanctified and obedient life. But those changes are not a *fruit* of justification, nor a *basis* for it, nor even an integral *part* of it. Holiness arises rather from the processes of sanctification that should occur as the next stage (after justification) in the believer's life.

So rid yourself of the idea that you cannot claim to be justified unless a moral change has happened in your behaviour. Especially, discard the notion that before you can declare yourself justified before God, you must effect a moral change in yourself by your own effort. Remind yourself always that your justification arises from a word God has spoken about you in heaven, not from a work God has done in you on earth.

The third limitation is this –

JUSTIFICATION IS A STRICTLY FORENSIC TERM

The constant meaning of *"justify"* (and other parallel words) in both Old and New Testaments, enforces the idea that it belongs without any moral sense in a strictly forensic setting. If justification contains anything more than a simple legal significance, then it differs in no material way from sanctification, and many biblical statements become meaningless. This can be seen in the following –

- In many places a strictly forensic sense is the only possible meaning of justify – to give the word a moral sense makes the statements ridiculous: De 25:1 Pr 17:15; Is 5:23; 53:11; Ro 3:20; 4:5,8; Ga 3:11; 5:4.
- The word *"condemnation"* is often used in antithesis to justification; but since condemning a man does not in itself make him wicked, neither does justifying him in itself make him righteous.
- Both terms express only a person's standing in the eyes of the law – in addition to some of the above references, see Ro 8:33-34; Ge 18:25.
- Expressions equivalent to *"justification"* clearly carry only a legal sense: see Ge 15:6; Ps 32:1-2; Ro 4:6-7; 2 Co 5:19; Ja 2:23.

A moving example of the transfer of guilt and innocence from one to another is found in *Philemon* (see vs. 17-18) –

- Onesimus had greatly wronged his master, Philemon; but Onesimus was Paul's friend,
- so the apostle asks that all *his* good qualities should be accepted as belonging to the slave; that is, Philemon should receive Onesimus as he would do Paul himself.
- In turn, Paul offers to take all the slave's guilt upon himself, and to discharge any wrong that may have been done to Philemon.

- Paul's innocence was to be given to Onesimus, and the guilt of Onesimus was to be charged against Paul. Neither Paul nor Onesimus experienced any inner change in this transaction; the change was only in the relationship of the slave to his master. So it is too between us and God.

So, we can state the meaning of justification as simply to set a person into a legally correct relationship either to the law or to another person. For us, this means the law of God and God himself. In the case of a person who is actually free from guilt, justification involves only a vindication of his or her innocence. But where there has been actual wrongdoing, as in our case, justification can be achieved only by some means that fully expiates that guilt. God has found that means in Christ.

Our position can therefore be summarised –

Although we are guilty and deserve punishment, God, in a legal and just response to the atonement Christ has made, clears us from all guilt, and calls us fully innocent in the sight of his law.

Thus, though your guilt may be _factually_ undeniable, your innocence is _legally_ undeniable. God must therefore deal with you as though you had never sinned.

Does this justification then mean that you can be content to remain guilty in fact and only innocent in law? Of course not! As I have said above, this change in *legal* relationship is emphatically intended by God to lead us into a change of *life* relationship. Justification does not in itself cause any moral change or inner transformation, but it does pave the way for such a change to be wrought later by the Holy Spirit.

Thus the outward imputation of *righteousness* in *justification* becomes the basis for an inward infusion of *holiness* in *sanctification*. So remember this – never base your claim of justification upon whether or not you have reformed morally, or upon whether or not you *feel* justified. Your justification does not depend upon any internal change, nor upon any *feeling*, whether wrought by you or by God; it is a wholly legal matter, based on the just acquittal God has secured for you in Christ.

That leads to a fourth limitation – your justification depends on

A HEAVENLY WORD, NOT AN EARTHLY WORK

I have already stated this: but do mark it again. Here is the single greatest thing you can understand about justification: it results from a *word* already spoken in heaven, not from an *act* being performed on earth. The entire transaction is a *heavenly* not an *earthly* one, based solely upon the merits of Christ and his substitutionary death on your behalf. Seeing the cross, and the victory over sin Christ gained there, the Father has spoken in heaven the sentence of acquittal for all who believe in Jesus.

If justification depended upon some ongoing work of mine on earth, then a thousand misadventures could undermine it. Happily, I know it is not my *work* but the Father's *word* that justifies; he has given me a verdict of acquittal entirely because of what Christ has done for me and, of course, for all who believe.

The cross is rooted in history, and cannot be changed; the justifying sentence is recorded in heaven, far beyond the interfering reach of men or demons.

So upon those unassailable guarantees I base my claim of innocence in Christ; which means that you and I are left with no other choice except to believe or reject the word the Father has spoken. Upon that simple choice our eternal destiny hangs.

Does that mean there are no earthly ramifications to justification? Of course not! It is expected of people who walk out of a courtroom as free citizens that they will at once resume all the rights and benefits that are rightfully theirs. Which is just what you should do before God. Peace and joy, access to the throne of God, answered prayer, all God's promises, are lawfully yours in Christ and cannot be lawfully denied to you.

Have you heard the Judge pronounce that sweet word, "Justified!"? Then boldly claim all that belongs to you as a freeborn citizen of the kingdom of God!

THE BASIS OF OUR ACQUITTAL

Our acquittal is not an arbitrary act of judicial capriciousness, or favouritism, but is solidly based in lawful practice –

TWO LEGAL RULES

DESTRUCTION OF THE EVIDENCE

It is not uncommon in our courts for a case to be dismissed, either because of lack of evidence, or because a crucial piece of evidence has been lost, or a key witness is missing (see Ps 103:12; Is 44:22; Mi 7:18-20). Even better, see *Jeremiah 50:20!*

Doubt it not! Whatever evidence may once have spoken against us, proving us overwhelmingly guilty, was altogether destroyed when Jesus rose from the dead. The prosecutor has been left with no case to bring before the Judge. The sentence cannot be either delayed or revoked. It reads: *innocent of all charges*. We walk out of the court unchallenged, able to resume life as free citizens with no shadow over our name or honour. No right that belongs to us as citizens of the Kingdom of God can be denied.

SUBSTITUTION OF A VICTIM

Sometimes it happens in a court that an anonymous benefactor will pay the fine imposed by the judge upon a convicted person. Further, it is not unknown for one person to offer to go to prison, or even be put to death, in place of another. Rather like Sydney Carton who took the place on the guillotine of his friend Charles Darnay. The last line of *A Tale of Two Cities*, by Charles Dickens, quotes the final words of Carton, which are among the most famous in English literature – "It is a far, far better thing that I do than I have ever done; it is a far, far better rest that I go to than I have ever known."

There used to be a legal doctrine that prevented even a guilty person from being punished if another had already born the penalty (e.g. if an innocent man had been executed, the guilty person could not then be put to death; the law was forbidden to seek a double satisfaction.)

That rule may have been abandoned, or at least modified, in our modern courts; but it still obtains at the bar of heaven for all who have fully embraced Christ as Saviour.

THE RULE OF "DOUBLE JEOPARDY" APPLIES

A still-valid legal doctrine states: "A person cannot be tried a second time for an offence of which he has been acquitted at a previous trial." [29]

So once you have been dealt with at God's bar and have found acquittal through Christ, you can never again be prosecuted for sin. And note that the work of Christ embraces your future as well as your past, because your offence against God was not so much the individual sins you may have committed as it was the sin-nature within you. Your very life was an offence! But God has dealt with that life in Christ, so that now, as long as you cling steadfastly to him, you can be as sure of tomorrow as you are of today.

WE ARE TRIED BY OUR PEER

Ever since *Magna Carta*, British jurisprudence has been built around trial by a jury of "peers" as demanded in the following excerpts –

> [21] Earls and barons shall not be amerced [30] **except by their peers**, and only in accordance with the degree of the offence.

> [39] No free man shall be arrested or imprisoned or disseised [31] or outlawed or exiled or in any way victimised, neither will we attack him or send anyone to attack him, **except by the lawful judgment of his peers** or by the law of the land.

> [52] If anyone has been disseised of or kept out of his lands, castles, franchises or his right by us **without the legal judgment of his peers**, we will immediately restore them to him ... and if a dispute arises over this, then let it be decided by the judgment of the twenty-five

---

(29) The rule has been modified somewhat in modern jurisprudence, but it still generally applies. The main exception is when new and compelling evidence of guilt has been discovered and presented to the court.

(30) Amerced = liable for punishment.

(31) Disseised = wrongfully dispossessed.

barons who are mentioned below in the clause for securing the peace ...

[56] If we have disseised or kept out Welshmen from lands or liberties or other things **without the legal judgment of their peers** in England or in Wales, they shall be immediately restored to them; and if a dispute arises over this, then let it be decided ... **by the judgment of their peers.** (32)

Trial by one's peers means that if you were obliged to appear before a court of law, and face a jury, you could object to a jury of dukes, or illiterates, or soldiers, or foreigners, or against any company of jurors whom you could show were not truly your peers. (33)

In the spiritual world, you could rightly object to the unfairness of being judged by God, and even more of being judged by Satan. But no one has grounds to protest against the One whom God has appointed the Judge of every person – Christ! This is because Jesus is peer to every human being –

- The **poor** – *"Foxes have their holes, and birds have their nests; but the Son of man has nowhere to lay his head"* (Mt 8:20).
- The **rich** – *"He owns the cattle on a thousand hills"* (Ps 50:10).
- The **high-born** – *"He is the image of the invisible God, the firstborn of the entire creation"* (Cl 1:15).
- The **low-born** – *"Is not this the carpenter, the son of Mary"* (Mk 6:3).
- **Soldiers** – *"Do you think that I cannot appeal to my Father, and he will at once send me more than twelve legions of angels?"* (Mt 26:53)

---

(32) The emphasis in the segments above is mine.
(33) "Peers" in this context means a person who is of equal standing with you in the social group to which you belong.

- **Artisans** – *"By him all things were created, in heaven and on earth, visible and invisible ... — everything was made through him and for him."* (Cl 1:16).
- **Judges** – *"Christ Jesus will Judge both the living and the dead"* (2 Ti 4:1).
- **Physicians** *"Jesus cast out the spirits with a word and healed all who were sick."* (Mt 8:16).
- **Children** – *"Jesus went with his parents to Nazareth, where he remained submissive to them"* (Lu 2:51).
- **Scholars** – *"In Christ are hidden all the treasures of knowledge and wisdom"* (Cl 2:23).
- **Leaders** – *"Great crowds followed him"* (Mt 4:25).
- **Servants** – *"The Son of Man came not to be served but to serve"* (Mt 20:28).
- The **lonely** – *"I trod the winepress alone, no one came to help me ... I looked, but there was no one to help"* (Is 63:3-5).
- The **popular** – *"The crowd was pressing in on him to hear the word of God"* (Lu 5:1).
- The **tortured** – *"They stripped him and twisting together a crown of thorns, they put it on his head and put a reed in his right hand ...and they spat on him and took the reed and struck him on the head. And when they had mocked him they led him away to crucify him"* (Mt 27:28-31).
- **Everybody** – *"God sent forth his Son, born of woman, born under the law"* (Ga 4:4).

He endured and overcome the temptations that tested all of them, and indeed of all classes of men and women in every possible profession, trade, or craft (He 4:15). In fact, because of that identification with every person, Christ is the only one fit to judge any and all of us; yet, prior to the Last Day, he refuses to do so! –

> *Who can bring any charge against God's elect, for is it not God himself who justifies them? Who can condemn them? Christ Jesus is the one who died! More than that, he was raised from the dead and is now at the right hand of God, interceding for us.* (Ro 8:33-34)

So do not allow anyone to condemn you. Who made your accusers your judges? God alone is truly the offended party; but for Christ's sake he has resolved to acquit all who believe. So we stand secure, because

- Christ <u>died</u> for our <u>pardon</u>
- Christ was <u>raised</u> for our <u>victory</u>
- Christ is <u>enthroned</u> for our <u>righteousness</u>
- Christ <u>intercedes</u> for our <u>access</u> to God!

THREE SPECIAL CHANGES

While there are plainly some striking similarities between God's justice and man's, there are also some equally striking differences –

WHEN GOD FORGIVES, HE FORGETS

In human courts a bad record can pile up against you! But there is no court record in heaven, except the one word: *"Justified!"* So stop reminding yourself, and don't let the enemy remind you, of that which God swears he has forgotten! (He 8:12; 10:17)

INNOCENCE DEMANDS ADMISSION OF GUILT

God's court is the only one in the universe where the judge will find you innocent only after you have declared your guilt! (See 1 Jn 1:7-10; 2:1-2.) Indeed, we must identify ourselves with the Crucified One in his *death* before we can share in the fulness of his *life*. And how much we need to admit our guilt! –

> *What is any human being, that he should be innocent, or any child of woman, that he should be justified? If God puts no trust in his holy ones, and the heavens are not innocent in his sight, how much less so are human beings, who are loathsome and corrupt and lap up evil like water!* (Jb 15:14-16)

THE AGENT OF OUR JUSTIFICATION IS FAITH

Two things you should note in connection with this faith -

- It is a boldness of belief, based on the truth of God's word (1 Jn 5:9-11); and

- It is neither a virtue nor a source of virtue; it is simply the means that links us to Christ. Always and only it is Christ who justifies, not our faith.

So we end where we began – *"Christ came so that we might be **justified** by faith"* (Ga 3:24).

Chapter Eight

LIFE

> *I have been crucified with Christ. So it is no longer I who live, but Christ who lives in me. And the life I now live in the flesh I live by faith in the Son of God, who loved me and gave himself for me* (Ga 2:20).

Georgio Vasari (1511-1574) tells a story about the Italian Renaissance artist Jacopo Pontormo, who upon seeing a self-portrait done by a vain fellow artist decided that it was a poor likeness. So Jacopo took up a brush and set to work on the picture. His changes were so successful that all who saw the transformed picture exclaimed that it seemed like a living person rather than a mere portrait. [34]

Thus, in our vanity, we too labour vainly to reach our own true likeness, but cannot hope to succeed without the touch of the Master Artist, Christ. That is the powerful idea expressed in our text. It is an important key to enjoying a limitless life in Christ! Indeed it goes a long way toward solving one of the most perplexing problems Christians face: *just how should we live as Christians?* Paul's solution requires us to take certain steps to actuate the new life God has given us in Christ. We can reduce them to two major propositions: <u>*capture the right identity*</u>; and <u>*make the right confession*</u> –

CAPTURE THE RIGHT IDENTITY

"It is no longer I who live, but Christ who lives in me!"

---

[34] <u>Lives of the Artists</u>, tr. by George Bull; The Folio Society, London, 1993; in three volumes; Vol. Three, "The Life of Jacopo Pontormo;" pg. 49. A number of Pontormo's splendid portraits still survive, along with other great works of his, among which the finest is probably an altar-piece in the chapel of St Felicita, in Florence.

From the earliest days of the French Foreign Legion (founded in 1831), it was understood that once a man joined the Legion he lost all identity except that of a Legionnaire. The doctrine was established in the first fortress built by the Legion in Algeria, when a soldier was sent to prison for calling a comrade a "dirty stinking swine of a German". The Colonel is said to have told the offender, in front of the entire regiment, "You are right to call him a dirty stinking swine, because he stinks, he is dirty, and he is a swine. You have no right to call a Legionnaire a German. Thirty days solitary." [35]

So too, have we been given a new identity – we are God's new creation in Christ, warriors now in the Legion of God, the Lord of Hosts! Therefore, all successful Christian life begins with a bold affirmation of the truth that

CHRIST IS IN ME!

Just before the Second World War, Julius Streicher, a senior member of the Nazi Party, addressed the German Academy of Education in Munich and said: "It is only on one or two exceptional points that Christ and Hitler stand comparison, for Hitler is too big a man to be compared with one so petty." [36]

His speech received a standing ovation from the presumably cultured audience of academics. Mr Streicher, of course, was thinking about Jesus only as the Man of Galilee, ignoring his resurrection, ascension, and enthronement. Yet even as a man, Jesus possessed a greatness that reduces every other mortal to a midget.

Then again, far beyond the humanity of Jesus there is his deity, and this fact remains: Hitler is dead and facing Judgment, while Christ is alive and reigns in Heaven! And of no one else has a

---

(35) International History Magazine #6; Editions Horizons, June 1973; article "Vive la Morte", by Pierre Martin; pg. 15.

(36) I have lost the source of this anecdote.

statement like this ever been made: *"Christ lives in me!"* (Ga 2:20) But what that means depends upon

- the **sense** in which Christ is **in** every believer; and upon
- the **identity** of this Christ who is in me –

THE IDENTITY OF CHRIST

If Jesus were but an ordinary (albeit sinless) man, then perhaps I can receive nothing more from him than was imparted to me by my earthly father, of whom I could also say, in a sense, that he *"lives in me"*.

But see who this Man truly *is!* – *Colossians* 1:15-20; *Hebrews* 1:3; *Revelation* 1:12-13; 19:11-16). And this is the Redeemer who lives in you and in me, simply because we have believed the gospel and have gained the pardon of God!

OUR UNION WITH CHRIST

With this Saviour you and I have come into union by faith, but this is much more than the kind of union, say, that a married couple enjoy. In this union with Christ there is –

- an impartation of **<u>all that Christ is</u>** –

Christ is in you, the hope of glory ... in him all the fulness of the Deity dwells bodily, and in him you too are filled with him, who is the head of all principality and power (Cl 1:27; 2:9, 10).

And in our union with Christ there is also –

- access to **<u>all that Christ has</u>**

Blessed be the God and Father of our Lord Jesus Christ, who has blessed us with every spiritual blessing in the heavenly places in Christ. (Ep 1:3)

"Spiritual blessing" should not be construed as applying only to ethereal bounties that are immaterial and angelic. No, they include every promise that is in the gospel of Christ – full pardon, bodily healing, daily victory, answered prayer, the supply of life's necessities (Mt 6:11; Ph 4:19); and a multitude of other good things; along with all that belongs to us in the supernal dimension.

Of course, none of this will happen independent of personal faith – that is, trust in the promise of God and a firm expectation of its fulfilment. This work of faith results from the reality that Christ is alive in every believer, and it brings us into full union with his endless life. Our appropriation of that life by faith then becomes God's answer to the problem of sin, and not just to sin, but to sickness and defeat as well –.

SIN

HOW TO OVERCOME SIN?

The old idea was one of passive dependence upon divine rescue, as in the hymn *Yield Not to Temptation* –

> Yield not to temptation . . .
> Ask the Saviour to help you,
> Comfort, strengthen, and keep you,
> He is willing to aid you,
> He will carry you through.
>
> – H. R. Palmer

But God has **already** acted in Christ, and done the best that even heaven can do to open the way to full victory over all sin, by bringing us into union with Christ through faith. What we need now is a **revelation** of the indwelling Christ. That is, give yourself no rest until you truly *know*, inwardly, dynamically, powerfully, passionately that you are *now* crucified and risen with Christ, and brought into union with him by faith. Change your thinking about your identity! If Christ is in me, how can sin prevail over me, or Satan defeat me, or death conquer me, or hell welcome me?

Sir Thomas Malory, in *Le Morte d'Arthur* (1469-1470), tells how the wizard Merlin, early in the reign of King Arthur, came to him and said –

> "Sir, see that ye keep well the scabbard of Excalibur, for ye shall lose no blood while ye have the scabbard upon you, though ye have as many wounds upon you as ye may have." But later, in great trust Arthur gave the scabbard to Morgan le Fay his sister. She loved another knight better than ... King Arthur, and she wished to have her brother Arthur slain. Therefore by enchantment she had

another scabbard made for Excalibur, just like the first, and she gave the real scabbard for Excalibur to her lover ... who later nearly slew King Arthur. (37)

Our "Excalibur" is the Word of God, housed in the scabbard of Faith. Don't give it away! Keep the sword and the scabbard so tightly entwined that they can never be separated. Stand with firm faith *in* the promise, so that you may stand firmly in faith *on* the promise! It will then be for you as Merlin promised Arthur – no matter how many wounds you receive in the battle, you will not, cannot, finally fall!

SICKNESS

Can you visualise the life of Christ at work in you? Unfortunately, we usually find it easier to imagine evil than good; but cp. *2 Corinthians 10:4-5* –

> *The weapons of our warfare are not man-made; rather, they are mighty in God to overthrow strongholds, banish imaginations, and to destroy every lofty idea that tries to exalt itself against the knowledge of God. Use those weapons to bring every thought into captivity and to make them obedient to Christ!*

Doubt, as Tennyson said, is perhaps inevitable, and may even be useful to stir faith; but in the end we must discard our doubts and fears, and allow them to be replaced by absolute confidence in the truth of God's promise –

> It is man's privilege to doubt,
> If so be that from doubt at length
> Truth may stand forth unmoved of change,
> An image with profulgent (38) brows
> And perfect limbs, as from the storm
> Of running fires and fluid range
> Of lawless airs, at last stood out

---

(37) Part One, Chapter Two, Sec. 11.
(38) Radiant.

> This excellence and solid form
> Of constant beauty. (39)

SUCCESS

The wisdom and mind of Christ are yours! Success in whatever the Father has appointed for you should therefore be assured. But there will be no triumph unless we fully yield to the life of Jesus, and also show boldness, and courage.

According to Sir Thomas Malory, in order to fulfil a knightly quest, and to aid a fair damsel, Sir Lancelot, the greatest of the Knights of the Round Table, had first to find and enter the *Chapel Perilous*, retrieve a magic sword, and overcome many dangers –

> Right so Sir Lancelot departed, and when he came to the *Chapel Perilous* he alighted and tied his horse to a little gate. As soon as he was within the churchyard he saw on the front of the Chapel many fair rich shields turned upside-down, and many of these shields Sir Lancelot had seen knights bear beforehand. With that, he saw standing by him there thirty huge knights, taller by a yard than any man that he had ever seen; they all grimaced and gnashed at Sir Lancelot. When he saw their countenances, he was sorely afraid; so he put his shield before him and took his sword in his hand, ready for battle. The knights were all armed in black armour, ready with their shields and their drawn swords. As Sir Lancelot would have gone through them, they scattered on every side of him and gave him the way. Therewith he waxed all bold and entered into the Chapel ... Then he saw a fair sword lying (there), and he got it in his hand and hurried out of the Chapel. ...
>
> (Beyond) the Chapel-yard a fair damosel met him and said, "Sir Lancelot, leave that sword behind thee or thou wilt die for it."

---

(39) Alfred, Lord Tennyson, <u>Supposed Confessions</u> (1830); lines 142-150. He describes truth emerging from troubled doubt as the beautiful earth emerged from its fiery and chaotic birth.

"I will not leave it," said Sir Lancelot, "for any threats." ...

"Now, gentle knight," said the damosel, "I require thee to kiss me but once."

"Nay," said Sir Lancelot, "the God forbid."

"Well, sir," said she, "if thou had kissed me thy life-days had been done!"

So Lancelot, having once again challenged and scattered the thirty black knights, escaped, and by use of the magic sword restored life and health to a dying friend, and made his way safely back to Camelot. [40] Think about that story and you will see there a useful parable of how we too should behave.

The second important proposition I want to pull out of our text is this –

MAKE THE RIGHT CONFESSION

The life I now live in the flesh I live by faith in the Son of God, who loved me and gave himself for me. (Ga 2:20)

How emphatic! How brave! How sure! Paul makes his bold declaration with absolute certainty, never for a moment doubting its unshakable truth! Our faith-confession should be the same. But on this matter of speaking out your faith, consider this –

AVOID EXTREMES

Because of some extreme ideas, the concept of holding to a positive confession has fallen into disrepute. But, despite human misuse, God's principles remain unchanged, and they are exemplified by Paul in our text. There are three essentials –

- **_perceive_** with your spirit that Christ is indeed alive in you by faith; then
- **_imagine_** with your mind his splendid victory over sin, death, Satan, through his mighty work at Calvary and by his glorious resurrection; and then

---

(40) Le Morte D'Arthur, Part Three, "Sir Lancelot du Lake," Sec. 15.

- ***confess*** with your mouth the reality of the promise and its sure fulfilment in your life!

BOLD CONFESSION

Making a proper and bold confession of your faith means that you should –

- ***Speak against Satan***, just as Subha did when (in 59 A.D.) he saw an opportunity, unseated the true king, and seized the throne of Ceylon –

  (The king) came to his end by his fondness for practical jokes. The palace doorkeeper, a man by the name of Subha, bore a remarkable likeness to the king, who frequently would change places with him and don his functionary's clothing in order to amuse himself at the sight of his ministers bowing down to a mere doorkeeper. But one day, when the real king was convulsed with laughter, Subha ordered that he be put to death for his lack of respect for the throne. The execution was carried out immediately, and Subha established his hold upon the throne and ruled well until his death. [41]

In the name of Jesus you too can usurp the mocker, and claim the throne that in fact rightly belongs to you in Christ. *"Resist the devil and he will flee from you!"* (Ja 4:7).

- ***Speak to Yourself*** – rebuking every doubt, fear, or anxiety, affirming all that scripture says about you in Christ, that you are in him already more than a conqueror, blessed with every spiritual blessing, and well able to do and to be all that the Lord has commanded you and spoken of you.
- ***Speak before the Father*** – his word and his promise, and your expectation that he will never leave you nor forsake you but will fulfil all that he has undertaken to do.

---

(41)   International History Magazine, # 13, pg. 23.

Thus, by establishing your _proper identity_ and by making a _proper confession_, you will assuredly discover abundant life in Christ, and you will shout with Paul, *"I live! Yet it is not I, but Christ who lives in me!"* (Ga 2:20)

Chapter Nine

WHIPPING

> *O foolish Galatians! Who has bewitched you? Was it not before your very eyes that Jesus Christ was publicly portrayed as crucified?* (Ga 3:1)

Ham House, in London, was built in 1610. It is said to be "unique in Europe as the most complete survival of 17th century fashion and power." It is also reputed to be the most haunted mansion in Great Britain! Many visitors say they have seen the ghost of Elizabeth, the 17th century Duchess of Lauderdale, and her dog!

I mention Ham House and the duchess because she was the eldest daughter of one, William Murray, who was the **whipping boy** for the prince who became King Charles I of England, Scotland, and Ireland. Charles was deeply committed to the principle of the *divine right of kings*, proclaimed by his father, James I, in a speech made to the English Parliament in 1609 –

> The state of monarchy is the supremest thing upon earth; for kings are not only God's lieutenants upon earth, and sit upon God's throne, but even by God himself they are called gods" (Ps 138:1; 82:1, 6).

He was partly right, but only partly, because *all* God's people are called "gods" by Christ! (Jn 10:34, quoting Ps 138). So James was a little narrow in his perspective. Nonetheless, he did give force to the doctrine of "the Divine Right of the King", and it led people to suppose that a king should not be touched. Hence it became unthinkable that a young prince should be flogged by his tutor. So a "whipping boy" was appointed to take his punishment. [42]

This boy was chosen while he and the prince were still infants, and they were raised and educated together in the royal palace. If the prince was good, his friend fared well; but if he was bad, the boy had a rather wretched life!

Nonetheless, whipping boys gained a fine upbringing and were often well-rewarded when they reached adult age [43] — thus Charles I gave Ham House to his former whipping boy, William Murray, and later made him Earl of Dysart. [44]

As one who took the punishment that belonged to another, whipping boys provide a fine illustration of what Christ did for us at Calvary. His death was

SUBSTITUTIONARY

Christ died for sins once for all, the righteous for the unrighteousness, that he might bring us to God, having been put to death in his body, but made alive by the Spirit!" (1 Pe 3:18)

The sufferings and death of the Saviour had power to atone for sin; that is, they freed believing sinners from the rightful punishment of their sins — DEATH.

Elsewhere it is called the doctrine of **propitiation** — that is, the wrath of God has been placated, and peace created between us and

---

(42) It is still considered ill-mannered and a serious breach of royal protocol to touch a monarch. Hence the furore in 1992 when Queen Elizabeth visited Australia, and the Prime minister, Paul Keating, put his hand on her back. One outraged British newspaper branded the Prime Minister "the Lizard of Oz".

(43) Because the prince and whipping boy grew up together they usually formed a strong emotional bond, especially since the prince usually did not have playmates as other children would have had. The strong bond that developed between a prince and his whipping boy dramatically increased the effectiveness of using a whipping boy as a form of punishment for a prince. The idea of the whipping boys was that seeing a friend being whipped or beaten for some wrong the prince had done, would likely ensure that the prince would not make the same mistake again.

(44) The family is still extant, the current earl (in 2015) being Lord Johnnie Grant (born 1946).

the Lord. Calvary is also described as an act of **expiation**, for Jesus fully atoned for our wrongdoing and appeased the wrath of heaven. Whatever debt we owed God has now been fully paid by Christ.

Only those can R.I.P who die in Christ and now await the resurrection!

EFFECTUAL

The sufferings of the Saviour are eternally effectual. He died once for all and for ever settled the sin question. The work of redemption was and is completed for everyone who believes. We can add nothing to it. We can take nothing from it. We may choose only to accept or reject the free gift of God, and so win heaven or merit hell.

VICARIOUS

Discipline was severe in the ancient Roman Army. One of the harshest punishments was "decimation", that is, the slaughter of every 10th man. This pitiless brutality was imposed upon an army when it was found guilty of cowardice. Usually the army would be broken into groups of 10, and then the victim would be chosen by lot. The remainder of his group then had to execute him, sometimes with clubs, sometimes with swords, or by hanging.

The 5th century BC consul, Appius Claudius, punished a company of cowardly troops in a particularly terrible way —

> The scattered soldiers were eventually brought back together, and assembled before the consul. He, with good reason, rebuked them soundly, and called them traitors to military discipline. ... Then he commanded that those soldiers who had thrown down their arms should be beaten first with rods and then beheaded. He did the same to the standard-bearers who had lost their standards, and to the centurions who had forsaken their posts. For the remaining soldiers, he commanded that

every tenth man should be chosen by lot, and then executed." (45)

There is a story told about a man and son who were soldiers together in a company that was condemned to decimation, though neither man was guilty of any wrong. In this case, the chosen men had to line up along the top of a cliff, and were obliged either to jump to their deaths, or be pushed over the edge; but the son manoeuvred, until he was able to die in place of his father.

In the same way, the death of Christ was substitutionary, except that in his case, a just man died for the unjust. *"The Lord has laid on him the iniquity of us all"* (Is 53:6).

Sometimes, perhaps, a rich man will choose to pay a poor man's fine, but then abandon him to poverty, and not make him part of the family. Not so Christ. He not only made himself a vicarious sufferer on our behalf, but having discharged all our debt he then chose to lift us into the heavenlies, enthrone us with him, and bless us with every spiritual blessing! (Ep 1:3; 2:5-7) He who knew no sin suffered in the place of those who knew no righteousness. And he died but once, never to die again; yet because of his true identity, this one death was enough.

Nor can there be any other suitable sacrifice for sin. We must rest in this one offering, or remain for ever burdened by sin.

RECONCILING

One might expect that the sight of his Son suffering would make God loathe us! Instead, through his death we have been brought near to God. The sin which alienated us has been removed. Friendship is now restored!

There are many examples where you need to have a "friend at court", who can sponsor you and gain admission for you. Think about joining a Rotary Club, and similar organisations. Or, suppose you wished to gain ready entrance to Buckingham Palace, or the White House. You would truly need a well-favoured friend!

---

(45)   Livy (BC 59 – AD 17), The History of Rome, Bk. 2.59. Simplified and paraphrased.

That idea is confirmed by the word "bring" (1 Pe 3:18), which was a technical word used of one who gained an audience at court for another, who introduced a friend to the monarch; or, especially, one who called the attention of the court to some favourable factors that had been overlooked.

Thus Christ has brought us to the royal court of heaven, and given us perpetual, free, and open access to the throne of God –

- *Legally*: by removing every legal barrier to our reconciliation.
- *Morally*: by changing our antagonism to God, and inspiring instead love for the Father and a desire to serve him.
- *Royally*: by giving us birth as the King's children, and clothing us in royal apparel.
- *Positionally*: by setting us in heaven with him, now and for ever.

PIACULAR

I was doubtful about using this word; but it is the only one in our language that fully expresses the idea of an atrociously bad crime that can find expiation only by the imposition of an extreme penalty.

This is important, because it highlights the reality of the death of Christ in contrast with some people over the centuries who have tried to deny his death. They hope to escape the demands made upon them by his emergence from the tomb by claiming that although his wounds were severe, he did not die. His disciples, they say, were able to rescue and resuscitate him. He then supposedly died years later in the normal fashion. An example of this sort of claim can be found in the Koran, which says that Jesus only appeared to die –

> The Jews said: Surely we have killed the Messiah, Jesus, the son of Mary, the apostle of Allah. But they did not kill him nor did they crucify him, it only seemed to them as if he died. ... Rather, Allah took him up to himself; and Allah is Mighty and Wise." (Sura 4:157-158; and see also Sura 3:55).

That Muslim belief is based upon an early Christian heresy called "docetism", which argued that Jesus only appeared to be flesh, and could not therefore truly die. But note how emphatically Peter speaks – *"Christ was put to death in his body!"* And Paul too insists that the death of Jesus was all too real and terrible –

> *You foolish Galatians! Who has bewitched you? Before your very eyes Jesus Christ was clearly portrayed as crucified* (Ga 3:1; NIV).

There can be no doubt about it. Jesus truly died, and was truly buried. And his pains were violent; his death came by brutal execution on a cross. It is a mark of the measure of our sin, the depth of wickedness that was in our souls, that such an extreme death alone could provide expiation for our iniquity. Indeed, it was a *piacular* atonement, freely offered to us by the love of God through his Son, Jesus Christ our Lord.

But the glorious good news is that death could not hold him; and the same Spirit who raised Christ will also raise all who die in Christ.

ETERNAL

There is a strange saying in *Matthew 27:57*, that when Jesus rose from the dead, a number of other godly people rose with him, presumably people recently dead, who were recognised by their friends, neighbours, and family. A later writing, known as the *Gospel of Nicodemus*, adds to the story, describing the descent of Christ into Hades, his resurrection, and the promise of his return. This account is said to have been written by the two sons of that Simeon who blessed the infant Jesus in the Temple (Lu 2:25-35). Their names, says the legend, were Karinus and Leucius, and they were among the dead who rose when Jesus rose, and walked into Jerusalem. They describe with passion and lively drama the joy of heaven and the despair of hell at the triumph of Christ. In one place they talk about the thief whom Jesus promised would that day go with him into Paradise –

And Joseph (of Arithamea) arose and said: [46] ...Truly and of right do ye marvel because ye have heard that Jesus hath been seen alive after death, and that he hath ascended into heaven. Nevertheless it is more marvellous that he rose not alone from the dead, but did raise up alive many other dead out of their sepulchres, and they have been seen of many in Jerusalem. And now hearken unto me; for we all know the blessed Simeon, the high priest which received the child Jesus in his hands in the temple. And this Simeon had two sons, brothers in blood, and we all were at their falling asleep and at their burial. Go therefore and look upon their sepulchres: for they are open, because they have risen, and behold they are in the city of Arimathaea dwelling together in prayer. ... *(so they journeyed to Arimathea, and the two young men told of their death and resurrection, and of the visions they had seen, and of the thief to whom Jesus had spoken on the cross)* ...

There came another man of vile habit, bearing upon his shoulders the sign of the cross; whom when they beheld, all the saints said unto him: Who art thou? For thine appearance is as of a robber; and wherefore is it that thou bearest a sign upon thy shoulders? And he answered them and said: Ye have rightly said: for I was a robber, doing all manner of evil upon the earth. And the Jews crucified me with Jesus, and I beheld the wonders in the creation which came to pass through the cross of Jesus when he was crucified, and I believed that he was the maker of all creatures and the almighty king, and I besought him, saying: Remember me, Lord, when thou comest into thy kingdom. And forthwith he received my prayer, and said unto me: Verily I say unto thee, this day shalt thou be with me in paradise: and he gave me the sign of the cross, saying: Bear this and go unto paradise, and if the angel that keepeth paradise suffer thee not to

---

(46) <u>The Gospel of Nicodemus</u>, XVII.1; XXVI; tr. by M.R. James, Clarendon Press, Oxford, 1924.

enter in, show him the sign of the cross; and thou shalt say unto him: Jesus Christ the Son of God who now is crucified hath sent me. And when I had so done, I spake all these things unto the angel that keepeth paradise; and when he heard this of me, forthwith he opened the door and brought me in and set me at the right hand of Paradise.

The legend adds that the true cross was planted in Hades itself, where it still remains, as a witness to all the denizens of hell of the absolute victory Christ has gained over them, and of their inability to detain even the weakest of the saints!

The story is no doubt fictitious, but the truth it illustrates is very real. Do you doubt your welcome into heaven? Simply carry with you the name of Jesus and the mark of the cross, and the angel who guards the Pearly Gates will see it, fling wide the doors, and joyously bid you to enter!

CONCLUSION

William Murray, the whipping boy for Prince Charles, was rewarded with Ham House, which remained in the family for 400 years, until in 1948 they gifted the estate to the National Trust. It remains one of the top London tourist attractions.

Murray was also given the surrounding farm lands, and later, the earldom of Dysart, along with a high position in the court. His eldest daughter Elizabeth became the Duchess of Lauderdale. A woman of vast wealth and high intelligence, she wielded enormous influence in the late 17th century. Her descendants have sustained their wealth and influence into modern times.

In a much vaster manner, the Saviour who volunteered to be our "whipping boy" has now been exalted to the highest splendour! (Ph 2:9; Re 5:12; plus several other references) –

> *Therefore God has highly exalted him and bestowed on him the name that is above every name, so that at the name of Jesus every knee should bow, in heaven and on earth and under the earth. ... "Worthy is the Lamb who was slain, to receive power and wealth and wisdom and might and honour and glory and blessing!"*

Let us then highly honour him! His death and resurrection, along with his exaltation to heaven's glorious throne. For us he was crucified.(Ga 3:1) For us, he rose from the dead and ascended back into heaven, to take his seat on the throne at the right hand of the Father. And for us he provided a salvation that is EXPIATORY – EFFECTUAL – VICARIOUS – RECONCILING – PIACULAR – and ETERNAL!

Chapter Ten

MIRACLES

> *Let me ask you only this: Did you receive the Spirit by works of the law or by hearing with faith? Are you so foolish? Having begun by the Spirit, are you now being perfected by the flesh? ... Does he who supplies the Spirit to you and works miracles among you do so by works of the law, or by hearing with faith?* (Ga 3:2-3, 5)

How naturally, without embarrassment or hesitation, Paul says it: *"God works miracles among you!"* Two powerful ideas at once spring to the fore –

HE IS A MIRACLE-WORKING GOD

In 1896 in Paris there appeared a young woman, Mlle. Henriette Couédon, who was credited with an amazing prophetic gift; she saw supernatural visions, and received revelations from the Archangel Gabriel. These revelations were of the most concrete nature. Some of them touched prophetically upon affairs of state, others descended to details of personal destinies. The fortunes of empires and republics, international complications, the rise and fall of individual statesmen, misfortunes and disasters innumerable, were predicted by the ingenuous young sibyl, who declared she had been entrusted with the divine mission of warning the world against the machinations of the Spirit of Evil. [47]

People besieged the house in which the Couédons rented an apartment, clamouring for oracles, until the neighbours and other tenants complained so vociferously that the landlord posted a placard proclaiming: MIRACLES PROHIBITED ON THESE PREMISES.

---

(47) International History Magazine, # 8, August 1973; article "Petite Histoire", pg. 78-79.

Many churches in different denominations could well place the same sign on their front door! At best they are suspicious of miracles; at worst, they spurn them altogether. But can any church claim to be true to scripture unless it enjoys the same experience of the supernatural as the early church did? – see *Mark 16:20; Acts 4:29-33; 5:12,16; 14:3; 28:8,9; Romans 15:18-19; 1 Thessalonians 1:4-5; Hebrews 2:4*.

We dare not allow an awareness of the supernatural, nor a desire for it, to slip away from our minds, or to become content with a situation in which miracles are sparse. Our unwavering conviction should be the same as the one expressed in scripture –

> *Ah, Lord God! It is you who have made the heavens and the earth by your great power and by your outstretched arm! Nothing is too hard for you.* (Je 32:17, ESV)

> *Nothing is impossible for God! ... Jesus said to them, I tell you the truth, if you have faith no bigger than a mustard seed, you will say to this mountain, 'Move from here to there,' and it will move, and nothing will be impossible for you. ... With God, everything is possible!* (Lu 1:37; Mt 17:20; 19:26)

Such miracles are possible because it is God's very nature to do wondrous things, he only does wondrous things, he cannot do other than wondrous things! (Ps 72:18; 86:10; 163:4; Je 33:3) Note, too, *Isaiah 28:21*, which declares that it is *"strange"* and *"alien"* when God has to act in judgment and bring destruction upon a people. His heart is rather always to do good and to save, especially by a miracle!

However, God seldom exercises his miracle-working power except through a believing man or woman. The Lord can and does, of course, act on his own initiative and exercises his own sovereignty, doing *"whatever he pleases in heaven and on earth"* (Ps 135:6); but he finds special pleasure in channelling a miracle through one of his servants. Which means, if we hope to see God acting for us as a miracle-working God, then we must first boldly set ourselves to act for God, declaring that -

WE ARE A MIRACLE-WORKING PEOPLE

Notice the astonishing sequence in *Matthew 17:21* and *19:26*, where the apostle, with a startling reversal of what would seem proper, places the idea that *"nothing is impossible for us"* <u>before</u> the idea that *"nothing is impossible for God"*. Why such an unseemly arrangement? Surely we can draw from it the truth that there will be no seeing the impossible things God can do until we stir up our own faith, believing that in God nothing is impossible for us! Certain steps must be taken to bring this to pass -

YOU MUST WANT YOUR MIRACLE

Despite what you might expect, there are many people who do not really want a miracle; they resist any real divine intervention. Why? Because –

MIRACLES OPPOSE THEIR REAL DESIRE

- A couple in a violent relationship may give lip service to wanting to escape it, yet will not allow God to help because (say) the husband is a sadist and she is a masochist, and so they both gain a twisted sexual thrill and carnal fulfilment from the pain they inflict and receive.
- When the disease becomes particularly nasty, a sick person may cry out for relief, yet not really want to be healed. Illness keeps people focussed on the sick person, who enjoys all the attention. Or perhaps remaining ill enables the patient to avoid resuming the responsibilities that health would bring.
- A person gripped by some sin or habit may go through the motions of seeking victory, but may not actually want it because sin is too pleasant.

The Lord does not force deliverance onto anyone; nor does he disregard his own injunctions (Mt 7:6); so miracles are usually given only to those who truly want them (cp. Mk 11:24, *"whatever you **desire** ..."* But this "desire" is no mere whim. The Greek word carries a strong sense of passion; it belongs in a context of craving, of yearning deeply for something.)

THEY PREFER PUNISHMENT

These people feel (consciously or unconsciously) that they deserve to suffer for their sins. Even if the Lord begins to bless them with healing or prosperity they cannot accept it, so they find ways to cast the blessing aside and to renew their pain. Some pastors are like this. Whenever their churches begin to grow they are smitten with a sense of being unworthy of such favour, and they find some way to whittle the congregation down to a more humble and (to them) acceptable size.

Some people cannot endure financial success. If a large sum of money comes into their hands they at once find ways to be rid of it, sometimes to the extent of punishing themselves for daring to prosper by plunging into miserable debt. Others, stricken with guilt, cannot endure happiness and seek to replace it with sorrow. And so on.

But the gospel demands that we find full satisfaction in the atoning work of the cross. We dare not insult the Father by suggesting that the grace of his Son is insufficient to remove all the guilt of our sin, along with all its penalty (Ga 2:15-16).

We must certainly be contrite for our sins (Ps 34:18; 51:17; Is 57:15; 66:2), even to the point of tears. (It may not be possible to be truly at *peace* by the cross until one has first felt the *pain* of the cross.) But then we are called to believe (1 Jn 1:9) and to rejoice (1 Pe 1:8-9). And then we are expected to reach out for all that God has ordained for us in Christ, allowing none of the Father's promised blessings to fall to the ground unrealised.

THEY DON'T WANT GOD TOO CLOSE

There are many people who prefer God to remain at a distance; they don't want him interfering too closely with their lives. They want a measure of blessing, but are content with enough to get them into heaven, and they care for little else. Yet the rule is immutable: those who don't press in for more will lose what they already have (Mt 13:12; 25:29). The old saying is true: "If he is not Lord of all, then he is not Lord at all."

YOU MUST WILL YOUR MIRACLE

One of the great painters of the early Italian Renaissance was Sandro Botticelli (1444-1510). On a certain day

> a cloth-weaver moved into the house next to Sandro's and set up no less than eight looms, which when they were working not only deafened poor Sandro with the noise of the treadles and the movement of the frames, but also shook his whole house, the walls of which were no stronger than they should be. What with one thing and the other, he couldn't work or even stay in the house. Several times he begged his neighbour to do something about the nuisance, but the weaver retorted that in his own house he could and would do just what he liked. Finally, Sandro grew very angry, and on top of his roof, which was higher than his neighbour's and not all that substantial, he balanced an enormous stone (big enough to fill a wagon) which threatened to fall at the least movement of the wall and wreck the other man's roof, ceilings, floors, and looms. Terrified at the prospect, the cloth-weaver ran to Sandro only to be told, in his own words, that in his own house Botticelli could and would do just what he wanted to. So, there being nothing else for it, the man was obliged to come to reasonable terms and make himself a good neighbour. (48)

Neither should we be bullied by the devil's clamour! So away with passivity! Miracles happen when believing people decide that they will happen; God gives little or nothing to wishful thinking, but everything to faith (He 11:6). So make a firm decision: "Whatever God has promised, I will have!" (Mt 7:7-8; 21:22; Jn 14:13-14; 16:23; 1 Jn 5:14-15)

YOU MUST WORK YOUR MIRACLE

This is particularly the function of the *charismata*, for by them the miracle-working power of God is released into the church through

---

(48) Giorgio Vasari, op. cit. Vol. Two, "The Life of Botticelli;" pg. 30-31.

gifts of revelation, healing, deliverance, and power. We should rise up in the Holy Spirit and stir up the gifts God has given the church in Christ and by the Holy Spirit (2 Ti 1:6-7).

Therefore Paul was emphatic and impatient with shrinking timidity, *"Since we have received these gifts* (Greek, charismata) ... **let us use them!***"* (Ro 12:6) The onus is upon us, not God. He is not reluctant; we are! Nor is it that we need to break through to God, but rather that we should allow **him** to break through upon us; after all, his name is **"Baal-Perazim – The Lord of the Break-through!"** (Ex 19:22, 24; 2 Sa 5:17-21; 6:8; Is 28:21; Mi 2:13).

CONCLUSION

The 19th-century English poet, Alfred, Lord Tennyson, in his poem *Ulysses* tells a story about the eponymous ancient Greek hero, and his band of intrepid mariners. At the end of his life, the aged Ulysses has become weary of indulgent ease at home, and determines to go on one last great voyage. He gathers his former comrades together, and urges them once again to embark on a stirring adventure –

> Come my friends,
> 'Tis not too late to seek a newer world.
> Push off, and sitting well in order smite
> The sounding furrows: for my purpose holds,
> To sail beyond the sunset, and to the baths
> Of all the western stars, until I die. ...
> Tho' much is taken, much abides; and tho'
> We are not now that strength which in old days
> Moved earth and heaven, that which we are, we are, –
> One equal temper of heroic hearts,
> Made weak by time and fate, but strong in will
> To strive, to seek, to find, and not to yield!

Now *that* is a motto for people like us, whom Paul himself bids to *"quit yourselves like men"* (1 Co 16:13). No matter what life has handed us, we will be one equal harmony of heroic hearts, resolved to be strong in will, to strive for the best, to seek the glory of God, to find and to fulfil his divine purpose, and never, never to yield!

Chapter Eleven

DYNAMITE

*God works **miracles** among you!* (Ga 3:5)

The key word *"miracles"* in Greek is *dunamis*, which means <u>power</u>. It occurs 118 times in the NT, and it is used in three ways –

- <u>**an inherent capacity to complete a task**</u>

This is power in an **attack** situation; taking the initiative; advancing against the enemy; strong to continue until the desired goal is fully accomplished. In this sense, *dunamis* has come into English as *dynamite*.

- <u>**an invincible strength against attack**</u>

This is power in a **defence** situation; creating impregnable strength against any and every assault by the enemy; preventing the enemy from diminishing the kingdom.

- <u>**an equipment of power to do the will of God**</u>

This is power expressed through signs, wonders, and miracles. It includes: a capacity to perform mighty deeds; an ability to display supernatural action; and a dynamic that sweeps every foe before it.

So *dunamis* provides a picture of the Spirit-filled believer, undefeated by sin, overcoming Satan, moving in the miraculous, completing every God-appointed task in supernatural power! In this study I want to deal with two important aspects of this *dunamis* –

"DUNAMIS" IS A HIDDEN POWER

We are not talking here about "power" as the world understands it; it is not brute force, nor tyranny, nor coercive strength. Rather, we are dealing with the strength and authority of the kingdom of God, which the world usually cannot either see or know. Indeed, in the eyes of the world we Christians often seem weak and defenceless; we certainly do not appear any different from any other group of unarmed people. Are we then defenceless? No, for sometimes (as Moses showed in Egypt, or Joshua on the plains of Gibeon, or David against the Philistines) one servant of God is more than a match for all the armies of the heathen.

However, there are other times when we show our real strength through apparent weakness (1 Co 1:26-29; 2 Co 12:8-10; and cp. also the remarkable contrasts in He 11:32-38, where some by faith gained life, while others, also by faith, gained death!)

For that reason, the power of *dunamis* may be expressed both through strength and weakness. Hence it can enable us to –

- prosper or to suffer
- be rich or poor
- live or die.

Pre-eminently, both aspects of *dunamis* can be seen in the life, ministry, death, and resurrection of Jesus – his *life* began with a miracle, and was supernaturally protected until his task was done; his *ministry* was replete with miracles, signs, and wonders; yet he yielded to *death*, and was still invincible, for no one could have taken his life unless he had allowed it; and of course, his *resurrection* showed indisputably that he was (and is) the Son of God with power! But in between those extraordinary events, he remained a man, with a full quotient of human needs and the normal range of human frailty. He had to grow and learn as any child must; he had to eat, drink, and sleep; he was made weary by toil; he sometimes found it prudent to retreat to the desert, where his enemies could not find him; he was dependent upon prayer and upon the Father's providence and protection. No one on earth could master him without his permission; yet he presented a gentle demeanour, kind and loving, *"holy, harmless, and undefiled"* (He 7:26, KJV). Actually invincible, yet weak in the sight of the world.

In our case, we show the full measure of *dunamis* not so much in the more spectacular aspects of the Spirit-filled life, but in those which display the character of Christ. That is, when we defy the influence and pressure of this world, and set ourselves to live by and for –

- *love* not hate

- *forgiveness* not revenge
- *purity* not licentiousness
- *spiritual* gain not material
- *sacrifice* not selfishness
- *gentleness* not violence
- *virtue* not vice
- *heaven* not earth, and
- *eternity* not time.

But who can possibly fulfil such a challenge? Who is equal to such a moral demand? Who has a spirit that can soar so high? None, except those who by the Holy Spirit have full access to all the strength that lies in *dunamis*!

"DUNAMIS" REQUIRES THREE THINGS

We are told not to grieve the Holy Spirit (Ep 4:30), which happens when we

- **<u>do what is forbidden</u> (vs. 25-31).**

People who violate the Lord's command mock both his <u>holiness</u> and the <u>power</u> he has given us by his Spirit to overcome sin.

- **<u>fail to do what is commanded.</u>**

People who ignore, whether carelessly or wilfully, the Lord's command, show a dismal perception of the future destiny appointed for everyone who faithfully fulfils his or her stewardship of the gospel in this life.

- **<u>do more than is commanded.</u>**

People who go beyond the Lord's command will lose access to his power, for the Holy Spirit lends strength only to doing the Father's will. You cannot gain righteousness by doing more than God actually requires any better than you can by doing less. So in such matters as prayer, witness, ministry, leadership, achievement, church service, giving, work, and the like, find out what the Lord wants, and do just that. People who allow themselves to be driven by the flesh, the world, the devil, a guilty conscience, or whatever, to go beyond what God requires, or to fall short of it, are on a pathway to frustration, exhaustion, and ruin.

Let the Lord teach you wisdom here, and how to be sensitive to his voice, so that you stay within the parameters of his purpose and therefore, in the power of the Holy Spirit, may fulfil all that God desires.

PRAY IN THE HOLY SPIRIT

See *Jude 20* –

Build yourselves up in your most holy faith by praying in the Holy Spirit.

Spirit-filled Christians have an enormous *dunamis* available to them through "prayer in the Spirit" (or perhaps, *"in the spirit"*, 1 Co 14:15). I take that to mean primarily (although not exclusively) praying in other tongues, or glossolalic prayer. It describes a vigorous use of glossolalia, pouring out a torrent of prayer to the Father (cp. 1 Co 14:2; Ro 8:26; 1 Co 2:11-16).

But merely speaking in tongues is not enough; the speaker must also stir up faith, and consciously release the power of God through that heavenly utterance (cp. 2 Ti 1:6-7).

WALK IN LOVE

See *1 Corinthians 13:1* –

I may speak in the tongues of men and of angels; but if do not have love, I am only a noisy gong or a clashing cymbal.

As surely as you yield soul and voice to the Holy Spirit, so must you yield spirit and heart. A loveless Christian is a terrible thing, an object of shame to heaven, of derision to the world, and of scorn to hell.

CONCLUSION

Holy Spirit baptism is a magnificent resource for effective Christian life and leadership. By fully employing this heavenly gift you can

- do all that God has given you to do
- overcome all the power of the enemy
- live in possession of the supernatural
- fit yourself to be an example to the saints

- equip yourself to be a servant of the church
- make yourself worthy to inherit the glory of the kingdom!

So by faith let God indeed *"work miracles among you"* (Ga 3:5). This is the "dynamite" of God, his heavenly *dunamis*, which transforms the church from a mere organisation into the power-filled body of Christ on earth.

Chapter Twelve

LAW

> *Everyone who relies for safety on obeying the law is under a curse; for it is written, "Cursed be everyone who does not abide by everything written in the Book of the Law, and keep it." Now it is evident that no one is justified before God by the law, for "The righteous shall live by faith"* (Ga 3:10-11).

Most people, if they are asked, will say that they want to go to heaven. Why then are they not Christians? The reason is not because they do not desire salvation, but because **they refuse to submit to God's way of salvation** (see Ro 10:3).

The scriptures set before us two ways of salvation, the one destined to fail, and the other to succeed. The first is –

THE WAY OF WORKS

A RIGHTEOUSNESS BASED ON WORKS

Paul defines a works-based righteousness in *Romans 10:*5 (which is based on Le 18:4-5) – "Moses says, 'The person who obeys laws will live because of the laws he obeys.'" (GW)

- The *"law"* here includes all our own *"good works"* – which may include honesty, gentleness, forgiveness, prayer, Bible reading, tithing, church-going, witnessing, even dying for the sake of the gospel – anything at all that people think gives them a claim upon God's favour.
- These things become a "law" particularly when they are set up as a rule of life, by which people hope to make themselves righteous in the sight of God, and acceptable to him.
- They are all summed up in the Ten Commandments (Ex 20:1-17).

Now, if you <u>could</u> keep those *"laws"*, then you could indeed *"live"* by them. However, the law (whether composed of our own rules, or God's, or some other set of commands) as a way of righteousness fails on four grounds –

- ***<u>Your past failures</u>***: nothing good you do today can change the evil you did yesterday. Yet despite the helplessness of the law to rectify our past guilt we still by nature resort to law rather than to grace, hoping to purchase pardon by good works. But the gospel is relentless in its demand that we discard Sinai and turn instead to Calvary (He 12:18-24).
- ***<u>The commandments are too broad</u>*** for any human being truly to encompass them (Ps 119:96) – for example, consider just one utterly impossible rule –

Jesus said, "You must love the Lord your God with all your heart and with all your soul and with all your mind, and with all your strength. This is the great and first commandment." (Mt 22:37-38; Mk 12:33; Lu 10:27)

Not one of us has ever come close to fulfilling that first and greatest commandment, not even for one moment in our entire lives. The quantifying adverb *"all"* slaughters us. I do indeed love the Lord with a large part of my heart, soul, mind, and strength; but *"all"*? That I cannot achieve. Hence I am marked by sin every moment of every hour of every day of my life, no matter what I am doing, even praying, preaching, and writing this book! For sin is simply falling short of the glory of God (Ro 3:23), and to attain to divine excellence in this life is quite beyond any mortal.

- ***<u>God has dismissed the law</u>*** as a way of righteousness, and insists that we submit to his new way. We dare not emulate those who refused to submit to divine righteousness and insisted upon going about trying to establish some righteousness of their own (Ro 10:3).
- ***<u>Even if I could obtain righteousness by the law</u>***, I would still be a fool if I did not discard that human righteousness and grasp the utterly perfect righteousness offered by Christ (cp Is 64:6). To do otherwise is to prefer menstrual rags to sparkling new raiment, a bucket of mud

to a truck full of gold, or the prettiness of a candle to the blazing glory of the sun!

So Paul declares boldly that Christ is the end of the law as a way of righteousness. He does not mean that the works of the law are bad, but that they must now be done as a response to grace, not as a means to obtain grace. Yet from the beginning the church has struggled with God's grace, and has constantly sought to add something to the merits of Christ, deeming his unaided grace to be insufficient. For example, the Venerable Bede, in his 8th century *"Ecclesiastical History of the English People"*, provides many examples of the common belief that people have to make atonement for their sins – the merits of Christ were drawn upon only to supply what was lacking in human virtue. Here are two out of many examples Bede gives of people endeavouring to attain sainthood by personal suffering and sacrifice –

- The first concerns **_Adamnan_**, an Irishman (date: circa 680) –

    During his youth he had committed some crime for which, when he came to his senses, he was thoroughly ashamed, and dreaded punishment by the strict Judge. So he visited a priest, from whom he hoped to learn a way of salvation, confessed his sins to him, and asked for advice how he might escape the wrath to come. When he had heard his confession, the priest said: "A severe wound calls for an even more severe remedy. Therefore spend your time as far as possible in fasting, reciting the psalter, and prayer, so that you may avert God's anger in confession, and deserve to find his mercy." Already deeply smitten in conscience, and longing for speedy release from the inward fetters of sin that burdened him (Adamnan) replied: ". . . I will readily undergo whatever penance you impose on me, if only I may be saved at Judgment Day. Even if you order me to remain standing in prayer all night, or to remain the whole week in fasting, I will do it." . . . (The priest then imposed a regime of fasting all week, except on Thursdays and Sundays, which Adamnan kept rigorously for the remainder of his life with) penitent tears and holy vigils. . . .

- The second story is an account of a prosperous householder who in his middle age became mortally ill, but was restored to life and health after seeing a vision of Heaven and Hell. He at once gave away all his goods, bade farewell to his wife and children, and entered a monastery. There he was given a remote cell, where he devoted his life to undisturbed prayer. Bede then writes –

Since this (monastery) stands on the bank of a river, he often used to enter it for severe bodily penance, and plunge repeatedly beneath the water while he recited psalms and prayers for as long as he could endure it, standing motionless with the water up to his loins and sometimes to his neck. When he returned to shore, he never removed his dripping, chilly garments, but let them warm and dry upon his body. And in winter, when the half-broken cakes of ice were swirling around him, which he had broken to make a place to stand and dip himself in the water, those who saw him used to say: "Brother Drythelm (for that was his name), it is wonderful how you manage to bear with such bitter cold." To which he, being a man of simple disposition, and self-restraint, would reply simply: "I have known it colder." And when they said: "It is extraordinary that you are willing to practise such severe discipline," he used to answer: "I have seen greater suffering." So until the day of his summons from this life he tamed his aged body by daily fasting, inspired by an insatiable longing for the blessings of heaven . . . [49]

---

(49)   Translated by Leo Sherley-Price; Penguin Books, London, 1990; pg. 251, 252, 289.

THE SCANDAL OF GRACE

The gospel is far removed from such religious distortions of divine grace, for God gives us his own true righteousness –

> If our souls have stained their first white, yet we
> May clothe them with faith, and dear honesty,
> Which God imputes, as native purity. (50)

So then, away with any dependence upon good works to gain you any better access to God than you already have in Christ. Which brings us face to face with what many feel to be the scandal of divine grace, the seeming licence it gives for sin. Thus a rapist, in theory, could walk away from his crime, realise that he had sinned, repent, and at once be as though he had never sinned. In practice, however, if there were no tears, no shame, no desire to make all possible restitution, his repentance might be doubted. There is truly a sorrow for sin that God honours (Ps 34:18; 51:17; Is 57:15; 66:2). Nonetheless, beware of turning even repentance into a works-based claim of righteousness. Indeed, almost *anything* can be turned into a law; so be warned against using any law to gain divine favour; such as –

- *"Won't I be a little more righteous if I read my Bible?"* No, you will only be spiritually weaker or stronger.
- *"Won't prayer make me more righteous?"* No, by the strength or weakness of your praying you will gain or lose answers, but not righteousness.
- *"Won't God reckon me righteous if I give sacrificially?"* No, you will reap prosperity or poverty, based on the measure of your giving, but not righteousness.
- *"Won't the practice of austerity make me righteous?"* No, you will turn flabbiness into toughness, but not righteousness.

So you need to examine your <u>motives</u>. Why are you doing these various good works? A lady once heard me speak against turning devotional discipline into a law, and reacted: "I had just made up

---

(50)   Lines 13-15 of John Donne's poem, *To Mr Robert Woodward*.

my mind to get up an hour earlier each day to pray and read the Bible. But now I doubt if it is worth doing." She was simply showing that her *motive* was wrong; she was hoping to extract some favour from God when she should have been motivated by her love of prayer and scripture.

If you are hoping to score points in heaven, to build up credit in God's register, to secure some righteous standing before God, to gain the favour of God by your efforts, then you have fallen under law, and you will incur his wrath rather than arouse his pleasure. Instead, abandon all attempts to build righteousness on your own good works, and depend only upon the merits of Christ.

Indeed, abandoning the law and turning to Christ is finally the only thing that can release you to find *life* in those same good works (such as reading your Bible, prayer, etc.) So *"stand fast in the liberty for which Christ has set you free, and never again allow yourself to be entangled in the yoke of slavery"* (Ga 5:1; the "yoke" referred to here is the law, especially when the law is seen as a way to build personal righteousness).

THE WAY OF GLORY

Where the Spirit of the Lord is, there is freedom, so that with our faces uncovered, we may all look upon the glory of the Lord. That glory, coming from the Lord, who is the Spirit, transforms us into his image, taking us from one degree of magnificence to another. (2 Co 3:17-18).

Paul says that as soon as we turn to Christ we are *"transfigured"* into the *"magnificence"* of Christ. He uses the same words that are found in the gospel –

Jesus was transfigured before them, his face began to shine more radiant than the sun, his raiment blazed with a dazzling brightness, whiter than any cleaner on earth could bleach them; and his disciples saw his magnificence (Mt 17:2; Mk 9:2, 3; Lu 9:29, 32).

Why does Paul connect that "transfiguration" language with a life in the Spirit?

- ***To give us a new view of each other***

Would you have dared to throw mud at the transfigured Christ? If not, then how can you do so to your fellow Christian, who is gloriously indwelt by that same Christ?

- **_To give us a new view of ourselves_**

He wants us to see that we are like Christ: that the same splendour is in us, as it was in him, even if it is ordinarily hidden –

> *Those whom he predestined he also called; and those whom he called he also justified; and those whom he justified he also <u>glorified</u> (the same word as before, "doxa") (Ro 8:30).*

- **_To give us a new view of the Spirit_**

It is the task of the Holy Spirit, beginning now and on through eternity, to carry us ever onward and upward into the magnificence of Christ. With such an inner grace working to transform us, who needs a beggarly law, which at best can only wash the skin while leaving the heart untouched? Let us rather seize the liberty of the Spirit and grow in our knowledge of the truth, and go on in the strength of his indwelling glory!

CONCLUSION

There has never been any other way to God except to cast oneself upon his divine mercy (Nu 15:27-31). Provision under the old covenant was made for *some* deliberate sins (Le 5:1-6; 6:1-7), but not for crimes like murder, adultery, or blasphemy. David, for example, was accused of all three, and had no hope left to him except to plead for mercy (see Ps 51). But mercy must have a firm basis of justice, and in Christ, God has found a way to forgive you and to impute righteousness to you, through faith alone.

What is this faith? Must it be strong or weak? No, it is simply a link of trust between the sinner and Christ. Faith is not a "work", it has no virtue, it is just an attitude of reliance upon the promise of God, an assurance that the merits of Christ are sufficient. So make sure your faith does not drift away from Christ and back to yourself, back onto something *you* have done. Let me ask: "How do you <u>know</u> you are saved?" Is it because you prayed, or responded to an altar call, or became a church member, or saw a vision, or made a truly sacrificial gift, or performed some really noble deed, or even because you invited Jesus to come into your heart?

Any "faith" that encourages you to look back to something you have done will fail you in times of doubt or of depression ("Was my profession of faith really genuine?" . . . "Did I really surrender to Christ?" . . . "Perhaps it was only an emotional experience after all?") One rock alone will remain unmovable in even the most awful storm – let all your faith be solely and for ever in the work of Christ (Ro 10:9-10).

Chapter Thirteen

GOSPEL

Long ago scripture foresaw that God would justify the Gentiles by faith, and it told how God spoke his promise to Abraham, saying, "In you shall all the nations be blessed." So then, those who are of faith will share the blessing of Abraham who was himself a man of faith. But all who rely on works of the law will find themselves under a curse; for it is written, "Everyone who does not heed everything written in the Book of the Law, and obey it, is accursed." Plainly, then, no one is justified before God by the law, for scripture says, "The righteous shall live by faith." (Ga 3:8-11)

The distinction between Law and Gospel is the highest art in Christendom, which should be grasped and understood by all who call themselves Christians. Where this is not done, a Christian may not be distinguished from a heathen or a Jew. So much depends upon this distinction ... Therefore, whoever has mastered this ability to distinguish the Law from the Gospel, place him at the head and call him a *Doctor of Holy Scripture*. For without the Holy Spirit it is impossible to make this distinction." [51]

Luther's opinion is perhaps a little extravagant. Other Christians may not feel obliged to endorse his claim that the separation of the law from the gospel is the key idea in the Bible, or that it warrants the award of a doctorate! Nevertheless, the distinction is a vital one, and failure to grasp it lies at the root of most spiritual poverty. And how passionately Paul declaims the contrast between

---

[51] From a sermon preached by Martin Luther, January 1st 1532; *The Distinction Between the Law and the Gospel*; tr. by Willard L. Burce; found on the web site of The Consortium for Classical and Lutheran Education (http://www.ccle.org/).

the law and the gospel; how vigorously he scorns a way of life based upon law while exalting the way of the gospel!

So let us too examine this contrast, beginning with the question why, after 20 centuries, do people still turn to the law? It is because of -

THE GLORY OF THE LAW

Before anyone can grasp the true glory of the *gospel* they first need to understand the quality of glory that *law* itself does bring –

THE ATTRACTION OF THE LAW

The glory of the ancient law cannot be doubted. Think about the awful majesty of its fiery setting on Mt Sinai (Ex 19:6-22; De 4:11-12). The mountain smoked and trembled as the finger of God carved his laws upon the hard stone, and the people ran away in terror. That glory has never departed from the law, which Paul himself acknowledged, even if the glory of the gospel surpasses it –

> *Carved in letters on stone, the law came with such* **glory** *that the Israelites could not look at Moses' face because it shone with* **glory** *... there was* **glory** *in the law ... the law had* **glory** *... the law came with* **glory** (2 Co 3:7, 9, 10, 11).

People still discover that ancient glory when they assay to achieve righteousness by observing a set of rules about eating, drinking, going, doing, dressing and the like. Of course, those things are all part of everyday life, and they must be done if life is to have any pleasure. But we may not do them as a way to be deemed holy or righteous by God, for if we do, we may find ourselves *"accursed"*. Nonetheless, the law's glory is so enticing that people do ignore God's warning and they do set themselves to gain heaven's acceptance by keeping one or another of various sets of laws –

KEEPING THE LAWS OF MOSES

Some churches have decided that no worship is valid unless it is based upon observance of the Sabbath, even to insisting on

Saturday as the only proper day. This is despite Paul's insistence that the Fourth Command has been abrogated (2 Co 3:7), [52] and that we should allow no one to judge us in respect to keeping one day above another (Cl 2:16-17). But they find glory in packing a set of rules around a particular day, and a feeling of enhanced righteousness, so they ignore grace and cling to law.

There are other Christians who insist upon keeping the food laws of ancient Israel (Le 11:1-47), which oblige them to reject pork, ham or swine products, and to eat only the flesh of animals that chew the cud and have cloven hoofs, and only fish with fins and scales. They scorn carrion birds, deem only hopping insects fit to eat, reject any reptiles, and the like. The glory, the feeling of righteousness, the glow of satisfaction they find in this legal observance blinds their eyes to Paul's injunction about the folly of rules that say, *"Do not handle; do not taste; do not touch"* (Cl 2:20-23).

LIVING BY THE LAWS OF A CHURCH

Many years ago I had reason to search for another church in which to worship and to serve the Lord. I visited several before finding one that fitted most of my requirements. Some churches I rejected almost at once, usually on the ground of their addiction to law. For example, in the lobby of one I found a brochure detailing the rules for membership. Among the usual demands (born again, baptised, agreeing to a Statement of Faith, and so on) the enquirer had to sign off on a long list of "do's" and "don'ts" – no smoking, no drinking alcohol, no going to the movies, no gambling, no dancing, no drugs, no illicit sex, and others; along with an obligation to tithe, worship regularly, pray, read the Bible, bear witness, and others. I put down the document, walked out of the church, and have never been back there.

Did I want to do all that was forbidden and spurn all that was required? Of course not. Indeed, I was already keeping nearly all their rules already. What I objected to was that they were *rules*,

---

(52) The phrase "done away" (2 Co 3:7, KJV) has the sense of "make void", "abolish", or, in a legal sense, "abrogate ... repeal ... annul". See below.

when they should have been voluntary expressions of the working of divine grace. The presumption behind the lists was that anyone who kept them could pronounce himself or herself "holy", which is nonsense. True holiness is an inner dynamic not some sort of outward conformity.

In another church that I truly wished to join, and did, I had to remonstrate with the pastor over a number of absurd rules, to which I refused to add my signature. They let me and my family become members anyway, and we spent several happy years there, until we had to move to another city. Here are some of the things I refused to sign, copied from a booklet published by the church, called *Constitution and By-Laws*. They are taken from a chapter on *Membership Requirements*, which begins by stating that all who wish to become members of the congregation must –

- *Disapprove of and refrain from participation in sinful amusements such as immoral drama, Hollywood type movies, gambling, dancing, secret societies, etc.*

How could I sign such a rule without perjuring myself? What is a "sinful amusement"? Who will define that for me? And suppose I disagree with his or her list of what is right and wrong?

What is "immoral drama"? Does it include Shakespeare? And what about the biblical *Song of Solomon*? What are "Hollywood type movies"? Even evangelical films have been made in Hollywood, using some of the same studios, technicians, and so on, that also make secular movies. Am I never to watch a film of any sort, for is not *every* film a "Hollywood type" movie? How, too, can I walk out my front door, drive on a freeway, or fly with Qantas without "gambling" with my very life? And may I never "dance" before the Lord, or share in a happy social gathering where dancing is integral to its success? The pastor could not give me a sensible definition of any of the items mentioned in that rule.

- *Abstain from drinking intoxicating beverages of any kind, the use of tobacco in any form, and the use of habit forming or mind bending drugs.*

Without much more detailed definition, which of course would then fill a large book, those rules are impossible to keep! As they stand, they would prevent me from using a number of medications that contain either alcohol or nicotine, or both. They would also forbid me the use of medications that use cocaine, morphine, or any other potentially addictive substance. I declined to put my life at risk by agreeing to keep any such rules.

The list of rules contained 15 such paragraphs, many of them subject to the same sort of criticism as I have voiced above. After hearing me, and being unable to offer a satisfactory reply, the pastor laughed and said he would accept my unsigned application for membership, and he would not oblige me to tell lies to join his church.

My family and I did join the church, and were glad to do so, for it was indeed a fine church, strong in worship, rich in the word of God, and delightful in fellowship. But that was despite their membership rules, not because of them. But after he had agreed to welcome us into his church, I asked the pastor what I thought was the most pertinent question – why such *superficial* rules?

If a church *must* make rules, why focus (contrary to scripture) on such peripheral matters as eating and drinking, touching and going? (Cl 2:20-22). Why not promise rather to feed the poor, clothe the naked, fight for justice, work for peace, oppose prejudice, and the like? –

> Guard the rights of the widow, secure justice for the ward, give to the needy, defend the orphan, clothe the naked, care for the injured and the weak, do not ridicule the lame, protect the maimed, and let the blind have a vision of my splendour. Protect the old and the young within your walls. When you find any who are dead, commit them to the grave and mark it, and I will give you the first place in my resurrection. (2 Esdras 2:20-23, NRSV)

LIVING BY THEIR OWN LAWS

Scorning the laws of Moses, rejecting laws devised by some ecclesiastical authority, other people, still hoping to buy the favour of God and gain better access to the throne, create their own rules. By various acts of devotion, of self-denial, of sacrifice of time, money, and effort, they expect to get a better hearing in heaven. Against all which, let these words stand –

> God whom I praise; how could I praise
> If such as I might understand,
> Make out, and reckon on, his ways,
> And bargain for his love, and stand,
> Paying a price, at his right hand? (53)

He means that the ways of God are beyond his comprehension, and that salvation is all of **grace**; good works cannot buy it, nor can evil works easily destroy it.

But despite all that scripture and reason tell us, multitudes of people still choose the way of law, of rules and regulations; and they will tell you about the *"glory"*, the satisfaction, that such law-keeping gives them. Paul recognises that *"glory"*, but nonetheless declares –

THE FAILURE OF THE LAW

No matter how much "glory" the law may contain, or seem to contain, in the end it fails dismally –

THE LAW FAILS IN HOLINESS

There are only two possible ways to holiness –

OUTWARD OBEDIENCE TO A WRITTEN CODE

See again *Colossians 2:20-23*, where Paul says that *"letting people dictate to you ... and submitting to human rules and regulations"* touches only the flesh. All those rules deal only with the outer frame, which is doomed to perish; but the Lord is looking for an *inner* transformation that will endure for ever. Even worse the law is deceptive, because although severity on the body (as a way to holiness) seems wise and pious, it is actually *"worthless as a means of combating sensuality"* (vs. 23); and, worse still, in the end, the law is a killer (2 Co 3:6, 7).

---

(53) From Robert Browning's 1836 poem, "Johannes Agricola" (the leader of an Antinomian sect, circa 1535; the words are Agricola's).

Paul does not mean that God's holy law itself actually kills; but it condemns to death, or at least it precludes from life, all who try by it to reach God.

So here is a paradox — a way of life that seems so pious (food deprivation, abstaining from all alcohol, not going to this place or that, denying oneself many pleasures, not touching, not tasting, not doing, not going) is in fact useless as a way of defeating sin or gaining righteousness. Far from flattening the flesh it fattens it! It is not a spiritual way of life, despite appearances, but carnal. It does not deny the flesh, but indulges it.

Those rules cannot ever do more than touch the surface of one's life, but the demand of the gospel is for an

INNER TRANSFORMATION TO THE CHARACTER OF CHRIST

No one can legislate, or reduce to rules, the kind of holiness God requires from each one of us! That holiness comes only from union with Christ by faith, and from the principle of *"Christ in you, the hope of glory"* (Cl 1:27; and see also Ga 2:20).

If law-keeping fails in holiness, is also true that -

THE LAW FAILS IN STRENGTH

Here is something that all law-keepers find, to their growing despair – the law's glory constantly fades, just as it drained away from the face of Moses (2 Co 3:13). Hence, to maintain the same level of satisfaction, the more you do, the more you have to do. Thus rule-makers find themselves making more and more rules, and keeping them more and more rigorously, yet still failing to achieve a lasting sense of inner holiness, of reconciliation with God, or of joyful delight.

The ancient monks display the tragedy of a church that had lost contact with the Spirit of life. Living alone in caves, standing outside in all weathers for years at a time, dwelling on top of tall stone pillars, curled into barrels, flogging themselves, eating bitter food, lacing their garments with thorns, depriving themselves of all worldly comfort – they strove to draw nearer to the Lord or to gain some assurance of salvation.

Reading the historical accounts of their awful self-imposed privations one would think they were crazy! Actually they were very logical – certainly more so than multitudes of comfort-loving yet law-keeping saints in our day! If the highest level of salvation, of closeness to God, can be obtained only by personal sacrifice, then the ancient hermits were perfect exemplars of the principle. As for us, we are mostly less honest than the hermits, for we allow *our* rules only so much severity; God forbid they should cause us any real discomfort! Some people resolve to get near to God by fasting for a day, or doubling their tithe one Sunday, or obliging themselves to go out street witnessing, or deciding to stay on their knees in prayer for an hour or two. They then suppose themselves to be heroes of self-denial, great warriors for Christ, who have surely put God deeply into their debt. How could he possibly reject their prayer when they have suffered such privations, endured such pain!

How absurd! What delusion! Surely a moment's thought would show any sensible person that the torments endured by (say) St Alypius, perching on a pole for 67 years, lifted him not even one centimetre nearer to God! If he was truly a "saint", his pillar had nothing to do with it! How then can any modern Christian suppose that their petty privations have advanced them one hair in righteousness? [54]

The mistake made by the old eremites in their caves and on their pillars was a failure to recognise that –

THE LAW FAILS IN LAWFULNESS

Here is a remarkable thing – the law is *unlawful*! Paul says it has been *"done away"* (vs. 11). The Greek word means to "render powerless . . . to bring to an end . . . to destroy, annihilate, abrogate." Once a law has been repealed it no longer has any force. It remains merely a historical curiosity. There is no penalty for violating it; there is no advantage in keeping it. That is what God has done to the ancient laws of Moses, all of them. He cancelled

---

(54) For more about Alypius and other examples of extraordinary anchorites see the *Addenda* following this chapter.

them at Calvary. He did this because he resolved that no one can gain access to him by law, no matter how rigorously the law is obeyed! But **_test yourself_** – do you feel that you will gain favour with God if you keep your rules, but will lose favour if you don't? If so, then *law*, not grace, has become the basis of your righteousness, and you have actually *cut yourself off* from the throne of God! (55)

THE LAW FAILS IN COMPARISON

Paul draws a striking comparison (2 Co 3:6-18) –

- the law is the letter that kills, the gospel is the spirit of life
- the law was preached by Moses, the gospel is preached by Christ
- the law was the old covenant, the gospel is a new covenant
- the law is a ministration of death, the gospel is a ministration of life
- the law was engraved upon stones, the gospel is imprinted upon hearts
- the law was a word of condemnation, the gospel is a word of the Spirit
- the law was a set of ordinances, the gospel is a source of righteousness
- the law was a cold letter, the gospel is a compassionate Man
- the law was impotent to heal, the gospel is a transforming power
- the law brings fear and bondage, the gospel brings faith and liberty
- the law has been legally abrogated, the gospel is established for ever

---

(55) There is, of course, a place for rules and discipline, both in the church and in personal life, for they help to maintain good order and to check the flesh. But this is a matter of <u>conduct</u>, outward behaviour, of living as good citizens of the kingdom, and has nothing to do with inner <u>righteousness</u>. Inner righteousness, of course, should lead to proper behaviour; but the reverse does not follow.

- the law was glorious, and still has glory; but the gospel is much more glorious, and possesses that glory without measure and for ever.

Since those things are all undoubtedly true, we must ask again: if the law compares so badly with the gospel, why then do people still cling to the law? Paul gives an extraordinary answer – it is because of –

THE DECEPTION OF THE LAW

Paul says that people have a veil over their eyes (vs. 14-15), which prevents them from seeing that the glory has gone out of the law (vs. 13; and see Ex 34:29, 30, 33, 34).

Did you notice the astonishing (and brave) change that the apostle makes to the ancient record? In harmony with the passage in *Exodus*, the Rabbis taught that Moses' face shone for the rest of his life, and is still shining in the grave. But Paul, with marvellous daring, asserts instead that Moses covered his face to hide, not the glory, but the *fading* of the glory! And he reckons that many people still in effect have a veil in front of their eyes, and they have never realised that whatever glory the law may once have had, it has dimmed almost to nothing. So, says he, tear that veil away, so that you can see that the glory has gone from the law, and then turn to Christ, and to ever-increasing liberty and splendour! (vs. 16-17)

THE GOSPEL

What a tragedy that the gospel promises so much, yet we are content with so little! We experience but a touch of glory, and are content, when we should press on and on. Chrysostom wrote, in a sermon on our text –

> Woe is me! for well is it that we should here even groan bitterly, for that we who enjoy a birth so noble do not so much as know what is said, because we quickly lose the reality, and are dazzled about the objects of sense. For this glory, the unspeakable and awful, remaineth in us for a day or two, and then we quench it, bringing over it the winter of worldly concerns, and with the thickness of those clouds repelling its rays. For worldly things are a

winter, and that winter more lowering. For not frost is engendered thence, nor rain, neither doth it produce mire and deep swamps; but, things than all these more grievous, it formeth hell and the miseries of hell. And as in severe frost the limbs are stiffened and are dead, so truly the soul shuddering in the winter of sins also, performeth none of its proper functions, stiffened as it were, by a frost, as to conscience." (56)

But Paul has shown us how to escape such a frigid state. The key lies in turning to Christ and unveiling the glory of God (vs. 17-18). Let us all then do as he bids us, and with *"unveiled faces"* gaze upon the glory of Christ and of the gospel, and be transformed into the glorious liberty of Christ, from glory to glory, for ever!

PRAYER ANSWERED

So here at last is God's answer to the age-old cry of Job –

> *If only I knew how to reach God, how to enter his court, I should state my case before him and set out my arguments in full; then I should learn what answer he would give me and understand what he had to say to me.* (Jb 3-5, WEB)

To that yearning plea, Christ has returned a stunning answer –

> *The way into the holiest has been made wide open to everyone who believes, through the blood of the everlasting covenant!*
> (cp. He 4:16; 10:19-23; Re 22:17; Jn 3:14-17)

So seize your birthright in Christ, abandon any dependence upon good works, and simply, in the name of Jesus, march boldly into the holy of holies, the very throne room of God, and up to his throne, and there receive abundant mercy and rich grace to help you in every time of need! (He 4:16)

---

(56)   St John Chrysostom, 4th century archbishop of Constantinople; <u>Homilies on Second Corinthians</u>, *Homily Seven*.

CONCLUSION

Have you now learned to distinguish between the law and the gospel? If so, as Martin Luther said, you may promote yourself to the top of the class and award yourself a doctorate in divinity! You have mastered the greatest art in Christendom!

ADDENDA

SUNDRY ANCHORITES AND EREMITES

ACEPSEMUS

Immuring himself in a cell, he persevered for 60 years, neither being seen nor speaking ... He received the food that was brought to him by stretching his hand through a small hole. To prevent his being exposed to those who wished to see him, the hole was not dug straight through the thickness of the wall, but obliquely, being made in the shape of a curve.

The food brought to him was mainly lentils soaked in water. At the end of 60 years he emerged from his cell, bent double under a weight of iron, which he had apparently borne throughout the entire period.

He looked so wild and shaggy, that he was once actually taken for a wolf by a shepherd, who assailed him with stones, till he discovered his error, and then worshipped the hermit as a saint.

Acepsemus declared that God had shown him that he would die within a few weeks (which happened). [57]

BARADATUS

I wish to record the life of the wonderful Baradatus, for he too devised new tests of endurance. First, immuring himself for a long time in a cell, he enjoyed divine consolation alone. From there, aspiring to the ridge situated above, and constructing out of wood a small chest that did not even match his body, in this he dwelt, obliged to stoop the whole time – for its length was not equal in size to the height of his body. It was not even fitted together with planks, but had openings like a lattice

---

[57] Theodoret, Religious History #15; tr. by R. M. Price, A History of the Monks of Syria, Cistercian Publications, Kalamazoo, Michigan, 1985; pg. 114-116.

. . . (so that) he was neither safe from the assault of the rains nor free from the flames of the sun, but endured both of them like the other open-air ascetics, whom he surpassed only in the labour of reclusion.

Having spent a long time in this way he later came out . . . (but now) he stands all the time, stretching out his hands and hymning the God of the universe, and covering his entire body with a tunic of skins – only round the nose and mouth has he left a small opening for breath, in order to receive and inhale the common air, since otherwise human nature cannot live. He endures all this labour, even though with a body not robust but much afflicted by numerous ailments; but his bubbling zeal, inflamed by divine love, compels to labour one who cannot labour. [58]

THALELAEUS

He made a kind of cylinder out of two cart wheels joined by planks and suspended in the air on chains. After he had been squatting in his "bucket" for ten years he was visited by Theodoret, who says that he was unable to straighten himself and "always sits bent double, with his forehead pressed against his knee" [59]

It is not known how much longer he remained there.

OTHERS

Theodoret describes other monks who lived in tiny huts or cells in which they could neither stand nor lie down full length, while others lived in disused cisterns, or dug deep holes in which they immured themselves. One hermit lived alone in a cave on the top of a mountain, and never once turned his face toward the west.

Such men became a pattern for many others who locked themselves alone in caves for life, slept on beds of thorns, laced their food with bitter herbs, twisted thorns and thistles into their

---

(58) Mid 5th century. Ibid. #27.
(59) Ibid. #28.

garments, burdened themselves with massive loads of iron, and embraced many other forms of self-torture.

Then there were **_James_** and **_Alexander_** of Cyr, who (like Baradatus) imposed upon themselves the sentence of standing in the open for the rest of their lives [60]. St. Gregory of Nazianzus speaks of a solitary who stood upright for many years together, absorbed in contemplation, without ever lying down. They too were copied by others, who stood in the open, sometimes for many years, using various tethers or props to hold themselves upright.

Sulpitius Severus tells of a hermit who for fifty years lived secluded from all human society, in the clefts of Mount Sinai, entirely destitute of clothing, and all overgrown with thick hair, avoiding every visitor, because, as he said, intercourse with men interrupted the visits of the angels.

One of the most renowned hermits was **_St Simeon Stylites_** (390-459) who sat on a 60-foot pillar for 36 years. I will return to him; but in the meantime note that he was outdone by **_St Simeon the Younger_**. The early historian **_Evagrius_** ("Ecclesiastical History") says that while Simeon was still a child he befriended and tamed a young panther, which he led to a nearby monastery – the preceptor, who was ensconced on a column saw in this a sign of special sanctity and invited the boy to join him on his column. This Simeon agreed to do, and then spent the next 68 years on pillars of ever-increasing height, including 45 years on his last, during which many miracles of healing, exorcisms, fulfilled prophecies, and the like, were attributed to him.

But both Simeons were exceeded by **_St Alypius_**, who combined the idea of standing with that of a pillar, and so stood on his pillar for 53 years, until he lost the use of both his feet, upon which he spent his last 14 years lying only on one side of his body.

Evagrius writes further –

> (There are some) who individually seclude themselves in chambers of so limited a height and width that they can

---

(60) Theodoret, Ecclesiastical History 17-21.

neither stand upright nor lie down at ease, confining their existence to "dens and caves of the earth" ... as says the apostle. Some too take up their dwelling with the wild beasts ...

Another mode has also been devised, one which reaches to the utmost extent of resolution and endurance; for transporting themselves to a scorched wilderness, and covering only those parts which nature requires to be concealed, both men and women leave the rest of their persons exposed both to excessive frosts and scorching blasts, regardless alike of heat and cold. They, moreover, cast off the ordinary food of mankind, and feed upon the produce of the ground, whence they are termed Grazers, allowing themselves no more than is barely sufficient to sustain life. ...

I will mention still another class ... persons who, when by virtue they have attained to a condition exempt from passion, return to the world. ... They (then) frequent the public baths, mostly mingling and bathing with women, since they have attained to such an ascendancy over their passions as to possess dominion over nature, and neither by sight, touch, or even embracing of the female, to relapse into their natural condition. It (is) their desire to be men and among men and women among women, and to participate in both sexes. In short, by a life thus all excellent and divine, virtue exercises a sovereignty in opposition to nature ... [61]

Consider also –

Cyprian de Mulverton, fifth prior of the monastery of Saint Francis, a prelate of singular sanctity ... vowed never again to behold with earthly eyes the blessed light of heaven, nor to dwell longer with his fellow men. ... He kept his vow. Out of the living rock that sustained the saintly structure, beneath the chapel of the monastery,

---

(61) "Ecclesiastical History"; Bohn's Ecclesiastical Library; London, 1854; pg 285, 286.

was another chapel wrought, and thither, after bidding an eternal farewell to the world ... the holy man retired.

... Ascetic to the severest point to which nature's endurance could be stretched, Cyprian even denied himself repose. He sought not sleep, and knew it only when it stole on him unawares. His couch was the flinty rock; and long afterwards, when the zealous resorted to the sainted prior's cell, and were shown those sharp and jagged stones, they marvelled how one like unto themselves could rest, or even recline upon their points without anguish. ...

His limbs were clothed in a garb of horsehair of the coarsest fabric; his drink was the dank drops that oozed out of the porous walls of his cell; and his sustenance, such morsels as were bestowed upon him by the poor. ...

No fire was suffered, where perpetual winter reigned. None were admitted to his nightly vigils; none witnessed any act of penance; nor were any groans heard to issue from that dreary cave; but the knotted blood-stained thong, discovered near his couch, too plainly betrayed in what manner those long nights were spent. ...

One morn it chanced that they who sought his cell found him with his head upon his bosom, kneeling before the image of the virgin patroness of his shrine. [62] Fearing to disturb his devotions, they stood reverently looking on; and thus silently did they tarry for an hour; but, as in that space he had shown no signs of motion, fearing the worst, they ventured to approach him. He was cold as the marble before which he knelt. In the act of humblest intercession - it may be, in the hope of grace - had Cyprian's spirit fled. [63]

---

(62) St Thecla of Iconium, who is reckoned the first woman martyr of the church. Her story is told in the apocryphal Acts of Paul and Thecla (circa 180), in which she is described as a convert of the apostle Paul.

(63) The above quote comes from W. H. Ainsworth's novel Rookwood, Book III, Ch. 10 (1834), which also contains a vivid description of the famous ride from London to

.... *continued from previous page.*

Likewise, in the 6th century, in convents, it was not uncommon for a <u>nun</u> to have herself bricked into a small space, leaving only a tiny slit through which food was passed, and there remain until death. Possession of such a "living relic" brought enormous prestige to a convent, and large numbers of pilgrims.

Consider also the ***female saints*** of the Middle Ages, who flogged themselves pitilessly; drank pus from the sores of the poor; laid themselves prostrate on the floor in a cruciform shape, and remained there for hours, arms outstretched, touching the floor only with their head and feet; crawled on broken glass; stood outside in winter, on the ice, until they were at the point of death; starved and beat themselves in sundry ways; weighed themselves down with heavy burdens; laced their clothing with thorns; and so on.

DANIEL STYLITES (409-493)

He first entered a monastery when he was only 12, but emerged some 25 years later to visit some of the more famous "athletes of God", as the hermits were sometimes called. He was especially inspired by St Simeon Stylites (see below) and, at 51 years of age, hearing that St Simeon had died, he resolved to emulate him. He built a small platform on top of a high stone pillar, and there lived for the next 33 years, coming down only once – to rebuke the emperor! He was visited by multitudes of people, including high officials, emperors, patriarchs, who came to hear him preach, to receive counsel, and to receive a miracle. He was renowned for the many healings he effected and for numerous prophetic oracles.

THEODORE OF SYKEON

Theodore was the son of a prostitute, who nonetheless in his boyhood was extraordinarily devout and ascetic. He flourished in the late 6th century. His devotion to Christ was so remarkable that

---

York by the highwayman Dick Turpin on his mare Black Bess (although it seems that the rider was actually another highwayman who lived a century earlier). As far as I can discover, the story is fictitious, but it remains an excellent picture of ascetic practice.

he was ordained a priest at 18 years of age. He built a small cage and had himself hung in it from a rock, loaded with chafing irons. He fasted for long periods, all the time following a strict regime of psalm-singing and deep devotion. He was soon famous for his many miracles of healing, exorcisms, and other signs and wonders that were attributed to him. By popular demand he was made a bishop and had to leave his cage, but after 11 years he tired of public life and returned to a hermit's existence, which he maintained until his death.

BENEDICT OF NURSIA

He too flourished in the 6th century. After going to Rome as a youth, to study, he became appalled by the vice that was everywhere practised. So, while he was still in his teens he became a hermit. He was soon famous for his piety and learning, and many sought his counsel and begged him to teach them. Among them were numerous wealthy people who brought their own sons to him to be educated.

Benedict built 12 monasteries (so it is said), each with 12 monks and a superior. At 50 years of age, he moved to Monte Cassino, half way between Naples and Rome, destroyed a pagan temple where Apollo was still being worshipped, and in its place built a large monastery. A twin sister, St Scholastica, built a convent nearby, and died just before Benedict himself passed away, *circa* 545. He had more influence than anyone else on the rise of monasticism in the West. (64)

But let me sum up all the hermits, ascetics, and the like, and their motivations, by returning to the best known –

ST SIMEON STYLITES

The son of a shepherd, when he was still but a boy of thirteen years, Simeon was powerfully affected by the beatitudes, which he heard read in the church, and betook himself to a cloister. On its threshold he prostrated himself for several days, without eating or

---

(64) The two latter biographies were gleaned from several sources.

drinking, and begged to be admitted as the meanest servant of the house. He accustomed himself to eat only once a week, on Sunday. During Lent he even went through the whole forty days without any food; a fact almost incredible even for a tropical climate. The first attempt of this kind brought him to the verge of death; but his constitution conformed itself, and when Theodoret visited him, he had solemnized six and twenty Lent seasons by total abstinence, and thus surpassed Moses, Elias, and even Christ, who never fasted so but once.

Simeon remained in that monastery as a servant for two years, after which, dissatisfied with its comparative laxity, he moved to a more austere monastery. There he practised harsher mortifications than any of the other inmates, until he nearly died after twisting a rope of palm leaves so tightly around his waist that it sank beneath his flesh. The monks had to work for three days to remove the rope by incisions after softening his skin with liquids. The abbot, appalled by his extreme pietism, then expelled him.

Not in the least discouraged, Simeon at once climbed to the top of a nearby mountain and chained himself to a rock for three years. Scores of pilgrims began to struggle up to his retreat, so he resolved to escape them by climbing onto the top of a stone pillar about 3 metres high. There he remained for 4 years, dependent entirely upon disciples for the meagre sustenance that was conveyed to him by a ladder. Deciding he was still too vulnerable to interruption, he mounted a column that was 6 metres high, where he spent 3 years. His third pillar was 10 metres high (for 10 years); and his fourth, 18 metres (his last 20 years).

During lent, Simeon fasted absolutely, spending the first two weeks standing upright praising God; the next two sitting; and last two (owing to growing weakness from the fast) lying horizontal. Every day he repeatedly bowed his body in prayer, prostrating himself more than 1000 times in succession, while wearing a heavy iron collar. For a long time he suffered himself to be tormented by twenty enormous bugs, and, to exercise himself in patience and meekness, concealed an abscess full of worms,.

Twice each day across the years he preached to the multitudes who thronged at the foot of his pillar, including emperors and princes; he healed the sick; thousands were converted to Christ; and he wrote influential letters and theology. Hearers testify that his preaching was practical and compassionate, and his doctrine was orthodox. He died while bowing before God on his pillar –

> From his original pulpit, as a mediator between heaven and earth, he preached repentance twice a day to the astonished spectators, settled controversies, vindicated the orthodox faith, extorted laws even from an emperor, healed the sick, wrought miracles, and converted thousands of heathen Ishmaelites, Iberians, Armenians, and Persians to Christianity, or at least to the Christian name.
>
> All this the celebrated Theodoret relates as an eyewitness during the lifetime of the saint. He terms him the great wonder of the world, and compares him to a candle on a candlestick, and to the sun itself, which sheds its rays on every side. He asks the objector to this mode of life to consider that God often uses very striking means to arouse the negligent, as the history of the prophets shows; and concludes his narrative with the remark: "Should the saint live longer, he may do yet greater wonders, for he is a universal ornament and honour of religion."
>
> Simeon died in 459, in the sixty-ninth year of his age, of a long-concealed and loathsome ulcer on his leg; and his body was brought in solemn procession to the metropolitan church of Antioch." [65]

Yet was it not all in vain? How deluded they were to suppose that such self-imposed suffering could procure them any better right to draw near to God than the humblest believer possesses fully in Christ.

---

(65)   From Philip Schaff (1819-1893) – <u>History of the Christian Church</u>, Vol. 3, Ch. 4, par. 34. Possibly the most moving account of the motives that drove St Simeon, and of his almost unimaginable privations, occurs in Tennyson's eponymous dramatic monologue (1842). The poet shows remarkable sympathy for the saint and for his deepest yearnings (see the following paragraphs).

Their error is well-exposed by Tennyson (1842) in his dramatic monologue *St Simeon Stylites*. Tennyson puts these words into the saint's mouth –

> I will not cease to grasp the hope I hold
> Of saintdom, and to clamour, morn and sob,
> Battering the gates of heaven with storms of prayer,
> Have mercy, Lord, and take away my sin.
> Let this avail, just, dreadful, mighty God,
> This not be all in vain that thrice ten years,
> Thrice multiplied by superhuman pangs,
> In hungers and in thirsts, fevers and cold,
> In coughs, aches, stitches, ulcerous throes and cramps,
> A sign betwixt the meadow and the cloud,
> Patient on this tall pillar I have borne
> Rain, wind, frost, heat, hail, damp, and sleet, and snow;
> ....
> Have mercy, mercy: take away my sin.
> O Jesus, if thou wilt not save my soul,
> Who may be saved? who is it may be saved?
> Who may be made a saint, if I fail here?

How dismally Simeon failed to grasp the message of the gospel. How dark was the blackness that overwhelmed his soul. Even after such suffering as scarcely any man has endured, he was still unsure of his welcome in heaven, still doubting whether or not he was truly saved, still wondering what more he might have to do. Yet all the time, at any time, during the years of his mortification, he had only to believe that Jesus had already died in his place, paying the full price of his redemption, and he would at once have been fully saved, sanctified, made holy in God's sight, and totally fit for Paradise!

According to Tennyson, Simeon cried, "Who may be made a saint, if I fail here?" The answer comes simply – anyone, from whatever walk of life or class of society, learned or ignorant, rich or poor, beautiful or ugly, brave or timid, will at once be saved and called a saint who openly confesses that Jesus is Lord and heartily believes that God raised him from the dead (Ro 10:9). ⁽⁶⁶⁾ Nothing more is needed; nothing more should be attempted. There are many good reasons for practising a measure of self-denial, for prayer and fasting, for making sacrifices in the service of God, but they do not and must not ever include obtaining salvation, or righteousness, or holiness, or free access to the throne of God!

The anchorites, the eremites, the hermits, the flagellants, the ascetics, the monks in all their misery were all a sign of a church that had turned its back on the gospel. Instead of simple faith, they were striving to merit heaven by good works and painful sacrifice. It was a situation that largely continued until the 16th century Reformation. The Reformers, with their emphasis upon the efficacy of scripture and the work of Christ alone, gained by faith alone, brought about a vastly better understanding of what Christ had wrought for his people at Calvary and by his resurrection.

Nonetheless, the dregs of that ancient stifling legalism still survive into the modern church. Against all such pestilent notions we must be constantly on guard, sternly defending our right to *"stand fast in the freedom for which Christ has made us free"* (Ga 5:1).

---

(66) For a further description of the ancient hermits, taken from Edward Gibbons' The Decline and Fall of the Roman Empire, see the Addendum at the end of this book.

Chapter Fourteen

FAITH

> *Just as Abraham was blessed because of his **faith**, so everyone who has **faith** will receive the same blessings. ... In Christ Jesus you are all sons of God, through **faith** (Ga 3:9, 26).*

Archimedes (c. 250 B.C.), the renowned Greek philosopher and mathematician, perfected the combined use of levers and pulleys to move heavy objects. He once boasted, "Give me a lever long enough, and a place upon which to stand, and I will move the Earth!" The tyrant Hiero heard this and challenged him to help his sailors beach a large warship. Archimedes (so it is said) arranged his mechanisms to such good effect that alone he pulled the huge vessel out of the water and onto the beach!

God, however, has given us a better way to move the planet! – **faith.** The word occurs 22 times in *Galatians*, 15 of them in chapter 3. It is our key to the impossible. By faith we can do whatever the Lord wants us to do, including overcoming

THE WORLD

> *Scripture tells us that the whole world is held captive by sin; but the promise that comes by **faith** in Jesus Christ belongs to those who **believe**. Now before **faith** came, we too were prisoners of the law, held in thrall until the coming **faith** would be revealed (Ga 3:22, 23).*

The "world" in our text is not the physical world, for after all, the earth is made by the hand of God, and was pronounced "good" (Ge 1:31; Ps 24:1; 1 Ti 6:17). Rather, it means the "world" that is against God and his church, this world's system, the scheme of things, the society fashioned by human beings, but now corrupted by Satan. It is the "world" that loves darkness rather than light (Jn 1:5; 3:19). This dark world opposes us in several ways –

SPIRITUALLY

It scorns the existence of God, mocks the idea of heaven, derides the concept of hell, and rejects the inspiration of scripture, insisting that at best religion is harmless if worthless, and at worst a deranged superstition. In any case, says the world, all religions are equal and can be dismissed as irrelevant.

MORALLY

The world never stops attacking the strictures of the church, striving to debase the moral tone of the community, using every means to incite men and women to ungodly passions. The world continually pressures the church to modify its moral laws, to allow free sex, to legitimise homosexual behaviour, even to endorse as valid lifestyles the practice of bestiality, cross gender dressing, and other conduct that violates biblical teaching.

INTELLECTUALLY

The world denounces the proposition that faith conveys its own authentication, and that faith can bring greater certainty than any other form of learning (cp. He 11:3, *"by faith we KNOW ..."*) It also denies the possibility of miracles, insisting that the world is absolutely controlled by natural law, and that even if there is a God he does not, and cannot, intervene in human affairs.

PHYSICALLY

Satan works in the secular world to produce disease and to enforce inequality and poverty, and whenever possible to undermine the influence of the gospel.

VIOLENTLY

The world inflicts persecution upon the righteous, sometimes covertly, sometimes overtly, but always continually and relentlessly (Jn 6:33).

Against such apparently overwhelming opposition what hope do we have? At first sight our case may seem hopeless, and our defeat inevitable. But then we raise a trumpet blast of **faith**, and suddenly reinforcements arrive, a Mighty Ally springs to our aid! We are a little like Robin Hood and his Merry Men – the outlaw leader had but to sound his horn and at once his men would rush to his aid! So too the angels are ready to war on our behalf (Ps 34:7; He 1:14) –

> *The angel of the Lord encamps around those who fear him, and he delivers them. – All the angels are ministering spirits, sent to serve those who will inherit salvation!*

And if they are not sufficient, then we have a Defender and Warrior in the Lord God himself (Ps 27:1-3). So we declare boldly that against this opposing world and all its enmity stands -

OUR FAITH

About this invincible faith that *"overcomes the world"* (1 Jn 5:4), we may say that

FAITH SEES VICTORY IN EVERY CIRCUMSTANCE

*In Christ Jesus you are all sons of God, through **faith** (Ga 3:26).*

Am I truly a son of God? Then I cannot be defeated! Oh! I may (and do) lose a skirmish or two, and perhaps even an occasional battle – but the <u>war</u> I cannot lose. Indeed, we must all believe unwaveringly in the inevitability of our triumph in Christ. The Christian's attitude should be like that of Alexander the Great, when some of his generals expressed alarm at the immense size of the Persian army. The Greeks, who numbered only 50,000, faced a host of two million Persian warriors. But Alexander laughed: "Is the butcher afraid, though he stands alone before a thousand sheep?"

Or like the warrior, Dienekes, described by the Greek historian Herodotus (*circa* 450 B.C.) –

> Of all the Spartans who fought so valiantly, the most signal proof of courage was given by Dienekes. It is said that before the battle he was told that when the Persians shot their arrows there were so many of them that they hid the sun. ... Dienekes, however, quite unmoved by the thought of the strength of the Persian army, merely remarked: "This is pleasant news! If the Persians hide the sun, then we shall have our battle in the shade." He is

said to have spoken many things of this kind, by which he will be remembered. [67]

The American president, Andrew Jackson (1767-1845), once said, "One man with courage makes a majority!"

So too, we who believe must hold bravely to our faith, no matter how dire our situation may seem to be. Those who believe in victory cannot ever be persuaded to give up, or surrender, or turn away from the battle!

Yet people often feel that they must blame themselves when troubles come upon them, as if they were lacking in faith. But troubles do not mean that you have no faith; rather, they are a signal to rise up and *use* your faith! Never doubt that Jesus has *"conquered the world"* – not for himself, but for you and me!

Yet that does not mean an easy path, nor that the battle will be without pain, nor that the warrior in the thick of the fight will always escape unscathed. Warfare is never pleasant, although many do seem to expect a pleasant ride to heaven, and are dismayed and run away when the going gets hard. But –

> It's easy to cry that you're beaten – and die;
> It's easy to crawfish and crawl;
> But to fight and to fight when hope's out of sight
> Why, that's the best game of them all!
> And though you come out of each gruelling bout
> All broken and beaten and scarred,
> Just have one more try – It's dead easy to die,
> It's the keeping-on-living that's hard! [68]

We who believe are resolved to *"quit ourselves like men and women of God"* (1 Co 16:13), never to surrender, to stand fast in the freedom for which Christ has set us free (Ga 5:1), and to hold unwaveringly to the faith that can and will overcome the world!

---

(67) Herodotus was referring to the Battle of Thermopylae, where the valiant 300 Spartans opposed the massive advancing Persian army. In the 2007 film about this event, "300", the line is attributed to someone else, but it was actually spoken by Dienekes. A street in modern Sparta (pop. 20,000) is named after him.

(68) "The Quitter", by Robert Service, st. 3.

FAITH TRUSTS IN THE GOODNESS OF GOD

*For through the Spirit, by **faith**, we ourselves eagerly wait for the hope of righteousness.* (Ga 5:5)

A legend is told about a German monk, whose only possessions were a donkey to carry him, a parrot to keep him company, a lamp to guide him at night, and a song to sing: *"Praise God from whom all blessings flow!"* As he journeyed, a lion killed his donkey; but he sang, "Praise God from whom all blessing flow!" An eagle seized his parrot; but he sang, "Praise God from whom all blessings flow!" He fell, and smashed his lamp; but still he sang, "Praise God from whom all blessings flow!" He sought refuge in a village and was roughly driven out; but as he went he sang, "Praise God from whom all blessings flow!" That night, while he slept in the forest, damp with dew, still murmuring his praises to the Lord, the village was attacked by bandits, pillaged, torched, and its inhabitants enslaved. He remained undiscovered and safe. He went on his way, still singing, *"Praise God from whom all blessings flow!"*

He had sustained his faith with unwavering praise, and so gained the honour and protection of God! How can we learn to confront the sometimes crushing burdens of life with such cheerful optimism? How can we begin each new day energised by the all-conquering dynamic of miracle-working faith? Simply make up your mind that you will cast aside all fear and **believe!** The promises of God are sure, sealed by the blood of Christ, guaranteed by his resurrection, and alive in him on his throne at the Father's right hand. But the victory of Jesus over the world can do you no good while you stay afraid and doubtful. So *"fear not, believe only"* and you will never fight alone, but always with Christ at your side.

FAITH TRUSTS IN THE LOVE OF GOD

*Dear friends, you have been called into freedom, but do not use your liberty as an excuse to gratify the flesh, but by **love** serve each other. ... For all the law is fulfilled in this one command –You must **love** your neighbour as yourself. ... The fruit of the Spirit is **love**.* (Ga 5:13, 14, 22)

Two of the characters in Oscar Wilde's play *A Woman of No Importance* (Act One) are a young man (Gerald), and a young woman (Hester). Gerald receives some good news and he asks Hester why she does not congratulate him on his fortune –

Hester: Are you very pleased about it?

Gerald: Of course I am. It means everything to me – things that were out of the reach of hope before may be within hope's reach now.

Hester: Nothing should ever be out of the reach of hope!

We are called to trust in the goodness and love of the Father, not because everything always goes right for a believer, but because many things will and do go wrong! But we who believe never abandon hope. Yet the only valid foundation for unshakable hope is unbreakable trust in the love of God offered to us through Christ. That love, we are told, is a *"fruit of the Spirit"*, which means that it comes from God and is indeed his very character. He cannot do other than act in love, for *"God is love!"* (1 Jn 4:8, 16)

The love of God is not always apparent. He sometimes acts in ways that seem to us unloving, allowing horrible things to happen. But that is only because our viewpoint is short-term, whereas the Lord has eternity in mind. For this reason, troubles may be inevitable, but they cannot crush us unless we have allowed fear to take mastery over us. Fear creates an impenetrable barrier to faith. So we must choose between fear or faith – the first pulls us toward ruin; the second pulls us toward a miracle of answered prayer.

FAITH RELEASES THE POWER OF GOD BY PRAISE

Never once in history has a conquering army been known to sit down and howl in despair! But scripture says that our faith already IS the victory; that is, those who believe are not <u>reaching</u> for victory; rather, they see themselves as already triumphant in Christ. Faith admits no defeat; in fact, faith cannot be defeated! Therefore we who believe, rejoice, for we can do no other.

In 1915, during the darkest days of World War I, a competition was held in London to find a song that would build the optimism and morale of the British army and people. The rules required the song to be one that would cause people to whistle and sing, even when German shells were raining down upon them! The winner was –

> Pack up your troubles in your old kit-bag,
> And smile, smile, smile!
> Don't let your joy and laughter hit a snag,
> Smile boys, that's the style!
> What's the use of worrying?
> It never was worthwhile, so,
> Pack up your troubles in your old kit-bag,
> And smile, smile, smile!

Yet the man who wrote those happy words, along with the song's lively melody, Staff Sergeant Felix Powell, later committed suicide by shooting himself through the heart with his own rifle. I don't know why Mr Powell took his own life. But it is hard to believe that he could have done so if he had been living in the genuine faith-drenched optimism that Christ conveys! Like Israel of old, we march to war singing the songs of Zion, hearing the rustle of angels' wings over us and around us, assuring us that our triumph is certain.

So in harmony with the scriptures that head this chapter, and with the promise of Christ, we should boldly believe that by faith we can overcome this world and all its opposition. We are, says Paul, children of God by faith alone (Ga 3:26), and as such we are assured of -

VICTORY

One occasion Jesus said, *"In this world you will experience suffering, but cheer up! I have overcome the world."* (Jn 16:33) He used a lively word, which is properly translated as *"cheer up"*. It could also be rendered, *"take heart ... be brave ... take courage"* – and the like; but "cheer up" probably best catches the vigorous sense of the original. The word is always imperative, and it occurs in 6 different settings (Mt 9:2, 22; 14:27; Mk 10:49; Jn 16:33; and Ac 23:11), where Jesus spoke his command to "cheer up" –

- To the PARALYSED man who was let down through the roof on a stretcher.
- To the WOMAN suffering from chronic bleeding who crept up behind Jesus and touched his robe.
- To the DISCIPLES at sea on a stormy night who were terrified when they saw Jesus walking toward them on the water.
- To blind BARTIMAEUS as he was shouting for mercy.
- To the DISCIPLES when they heard that Jesus was to be taken away from them.
- To PAUL when he had been rescued by the Romans from a riot in Jerusalem and had been dragged off to prison.

In each case, the people faced impossible odds, more conducive to despair than to laughter. So why did Jesus make such an unreasonable demand?

He understood this principle: the miracle you need does not begin in God, but in your own spirit. He wanted them all to be like Veronica, [69] who walked 75 km from Caesarea-Philippi to lower western Galilee, and all the way kept *"saying to herself, 'If I can just touch his cloak, I will be cured!'"* (Mk 5:28)

So before Jesus gave those people any *promise*, he gave them a *command*: *"Cheer up!"* (the verb, once again, is strongly imperative in Greek). We too must learn, in <u>every</u> circumstance, to be cheerful – that is, ready to praise God with all our heart! There is *always* something for which to praise the Lord, even when the crisis has been precipitated by satanic action. There is always a promise to claim, an assurance to be grasped, a hope to be seized, a strength to be drawn, a light to shine, or the love of God to know!

---

(69) According to ancient church tradition the name of the lady whom Jesus healed of an *"issue of blood"* was Veronica. See *The Gospel of Nicodemus*, etc. See also *Wikipedia*, art. Saint Veronica.

In each of the examples given above, the people drove away their fears, set themselves to <u>believe only</u>, and they all gained the miracle they desired.

I do not mean to minimise or trivialise suffering, or to mock someone's pain, for no doubt their hurt is very real. Nonetheless, even in the darkest midnight of the soul we should reckon the glory of God is so much greater that beside it our troubles seem small. And again, in every circumstance we can *always* find some cause for praise.

In all these things, we have an astonishing example in the Saviour himself! —

TRIUMPH

How astonishing is the declaration Jesus made! Golgotha and all its horrors still lie ahead of him, yet so confident is he of victory that he asserts an existing triumph: *"In this world you will have many troubles. But cheer up! For I <u>have</u> overcome the world!"*

Although his death and resurrection were still ahead of him, he knew within himself that he would triumph, and boldly asserted his victory! That was a faith-statement! Thus he himself set the example that we should follow. So then, let us all resolve now to heed the Master's injunction and "Cheer up!" for Christ has utterly conquered the world!

We may have to contend with a few troubles; but Christ has given us his endless peace to quench every fear, and his limitless strength to carry us into invincible victory, *both now and for ever!*

Chapter Fifteen

REDEMPTION

*Christ has **redeemed** us from the curse of the law, having become a curse for us, for it is written, "Everyone who is hanged upon a tree is accursed." ... God sent his Son, born under the law, born of a woman, so that he might **redeem** those who were under the law* (Ga 3:13; 4:5).

On the evening each year when a Jewish family celebrates the Haggadah, [70] the youngest child asks these questions – *"Why is this night so different from all other nights, and why do we eat unleavened bread? ... On this night why do we eat bitter herbs?"*

Everybody present answers –

"We eat unleavened bread to remind us how our ancestors had to bake their loaves quickly and leave Egypt without delay. ... We taste bitter herbs to remind us of the bitter life they lived there."

This is done in obedience to the words of Moses in *Exodus 12:3-13, 23*, and in particular to his command that devout Jews must tell their children about the miracle of the exodus, and what it should mean to them (vs. 26-27; 13:8-14).

At the beginning of the meal, and in between the questions, the father at the head of the table is expected to tell the Passover story, and three things absolutely must be mentioned: the *Unleavened Bread*, the *Bitter Herbs*, and the *Passover Lamb*, along with the manner in which the avenging angel was compelled by God to

---

(70) The Haggadah is both the name given to the exodus of the Hebrew slaves from Egypt and the book that describes it. Reciting the story, the questions, and the answers, is all part of the Seder, a ceremony that is held around the end of March or early April each year. In the account above I have abridged the questions and answers, and simplified the ceremony. In a Jewish home the Seder would include several more rituals and much longer questions, answers, and commentary.

leave unharmed every household that had lamb's blood sprinkled on its doorway.

This study focusses on the third element – the Blood of the Paschal Lamb. Once every year the Seder reminds devout Jews of how the blood of a lamb secured their safety on that dreadful night of death throughout ancient Egypt. We too are regularly reminded of the death of our Saviour, the Lamb of God, when we break bread together in his name (1 Co 11:26). But much more than that, scripture urges us to think about what we are doing, and especially to understand the meaning of the blood spilt for us at Calvary.

If you are not experiencing the full potential of Christian life, perhaps the reason lies in a failure to grasp how you should relate to the blood of Christ. For example, consider the popular hymn, *Power In The Blood,* with its throbbing refrain, *"There is wonder working power in the precious blood of the Lamb."* No doubt that is a joyful song, and a delight to sing, but you should realise that its main idea does not occur in scripture! That is, nowhere in the Bible is any particular energy or strength ascribed to the actual blood of Jesus. It was, after all, simply ordinary human blood (albeit unstained by sin).

How then does the blood work? Has it no power at all?

Think about the first Passover. Note that the sprinkled blood itself did not drive away the Angel of Death. Rather, the dark Spirit was prevented *by the hand of God* from harming anyone in a house that was sprinkled with blood. In other words, this event was called the *Passover*, not because the *Angel* "passed *by*" the sprinkled homes, but because *God* "passed *over*" them – that is, he overshadowed and protected them by his own presence – *"When I see the blood, I will pass over you, and no plague will befall you to destroy you"* (Ex 12:13, ESV).

The Israelites did not expect the blood of a lamb to protect them; but, after the blood was applied, they did expect *God* to see it, and then to cover them himself, and to save them from the Avenger.

We too must see that the Blood of the Cross marvellously gives God a legal and righteous basis upon which to forgive us and to treat us as though we had never sinned. But the blood of Christ is not a kind of lucky charm, able by itself to ward off evil. Such ideas tend to reduce the atonement to the level of superstition, rather than exalt it into the realm of faith.

The blood of Christ is therefore not a weapon, whether of attack or of defense; by itself it cannot give you victory or protect you. But the blood does enable God to impute to you the righteousness of Christ (Ro 4:22-25). Standing in that righteousness then brings us two wonderful boons –

- It enables God to act on our behalf, to protect and prosper us.
- It enables us to speak boldly in Jesus' Name against all the works of Satan.

So let us remember the Paschal Lamb – Christ our Lord, who did indeed die for us, but who rose again from the dead, and now lives forever — God's guarantee that we too shall live and reign with him! But before going any further in a study of the redemption we have found in Christ, let us return to the Exodus. The number of people who marched out of Egypt may have been as many as two million! (Ex 12:37-38). Further, we are told that they were riotously healthy – not one feeble person among them! (Ps 105:37; Ac 13:12) They were all strong and well. Imagine a community of that size (twice the population of Adelaide, or, in the USA, of Tulsa) completely free from all disease, poverty, or weakness! Was this arbitrary? Can it happen now? Well, it certainly stretches one's credulity, yet there is no reason to suppose that the same degree of supernatural intervention is not available now. Why then do we so seldom see it? Perhaps because people fail to understand just what *redemption* means!

THE MEANING OF REDEMPTION

The original (but now archaic) meaning of "redeem" was to purchase freedom for someone who was a slave, or in prison. The word more commonly used today for such a transaction is "ransom"; but in biblical usage "redeem" still carries its ancient meaning. We were slaves, in bondage to sin, the moral law, and death; but Christ, by being made a curse for us, has redeemed us from the curse of the law (Ga 3:13). The Israelites were redeemed from Egypt — we have been rescued from the grip of Satan.

Something of what it means for one person to substitute himself for another is found in the ancient story of *Damon and Phintias* –

> Phintias had been condemned to death for treason by the ruler of Syracuse, Dionysius I (B.C. 432-367). Before the sentence was carried out, Phintias asked permission to return home to settle his affairs and bid farewell to those he loved. The tyrant refused. But then Damon, a close friend of Phintias, stepped forward, and offered himself as a hostage.
>
> Dionysius agreed, so long as it was understood that Damon would himself be executed if Phintias failed to return. Damon accepted the terms, and was sent off to prison. Phintias set sail for his home, and was not seen again until the day of execution had come. Just as Damon was being led out to his death, Phintias finally arrived, breathless from haste. He apologised for his lateness, explaining that his ship had been delayed by pirates, but he was now ready to submit to his punishment.
>
> Dionysius was so moved by this example of selfless love and friendship that he at once granted Phintias his freedom, and begged to become himself a friend to the two men. [71]

So Jesus proved himself our Friend, except that in his case no one came to his rescue. He had to tread the winepress of heaven's wrath alone (Is 63:3), all stained with blood, until the work of redemption was done. Paul uses an uncommon verb in our texts, *exagorazo*, which means literally "to buy out of slavery". Christ was driven by love to the cross, by love he held himself there, until he was able to cry, *"It is finished!"* The price was fully paid. The slaves can shake off their chains. The taskmaster no longer has any authority over them. Let them now learn how to stand fast in the

---

(71) The account given here is based mainly on the story as it is found in <u>A Smaller Classical Dictionary</u>, by William Smith, 19th edition; pub. By John Murray, London, 1882; article *Damon and Phintias*.

freedom for which Christ has so wonderfully set them free! (Ga 5:1)

TWO QUESTIONS

Two questions are provoked by the idea of redemption – what price was paid; to whom was it paid?

The price was manifestly the death of Jesus, who at Calvary took upon himself your sins and mine, and substituted himself for us. We should have died. He perished instead. Our sin should have destroyed us. Instead, it destroyed him. Our failure to keep the law of God condemned us to outer darkness for ever; but he obeyed the law in our place, and then accepted our punishment as if he himself were the guilty one. Now we no longer shrink from the presence of God, but rather rejoice before him, because through our Lord Jesus Christ, we have received full atonement (Ro 5:11).

None of this means that Jesus became sinful in himself, or that he was ever shadowed by guilt, but only that he was willing for sin to be attributed to him so that righteousness might be attributed to us. He might have been *"made a curse"* but he was never *in himself "accursed"*; he simply suffered vicariously, the innocent for the guilty, the ever-living for the dying, bearing the curse of death that should have fallen upon us sinners.

The recipient. Never suppose that the redeeming blood of Christ was offered to Satan to buy our freedom from him. God owed no debt to the devil, nor any need to pay even the smallest price to him. In this the divine transaction differs strongly from earthly actions. A benefactor who wants to free a slave from his manacles will offer a price to the slave owner. But the devil, although he held us in thrall, did not own us. We were and are always God's possession, even when we were still *"dead in our sins"* (Ep 2:4-5).

Nor was the price of our redemption paid to God, for the Father in love would gladly have pardoned all sin and welcomed us back to eternal life. But because the moral order of the universe had been disrupted by human sin, and because his offended law had to be requited, the Father had to find a legal and holy way to redeem us before he could seat us at his table (Ep 2:18-19).

In a sense, the price was paid to the Law itself. The broken commandments of God demanded satisfaction. But law is not an entity that can receive a payment of any sort. Nor can payment be made to sin, or to death. So when the Bible speaks about "redemption" and "ransom", we should see the words as metaphors, which mean only that whatever had to be done to satisfy all the penalties imposed by the broken law *was* done at Calvary. There, as our substitute, and in our stead, Jesus bore all the wrath of the violated law of God, loosing us from its threats, and releasing us to serve God in liberty as his free-born sons and daughters. There his blood purchased our deliverance from death and gave us a sure promise of everlasting life in Paradise.

CONCLUSION

Six weeks after she was born in New York in 1820, Frances became blind because of medical incompetence. Despite this handicap, she went on to a successful career as a teacher, particularly in English grammar, rhetoric, and American history. She was the first woman ever permitted to address the US Senate in Washington. In her mid-30s she began to write poetry seriously, and later, hymns, of which she composed more than 4,000, which were so well-loved that from her mid-40s onward she was able to support herself on royalties alone. She is also said to have written some 4,000 poems on diverse subjects. Perhaps 50 or 60 of her hymns are still regularly published in collections worldwide. She is known today as Fanny Crosby, and among the more popular of her hymns is *Redeemed* (published in 1882) –

> Redeemed, how I love to proclaim it!
> Redeemed by the blood of the Lamb;
>
> Redeemed through his infinite mercy,
> His child and for ever I am.
>
> Redeemed;
> Redeemed by the blood of the Lamb;
> Redeemed;
> His child and for ever I am!

That is a song the ransomed sons and daughters of God will still be singing in the halls of Paradise for ever!

Chapter Sixteen

HEIRS

And if you are Christ's, then you are Abraham's offspring, **heirs** *according to promise. I mean that the* **heir** *... is the owner of everything* (Ga 3:29-4:1).

Twice in my life I have been confronted by a loaded gun. On the first occasion, an irate husband sent a message to me by his wife that he had a shotgun standing beside the front door, and he would blast me with both barrels if I dared to visit his home. Well, of course, that was a challenge I couldn't possibly ignore. So up to the front door I went, rang the bell, and was admitted by his anxious wife. I confess I was a little worried myself when I saw the shotgun standing just inside the door! However, summoning all courage, in I went and confronted the angry householder, who turned as meek as a lamb. The visit concluded, I went safely home to my wife.

The second time a gun was poked at me happened one Sunday morning. Our church service was well under way when a deacon came up to me and whispered that there was a fellow outside with a rifle. He was threatening mayhem on anyone who showed a face, especially me, the pastor. I bade the deacon to lock the front and rear doors to prevent anyone from leaving the building, and then went outside to confront the would-be slaughterer. Walking straight up to him, I grabbed the rifle (which was pointing at me), yanked back the bolt, took out the bullets, and handed the disarmed weapon to him. This was all done so quickly he had no time to react or to stop me! Then I sternly warned him to leave the property at once or I would call the police and lodge so many charges against him he'd be lucky ever to get out of prison. He hurried away, and I have never again laid eyes on him.

I cannot deny that I look back on those two occasions and wonder if I was out of my mind! But still, that is what I did, and all the time I was trusting that the Father would protect me, his son and heir. Why? Because God is good, he is indeed my Father, I am surely his heir, and I do indeed trust him to care for me. Yet I know that supernatural protection is not always assured – or at least it can take different shapes at different times. The best of us may sometimes find ourselves dealing with misfortunes of various kinds. Any of us can suffer bitter loss – like the three travellers whose car broke down far from any town. One of the men was smart, one average, and one a bit dim. Having no other choice, they began the long walk back home. As they trudged along they came upon a large owl sitting atop the fence. To their astonishment, the owl suddenly spoke – "Weary Travellers, I will give you each one wish." At once the smart one cried, "I want to be home and rich beyond the dreams of avarice." "Wish granted!" said the owl, and the man vanished. Then the average man said, "I want to be home and married to the most beautiful girl in the world." "Wish granted!" said the owl. The dim fellow looked around and felt lonely. "I wish my friends were back," he said ... [72]

Just so, sudden reversals in fortune can overtake any of us. A prince today may find himself a beggar tomorrow, and a beggar may find himself a prince (Ec 10:7; Pr 30:22). So too, across more than 60 years of ministry together, my wife Alison and I have been through several dark vales shadowed by death – but like the psalmist of old we finally emerged from them safely (Ps 23:4). Now I can say with David –

> *I have been young, and now am old, yet I have not seen the righteous forsaken or his children begging for bread.* (Ps 37:25, ESV)

Are the righteous never obliged to beg? I suppose they sometimes do find themselves naked and hungry, and desperately in need. But I also know this – if they trust God, and hold to their faith with unwavering confidence, and keep on rejoicing, the Father will carry them through the trial and restore their prosperity.

However, many people, like the Israelites of old, are prone to blame God when everything goes wrong, and to accuse him of tyranny, indifference, or weakness!

---

(72)   I regret that I have no idea of the origin of this joke.

But he remains our Father and we are his children and his heirs. Every time we repeat the *Lord's Prayer* we are reminded of this. Yet how easily we forget. And if, in the midst of our complaint, we tune our ear to heaven, you will hear the voice of God speaking with plaintive sorrow –

> *I thought you would call me "Father!"* (Je 3:19)

How poignant those words are! What do they mean? Simply this: if I wish to be in truth an heir of God, and to be his true son, then I must learn how to affirm his Fatherhood boldly, and with brave assurance. I must learn to live as a child and heir of the Living God. And that means –

SUBMIT TO HIS DISCIPLINE!

Does that seem a strange place to begin? Yet there is no fatherhood without submission! –

> *Endure your discipline. God corrects you as a father corrects his children. All children are disciplined by their fathers. If you aren't disciplined like the other children, you aren't part of the family. On earth we have fathers who disciplined us, and we respect them. Shouldn't we place ourselves under the authority of God, the Father of spirits, so that we will live? For a short time our fathers disciplined us as they thought best. Yet, God disciplines us for our own good so that we can become holy like him.* (Hebrews 12:7-10, GW)

However, sometimes, like Absalom scorching the fields of Joab, God has to *"burn a barley field"* to get our attention (2 Sa 14:28-33). Let us then stop apologising for the dealings of God, and submit to them. Even better, let us try to hear what the Lord may be saying to us in the valley, heed his words, and allow him to lead us out of it! After all, the psalmist did not expect to remain in the valley of the shadow of death, but to walk *through* it, and in the meantime, to be comforted by the Good Shepherd's rod and staff.

BELIEVE IN HIS LOVE!"

The Hebrew text of the oracle from *Jeremiah* (3:19, quoted above, has two singularly strong expressions –

- *"I myself deeply thought ..."* – it is hard to express in English the heavy emphasis that is contained in the original.
- *"Treat you ..."* – the verb is feminine; the sense being that he is addressing Israel as a daughter, yet contrary both to law and custom, he wants to offer her the inheritance of a favourite son.

It reads as if, say, a lesser daughter were to replace a first-born son as heir to the British throne! How strongly then the Father wants to bestow upon us his rich promise! –

> *Oh what a joy it would be for me to treat you like a son! What a joy it would be for me to give you a pleasant land, the most beautiful piece of property there is in all the world!* (vs. 19a, NET)

But they would not receive it, nor call him "Father" – perhaps because of pride, sin, unbelief, or maybe just disappointment with the way the Lord had dealt with them. Don't be like them. Whatever circumstance we find ourselves in, we must learn how to affirm and cling to the love of God. No other knowledge can surpass knowing that God is your Father, and that he loves you with an everlasting love.

ACCEPT HIS PROVIDENCE

We can have free will or divine control, but not both! Thus we find scattered through the Bible, passages like these –

> *Dear friends, don't be surprised or shocked that you are going through testing that is like walking through fire.* (1 Pe 4:12, CEV)

> *You will start hearing about wars and threats of wars, <u>but don't be afraid</u>. These things must all happen first, <u>but this isn't the end</u>. Nations and kingdoms will go to war against each other. People will starve to death, and in some places there will be earthquakes. But these things are just the beginning of troubles, for you yourselves will be arrested, punished, and even killed.*

> *Because of me, you will be hated by people in every nation. Many will give up their faith, and they will betray and hate each other. False prophets will appear and deceive many people. Wickedness will spread and cause many people to abandon even the pretence of love. <u>But if you keep on being faithful right to the end, you will be saved</u>.* (Mt 24:6-13)

In the presence of such scriptures, we should hardly be surprised when evil things happen in the world, when sin and Satan are prevailing, when it seems that all goodness is gone and that God has lost interest in us and our hurt. But how can we despair? For to us who believe is given the wonderful promise –

> *We know that God is working in every circumstance, to turn it into good for those who love him, and who are called according to his purpose.* (Ro 8:28)

Which leads us on into our next thought. If you call God Father, then you will –

REJOICE IN HIS BENEVOLENCE

Despite heaven's invitation, ancient Israel never discovered this truth, they never learned to say to God, *"My Father!"* They failed to discern God's heart, and could see him only as Creator, Judge, Ancestor, King. He was "Father" only in a tribal or national sense, as in –

> *You should be my people and I should be your God. You should be my children and I should be your father* (2 Esdras 1:29).

The idea in that passage is much like the old British use of "Sire" when addressing the king. He was deemed the "father" of the nation; but the title lacked any element of personal relationship, of charm, or of fellowship.

Not until Jesus came (Lu 2:49; 11:2) did the warm, personal meaning of the old scriptures become clear. He was probably the first person ever in Israel's long history to say to God, *"My Father!"* People were amazed when they heard Jesus addressing the Lord in such a personal and intimate way. And still today many people find it difficult to accept that God loves them individually, and yearns for them to call him *"Father"* personally and lovingly.

One reason for this reluctance is that it takes a certain toughness of mind, a vigour of faith, to believe in divine benevolence, especially when you have been driven into a deep vale of sorrow. Often it seems that God has forgotten we exist, that he cares nothing for our pain. But those are the very times we need to affirm his Fatherhood loudly, bravely and persistently refusing to doubt his goodness. When the hour is blackest is just when we most need to be absolutely sure of his love and his benevolence.

To help us, we have a great asset in Holy Spirit baptism –

> *You have received the Spirit of adoption as sons, by whom we cry, "Abba! Father!" ... The Spirit helps us in our weakness. For when we do not know what to pray for ... the Spirit himself intercedes for us with groans that cannot be expressed in ordinary words.* (Ro 8:15-17, 26)

How beautiful is the word *"help"* – *"the Holy Spirit helps us!"* No Spirit-filled Christian is ever helpless, or lacking in help. Always, in every time of need, the Holy Spirit, the divine Comforter (Jn 14:16, KJV), is ever ready with assistance that is abundant, relevant, invincible, and supernal.

CONCLUSION

According to God's own promise we are his heirs and the owners of everything (Ga 3:29-4:1). And because we are his heirs, this is what the Father would like to say to you and to me today –

*"How gladly would I treat you as a first-born son!
How gladly would I give you a splendid inheritance!"*

What will your response be? Acceptance or rejection of the divine offer? For the one, there is a promise of bountiful love, life, and joy. For the other, nothing but a sad echo following each receding footstep –

"I thought that you would call me Father!"

Chapter Seventeen

TIME

*But when the fulness of **time** had come, God sent forth his Son, born of a woman, born under the law, to redeem those who were under the law, so that we might receive adoption as sons.* (Ga 4:4-5, ESV) [73]

Toward the end of the first century an unwanted infant boy was left on the roadside by his parents. He was picked up by a person who made a living out of collecting and selling abandoned children. In Rome the boy was sold to a wealthy matron, Rhoda, who eventually freed him. He soon displayed remarkable business acumen and began to amass a fortune. He also married, had several children, and, along with his family, began to attend church. His name was Hermas, and he and his family prospered until a time of persecution fell upon the church. His wife and children recanted and denounced Hermas, who was arrested and imprisoned. There he became aware of many personal faults, deeply repented, and resolved that if he were freed again he would devote his life, not to getting rich, but to the service of Christ. Upon his release he set about regaining the love and respect of his wife, who herself repented and returned to the faith. His children, it seems, remained rebellious against the gospel, but Hermas stayed true to his vow and was content to serve the church in Rome as a deacon for the remainder of his life.

Somewhere around the year 130, Hermas began to compose an allegory, *The Shepherd*, which, in a series of visions, similitudes, and other devices, presents a body of teaching about Christ and the church. For several centuries it was enormously influential and Hermas himself was named one of the Fathers of the Church. In

---

(73) This chapter closely resembles a section in my book *Emmanuel – Part One*. But the text is so central to Paul's argument in *Galatians* that I felt obliged to include it here as well.

many parts of the early church his book was treated and quoted as scripture. It was finally dropped from the canon in the fifth century, but it is still in print today, usually titled *The Shepherd of Hermas*.

It contains the first known reference to an ancient piece of theology known as **_adoptionism_**, which raises the question: has Jesus always existed as the Son of God with the Father, or did he have no existence prior to his birth in Bethlehem nearly 2000 years ago? Adoptionism argues that Christ was an ordinary man who, because of his extraordinary virtue and amazing works, was *"adopted"* by God – that is, elevated to deity by an act of the Father. Because of the many contemporary myths about humans who had been apotheosised, this was an easy view for the ancients to accept. The doctrine eventually assumed the following outline –

- Jesus was born of a virgin by an act of the Holy Spirit.
- After his virtue had been proved through 30 years of testing, the Holy Spirit fell upon him, and he became the *Christ*.
- But he was not yet divine, until by his resurrection the Father transformed him into the Son of God (Ro 1:4; and cp. Ac 2:32-33).

The purpose of the doctrine was to explain the mystery of how Jesus could be both God and Man, and how he could suffer and die if he is divine. It failed because scripture plainly shows the doctrine of Christ's –

PRE-EXISTENCE

The pre-existence of Christ is demonstrated in many places –

"Jesus knew that he had come from God." (Jn 13:3)

"I know where I came from ... I came from God." (Jn 8:14,42; and cp. 12:27; 18:37)

"The glory I had with you before the world began." (Jn 17:5)

"Christ is the Lord from heaven." (1 Co 15:47)

"Although Christ was rich, yet he became poor for our sake." (2 Co 8:9)

"Although he had the very nature of God ... Christ emptied himself, and ... took on human likeness." (Ph 2:6-8)

"All things in heaven and on earth were created by Christ." (Cl 1:15-16)

"Before Christ ascended into heaven, he first descended onto the earth." (Ep 4:8, 9).

"God sent his one and only Son into the world." (Jn 3:16; 1 Jn 4:9-10).

Or, as Paul puts it in our text, *"<u>God sent forth his Son</u>."* (Ga 4:4)

"Adoptionism" then must be rejected. We who believe have been *"adopted"* as the children of God (Ga 4:5), but not Jesus. Before time began he was the eternal Son of the everlasting Father, and he will still be so when time ends. The biblical proposition is that through Christ humanity has now been added to deity; but adoptionism turns scripture around and says that deity was added to humanity. But that would exalt man above God, for only the *lesser* can be added to the *greater*!

However, although Christ as the Logos dwells in eternity, his work of redemption was completed within the years of time – *"When <u>the time was fully come</u> God sent his Son to redeem us"* (Ga 4:4-5, ESV). [74] That double marvel – the virgin birth of Jesus, and his confinement within time – has often been raised by critics as proof that the gospel is absurd. They claim that

- the events are discontinuous with history, unlike anything God had done before, and are too improbable to be believed; and furthermore,
- it defies reason that deity can be confined to a womb and then circumscribed by time and flesh.

---

(74) This chapter closely resembles a section in my book *Emmanuel – Part One*. But the text is so central to Paul's argument in *Galatians* that I felt obliged to include it here as well.

No doubt the virgin birth of the Son of God is an amazing event; but it is not incredible, nor is it disconnected from history, for it had been long -

FORETOLD

INCREDIBLE PROPHECIES

It has been claimed that there are more than 300 predictions in the OT that were fulfilled in Jesus of Nazareth. Whether that is so or not, Jesus himself did tell us to *"search the scriptures"* (Jn 5:39).

Peter Stoner lists only 8 of those 300 prophecies (Ps 22:16; Is 53:7; Mi 5:2; Zc 9:9; 11:12,13; 13:6; Ma 3:1). [75] He then calculates that the chance of any one man (from the time the OT was completed until Jesus was born) fulfilling all 8 prophecies is 1 in 10^{17}. Here is some idea of what that means: cover the whole of NSW [76] with 20c coins to a depth of 2 metres; throw into the pile one marked coin; stir up the heap; then ask a blind man to find the marked coin! His chance of finding it on his first try is 1 in 10^{17}.

Add another 8 prophecies, and the odds increase to 1 in 10^{45}, which would equal enough 20c coins to cover a circle with an area 30 times greater than the distance from the earth to the sun – that is, more than 4 thousand million kilometres.

If you increase the number of prophecies to 48, the odds then become an astonishing 1 in 10^{157}, which I have heard said equals to the number of the grains of dust in the entire universe!

Contrast that prophetic boldness on the part of scripture with (say) the *Qur'an*, which scorns the need for any predictions, save those of the coming resurrection and judgment. The Bible staked its reputation on the reliability of its oracles, and is yet to be embarrassed by the failure of any of them!

---

(75) Science Speaks, by P. W. Stoner & R. C. Newman; Moody Press, Chicago; 1976; ch. 3, "The Christ of Prophecy".

(76) One of the larger states in Australia, about twice the size of California.

As one example, consider the astonishing miracle of the prophecy of *Daniel* (9:24-27). This oracle deals with "70 weeks", which are usually taken to represent 490 years (70x7), divided into three groups, thus –

7 weeks	=	49 years
62 weeks	=	434 years
1 week	=	7 years

The main ideas are –

- **<u>The Jewish captivity in Babylon was to end</u>** (vs. 1-23), and a command given for the people to return to Palestine, and to rebuild Jerusalem and the Temple (vs. 25).

This restoration of Israel was to take place during a period of "70 sevens" (= 490 years), which would begin with the issuing of a "decree" (vs.25). Many dates for that decree have been suggested, but the most common are linked with two announcements concerning the Jews, made by <u>Artaxerxes</u> in the 7th and 20th years of his reign, namely, 457 BC (Ezr 7:7 ff), and 445 BC (Ne 2:1-8).
So –

- **<u>From the date of the decree</u>** to rebuild Jerusalem, 490 years would elapse until the time when the messiah would come and be *"cut off"*.

During the first 49 years, the streets and walls of the city would be rebuilt, though the times would be *"troubled"* (see *Ezra* and *Nehemiah*). Following this, another 62 weeks (= 434 years) would elapse before the appearance of the Messiah; which leads to the following calculations (among other possible variations) –

$$457 \text{ BC} + 483 \text{ solar years} = 27 \text{ AD}$$
$$445 \text{ BC} + 483 \text{ lunar years} = 32 \text{ AD}$$

Given the fact that authorities differ by as much as 10 years in the date when they reckon Christ began his public ministry, the above dates represent a miracle of accurate prophecy.

- *"After"* the *"69th week"* (that is, after 481 years) the Messiah would be *"cut off, but not for himself"* – a vision of the cross, which again was wonderfully fulfilled.
- A **<u>great war</u>** would then begin (vs. 26, 27b).

"The prince" was Titus, and the prophecy was basically fulfilled in 70 AD, except that *"the war"* and *"desolation"* are to continue until *"the end"* (of the age) (cp. Mt 24:15-16; Lu 21:20-24).

Many other biblical oracles offer detailed specifics, thus leaving no doubt of the actual event when they occurred. This is particularly true of the messianic oracles, which predicted that the Christ, when he came, would —

- be born in Bethlehem (Mi 5:2),*of a virgin. (Is 7:14)*
- live in Nazareth of Galilee. (Is 9:1-2)
- minister and preach to the poor and the needy. (Is 61:1-2)
- preach to the Gentiles. (Is 42:1)
- be rejected by the rulers. (Ps 118:22)
- be betrayed by a friend for 30 pieces of silver. (Zc 11:12-13)
- be pierced (Zc 12:10) in his hands and feet (Ps 22:16). This latter oracle was spoken several centuries before crucifixion was invented by the Romans.

See how detailed Jesus himself found the prophecies to be: *Luke 18:31-33; 24:27, 44-47*; etc. Therefore, as Peter said, we should be encouraged (2 Pe 1:19-21).

WHY THEN DID THE JEWS REJECT CHRIST?

Some, of course, did accept Christ (Lu 2:25-28, 36-38.

Others were blind, being confused by the mixture of first and second advent oracles that exist in the OT. They wanted a political revolution, not a moral reformation; they wanted a Jewish Empire, not a Gentile Church; they wanted to confirm the establishment, not to destroy it. In any case, the prophecies could be understood only by revelation (Lu 24:45). But nothing anyone could do could hinder –

THE GREAT PLAN OF GOD

"When the time had fully come God sent his own son to us, born of a woman." (Ga 4:4)

Why did Jesus not come earlier? Because the time was not yet ripe. But when Octavian Caesar made himself the first emperor of the Romans, the scene was finally set, as it had never before been set, for the appearance of the Messiah. The ancient western world, for the first time in history, was then ready –

- **_Spiritually_** –the old religions were worn out, paganism was dying, and people were ready for a new faith. The Jews indeed had built synagogues in every city (Ac 15:21); but while their monotheism was appealing, it was too exclusive for most people. So around the world, there was a wide hunger for a better way to God.
- **_Culturally_** – the Greek language was familiar throughout the civilised world, and so provided a vehicle of communication that could be understood everywhere. This process began three centuries earlier, with the conquests of Alexander the Great. By the time of the apostles, Greek had become the *lingua franca* of the Roman Empire and beyond. For the first time in history, a tool was available to carry the gospel throughout a weary world longing for good news.
- **_Conceptually_** – Even more, the Greeks invented abstract thought, and therefore the capacity to contemplate and explore such concepts as love, truth, justice, and the like. Elsewhere in the ancient world, prior to the Greeks, people thought in pictures, shown notably by the Egyptian hieroglyphics, but also in the pictographs that comprised the Hebrew alphabet and the cuneiform letters used by the Assyrians, Babylonians, and so on. Within those cultures, love, for example, could be understood only in concrete terms, as a relationship between a person and beloved object. It was never seen as something that could be abstracted from actual happenings, and thought about as an independent concept. And the same was true of other notions, such as law, holiness, truth, and so on. Yet without those concepts the evangel would never have been developed, nor could it have been preached.
- **_Philosophically_** – Egypt, Israel, Babylon, and their neighbours, could never have produced an Aristotle, a Plato, a Socrates, or anything comparable to the philosophies developed by such thinkers. The abstract notions and universal entities of the Greek philosophers

would never have entered the head of a Hebrew prophet. But by the time of the apostles such abstract thinking had become widespread, and the apostles were easily able to talk about universal justice, holiness, goodness, and apply them to both God and man. But had he lacked this capacity to handle the abstract Paul could not have written his life-changing letters, nor could the gospel of justification, reconciliation, redemption, salvation and eternal love have been preached.

- **_Politically_** – the great contribution of the Romans to human civilisation, and to the church, was their understanding of the rule of law. Prior to the Romans, the law was whatever the king said it was! But, adopting Greek abstract thinking, the Romans began to conceive of law as a universal absolute in its own right, and to exalt it above the whim of a mere monarch. In theory, at least, and often in practice, even the emperor was subject to the rule of law. Consequently, the patterns of Roman government and law provided an example that made the forensic ideas of the gospel (with its message of justification by faith) everywhere comprehensible. Both God and the church had to accept the rule of the divine law, which would have been an absurd idea to most of the ancient world prior to the Romans. But when the apostles began to preach their forensic gospel of the acquittal Christ has gained for us, the idea of the rule of law was already firmly established throughout the Roman dominions.
- **_Practically_** – the Caesars bore the title *"Saviour of the World"*, because they had more or less brought peace to nations that had been warring for centuries. A divided world had become one empire under the Caesars, and the Roman roads and the Roman fleet made travel safe for everyone, including the apostles as they carried the gospel everywhere. (77) In reality, of course, the emperors often dismally failed to live up to their title. So the proclamation that Christ alone was truly Saviour, and the eternal Prince

---

(77) By contrast, note Sirach's brave comment, only two centuries earlier, Sir 34:10-12.

of Peace, gave new hope to a world disillusioned by the follies of kings. (78)

- **_Sacerdotally_** – the priesthood, both in Jewish and pagan circles, was mercenary, with the office being bought and sold, and priests susceptible to bribery and corruption. The time was right for a new priesthood to be established, the priesthood of every believer, under a new High Priest, Christ himself.
- **_Socially_** – with Caesar Augustus there began an era of 300 years of comparative peace unparalleled in the ancient world. (79) This world-wide peace, along with the protection afforded by the Roman authorities, and the laissez-faire structure of Roman society, were the main reasons why the apostles were able to travel freely, and to carry the gospel to the ends of the empire and beyond. (80) Even one century earlier, this would have been, if not impossible, at least vastly more difficult.
- **_Prophetically_** – the *Seventy Weeks* oracle spoken by Daniel (9:20-27), plus other prophecies, all suggested that the time had come for Messiah to be born.

So, *"God sent forth his Son"* –

- To reveal God – *John 6:38*; and Christ showed indeed that <u>all</u> could freely address God as Father.
- To save the lost – *Luke 19:10*, which is a picture unique in sacred literature, of *God* seeking man; for in all other religions the picture has been, and is, that of man seeking after God (with the

---

(78) For example, a hundred years earlier Paul could not have written in *Romans 7:1* the words: *"Certainly you will understand what I am about to say, my brothers, because all of you <u>know about law</u>!"*(GNB) Note also the idea of the rule of law in *Acts 25:16*.

(79) The "Pax Romana" brought to an end centuries of endless warfare. The citizens of the empire were so grateful for its benefits, that they readily called Caesar the "Saviour" of the world (which is perhaps one reason why the term is seldom used in the New Testament).

(80) The occasional bursts of imperial persecution of the church did not significantly alter this situation.

consequence that their gods become made in a human image, instead of the reverse).
- To ransom the slaves – *Matthew 20:28*.
- To destroy the works of Satan – *1 John 3:8*.
- To build his church – *Matthew 16:18*.
- To be crowned king – *John 18:37*.

Let us then never doubt that God is in final control of all events, both great and small. Likewise, his decrees are irresistible – Satan failed to prevent the birth and life of Christ, nor can he ever thwart the divine purpose. Thus, when the time is again fully come, Jesus will return in the clouds of heaven, and take us to himself for ever. (Ac 1:10-11; Mt 24:30-31)

Chapter Eighteen

"ABBA!"

> *Because you are sons, God has sent the Spirit of his Son into your hearts, crying, "Abba! Father!" So you are no longer a slave, but a son, and if a son, then an heir through God. (Ga 4:6-7)* [81]

"Riches rule the roost" says an old English proverb, expressing a sad truth. Hence people envy the rich and yearn to possess great wealth of their own. They desire riches, not for the sake of mere possessions (of which they mostly already have enough), but because they feel that wealth will make them strong, and no longer helpless. By amassing riches they feel that they can stave off enemies and get better control over their lives; they will no longer feel vulnerable to every vicissitude. Yet no sense of weakness can ever overwhelm anyone who has discovered the reality of our text. It declares that God has sent us his Spirit to help us, to break every chain of slavery, and to enable us to live as the free-born sons and daughters of the living God.

THE SPIRIT HELPS US TO GO FORWARD

We humans are always prone to fall back into fear and slavery (cp. Ro 8:15). But the Holy Spirit never pulls people into slavery; rather, he bonds them to the Father as his own dear children. This then enables us to offer a special kind of prayer. He says that ***"we***

---

(81) I have left the word "sons" in these verses, rather than use "children", or some other generic cognate, because "sons" has a theological sense. It conveys the idea that each believer, whether male or female, will be treated like a first-born son. The context, of course, is the ancient world, where Salic law prevailed everywhere except, says Paul, in the church. There, and before the throne of God, female believers have exactly the same legal rights as male believers. They are all treated as they would be if they were "sons" under Salic law. ("Salic" is a 5th century term, used to describe laws that explicitly prevent a woman from inheriting a throne, even if she is the firstborn child.)

cry, 'Abba! Father!'" That is, the first thing the Spirit enables us to do is to pray, and to call God *"Papa"* ("Abba") and *"Pater"* ("Father"), and to do so with a *"cry"*.

What is the meaning of that remarkable combination of a passionate Greek verb, an Aramaic diminutive, and a Greek noun? Did the early Christians truly go around shouting *"Abba! Father!"* in church? Was that couplet part of their public liturgy, or was it restricted to private use? Did anyone use the expression at all, whether in public or private worship? I have not been able to find any example of a liturgical use of the phrase, nor of its use in private devotionals. Indeed, it does seem improbable that the phrase ever was used literally. Why then does Paul say that *"we cry, 'Abba, Father'"*? There is a clue in the three Greek words, translated in our text as *"cry"*, *"Abba"*, and *"Father"* –

INARTICULATE PRAYER

The word "cry" is *"krazo"*, [82] *which* is an onomatopoeic word, that is, a word that sounds like the thing it represents – such as, hiss, bubble, bang, sigh, sizzle, ping, slap, croak, babble, pop, swish. Such words are sometimes also called "echoic" or "imitative". The Greeks used the noun *krazon* to represent the hoarse croak of the raven, and from that to indicate any sound of despair, or a haunting sound of helplessness. [83] The lexicons say –

- Brown: "a cry arising from great human need, a cry for help, as, say, in sickness or despair."
- Arndt: "cry out, scream, shriek – as when one utters loud cries, but no words capable of being understood (an inarticulate cry)."
- Kittel: "croak, or cry with a loud raucous voice."
- Strong: "croak like a raven, scream, cry out, shriek, entreat."

---

(82) Pronounced KRAHdzo. That is the verb form; as a noun, it is *krazon*.

(83) Alexander Poe captured the same idea in the sound that ends each stanza of his poem *The Raven* – "more!" ("nothing more" or "nevermore"), which should be spoken with a hoarse, croaking sound of despair, like the haunting "caw" of a raven.

Those are primary meanings, and if you speak *krazo* in a certain rough way it does indeed sound like a despairing croak. It was also used in a milder and derivative sense. In the LXX it occurs in Job 38:41 (*"The young ravens wander, and they cry to the Lord, in search of food"*); Psalm 34:16 (*"The righteous cried out, and the Lord listened to them"*); Isaiah 26:17 (*"A woman in travail cries out in her pain"*); and in the gospels in *Matthew 14:26, 30; 27:50*; plus other references.

Commentators offer diverse reasons why Paul uses the word in our text, in connection with *"Abba! Father!"* But let me make a brave suggestion: perhaps he intends it to be a synonym for glossolalic prayer, and to indicate the nature and content of such prayer. This may be confirmed by the context in which the apostle uses the same phrase in *Romans 8:15* (see vs. 26; and also 1 Co 14:15; Ep 5:19; Cl 3:16, which also comprehend glossolalic prayer and song).

It is a cry from the depths of the human heart for help.

In other words, when you speak in other tongues to the Father, from the depths of your spirit, pouring out your desire toward him, that is how he hears your words – as a *krazon* of the soul; he has no need to comprehend the words, but hears the passion of the heart. That is confirmed by the next word –

WE CRY "ABBA!"

Abba was an Aramaic diminutive, roughly equivalent to our "Daddy" or "Papa"; it was the word used in the lisping chatter of an infant, and in the intimacy of the family bosom. It was forbidden to slaves, belonging only to free-born members of the family.

In real life we grow from *Abba* to *Pater*, that is, from "Daddy" to "Father"; our relationship with our parent matures and we are no longer little children. But in spiritual life we maintain both together; that is, although we may reach maturity in some areas, in others we remain infants. So we are sometimes childish and sometimes adult; sometime very grown up in Christ, sometimes more like a helpless baby! Hence we need a way to pray in both an infant and an adult way. Thus, sometimes our cry is *"Daddy!"* (we address the Lord in glossolalia). But on other occasions, it is more properly *"Father!"* (we address the Lord in our vernacular tongue).

So then, if it is not too bold to suggest that in our text Paul is using *"Abba"* as a digest for glossolalia, then *"Abba!"* indicates how God hears us when we pray in other tongues. He catches our cry –

- as a **mother** hears her baby's cry: inarticulate, yet full of meaning, telling of joy or pain, of hunger or loneliness, of weariness or fretfulness. What mother needs intelligible words to tell her what her baby needs? The moment she hears its *krazon*, will she not run to nurture the little one?
- as a ***father*** hears the call of his infant son or daughter: irresistible in its plea for masculine protection, provision, nurture and strength!

Thus, when I speak in tongues, especially as a cry in a time of weakness, crying *"Abba"*, I am throwing myself as a needy child into the arms of my heavenly Father. It shows my –

- **_helplessness_** (this gift is not for the proud); and it shows my
- **_happiness_** (that I belong, I am home, I am with my Father).

Note also: *"Abba"* and *"Pater"* probably summarise the two kinds of prayer mentioned by Paul in *1 Corinthians 14:15*, namely, *"with the spirit"* ("Abba!"); and *"with the understanding"* ("Pater!") Which brings me to -

ARTICULATE PRAYER

Since we are not always in an infant state, Paul also says that, *"We cry, 'Father!'"* The Greek word is *pater*. It was the word of formal, adult discourse, the way a grown-up child would address a parent. It expresses the height of the communion to which the Father elevates us by the power of the Holy Spirit – he wants us to address him as mature children, as "adults" – cp. *Romans 8:14, 16-17*.

Once again, in real life, in our relationship with our parent, we grow from *Abba* to *Pater* – that is, from "Daddy" to "Father"; but in spiritual life we maintain both together. So let us then *"pray with our understanding"* (that is, in our vernacular tongue); but also *"pray in the spirit"* (that is, in other tongues imparted by the Holy Spirit). No one who is so rich in the Spirit will ever again be vulnerable or helpless, but will every day be able to cry with passion to the Lord, either in pleading or praise, calling to God both as *"Abba"* and *"Father"*.

So, while no one can say with any certainty whether or not the early church built an actual *"Abba, Father"* into either their public liturgies or their private devotions, I choose to see it as a metaphor of how the Holy Spirit worked a miracle in the church and in the lives of its people (Ga 3:5). The expression, *"we cry Abba, Father,"* stands therefore as a summary of Spirit-filled people praying passionately in other tongues (*"groans too deep for words"*), and in their native language, expecting to find *"help in times of weakness"* –

> *You have received the Spirit ... by whom we cry, "Abba! Father!" This is the Spirit himself, bearing witness with our spirit that we are children of God ... The Spirit also helps us in our weakness; for when we do not know what to pray for or even how to pray, the Spirit himself intercedes for us with groans that ordinary words cannot express.* (Ro 8:15-16, 26)

Christian people who strongly affirm their sonship in Christ, whether by *"Abba!"* or *"Father!"*, that is, who pray earnestly either in glossolalia or the vernacular, or both, will find that all the clamour of the law, sin, and the devil will be swiftly stilled. And we must do this despite all contrary evidence of the senses, which will mock our sonship, or try to drag us back under law, or accuse us of foul sins. But an *"Abba!"* or a *"Father!"* or better still, both together, will silence them! Or, as Paul says elsewhere, let us pray, not only *"with the spirit"* (that is, speaking in tongues), but also *"with the understanding"* (that is, in one's native tongue). (1 Co 14:15). This, he says, is indeed *"giving thanks well!"* (vs. 17)

Added to all this is the promise of a glorious inheritance. Strong joy in that glittering prospect will swamp every instinct to be afraid and to fall back into slavery. So our text declares that –

THE SPIRIT SEALS OUR SONSHIP

You are no longer a slave, but a son, and if a son, then an heir through God. (Ga 4:7)

Now here is a paradox! An heir cannot usually come into his or her inheritance until the testator has died. Yet God still lives, and will do so forever! Shall we then never inherit? Of course we shall, for as soon as we have passed by the Judgment Seat of Christ the prize will be ours (2 Co 5:10).

Paul, then, is speaking metaphorically. He simply means that there is an astonishing wealth awaiting those who stand firm until the end in their identity as children of God. As if he had said, *"Keep behaving as a son of God should behave, and you will receive the glorious crown he has promised to all who believe and serve. The full inheritance of a first-born son will be given to you freely."*

Or, perhaps we should understand it this way: since Christ is God's first-born son, and therefore heir to all that belongs to the Father; and since he has now gained his inheritance by his death and resurrection; and since we are in union with him by faith, then we too have become possessors of all that he possesses.

But do you grasp what it means to be a *"son of God"* ? Can you span the wonder of it? Can you measure its splendour? As Martin Luther said –

> If a man could comprehend the great excellency of this matter, that he is the son and heir of God, and with a constant faith believe the same, this man would esteem all the power and riches of all the kingdoms of the world but as filthy dung, in comparison of his eternal inheritance. He would abhor whatsoever is high and glorious in the world: yea, the greater the pomp and glory of the world is, the more would he hate it. [84]

---

(84) From a 19th century translation of Luther's 1535 *Commentary on Galatians*, in. loc.

Well spoken! For truly we who may call ourselves sons and daughters of the living God hold riches beyond measure. Further, whoever is able to cry from the heart, *"Abba! Father!"* cannot doubt the reality of their sonship. Can I call God *Father*, but then wonder if I am truly his son? Hardly! I call him Father, because I know I am his free-born son in Christ. And I know I am a free-born son of God in Christ, because I call him Father. Even better, in my spirit and by the Spirit I also cry to him (in glossolalia), *"Abba!"* That cry dispels any doubt I may once have had about my sonship or about his Fatherhood. Does a child who shrieks "Daddy!" in a time of need ever doubt that his father will hasten to his aid? Nor can I doubt when I cry, *"Abba! Father!"*

NO MORE A SLAVE

Paul asserts, not only that we are sons, but also, as a corollary, that we are no longer *"slaves"*. That is, we have been freed from the bondage of law, which insisted that we could not be saved except by sweaty personal struggle. Rules had to be kept. Works had to be done. Toil had to be undertaken. We had to refrain from certain foods and drinks, and had to prove ourselves righteous by our own endeavour. All this has been undone in Christ. Now, if ever I am disposed to fall back under the law, to think myself a slave, chained by sin, imprisoned by death, flogged by guilt, then this cry of *"Abba!"* will liberate me gloriously. I am no longer a slave! I am a son, and rightful claimant to all that appertains to that relationship with the Father. I am near to him, not far away. No longer rebellious, I delight to obey him. He himself bids me ask him for my *"daily bread"* (Mt 6:11), which includes everything ever promised in the gospel – victory over sin, healing in times of sickness, prosperity in place of poverty, hope instead of despair, light in place of darkness, salvation in place of death, and happiness for ever in Paradise!

Mark, too, that sons are heirs, not by some meritorious achievement, but simply by right of birth. Am I born again by the Spirit of God? (Jn 3:1-8), then my sonship cannot be questioned, and my inheritance is sure. Nothing more is required, except that I believe it and live it out day by day.

Can my relationship with my earthly father ever be less than that of his son? No, whatever I do, good or ill, at home or away, I remain his son. Nothing can undo that, nothing can change it, by his seed and his alone I came into this world, and I cannot reverse it. That _relationship_ is fixed for ever. I can however weaken or strengthen my _fellowship_ with him. Worthy behaviour will bond me to him more closely; dishonourable actions will cause him to drive me away. Yet I remain his son.

In the same way my status as a son of God is fixed irrevocably, except for one demurral. If backsliding is taken to the extreme of actually despising the blood of the covenant, mocking the grace of God, and renouncing Christ, sonship can be lost. After all, I am God's son only by virtue of what Christ has done and by my union with him by faith. If that faith is wilfully abandoned, if that union is blasphemously destroyed, then sonship and inheritance will also vanish. (85)

But for everyone who maintains his or her union with Christ, that person's "sonship" is established in God the Father, fixed and sure for ever. So I cannot doubt my filial relationship with God. Throughout the years of time and across eternity I am his true-born son. The thing to be determined now is how closely I walk in fellowship with the Father.

So cling to Jesus! The more firmly one perceives the spiritual reality of the believer's *"sonship"* in Christ, the more certainly that person will stomp on Satan, sin, disease, the law, and even death. We are sons of God, who can defeat us? We are sons of God, who can deny us? We are sons of God, who can deprive us? –

---

(85) Plainly, I do not accept the dogma, "Once saved, always saved"? Let me say this again: sonship depends altogether upon my union with Christ by faith. If that union is broken, then I am a son no more, but an outcast – see *Hebrews 6:4-6; 10:29*, along with many other NT warnings about the perils of backsliding and of being cut off from Christ.)

> *No, in all these things we are more than conquerors through him who loved us. For I am sure that neither death nor life, nor angels nor rulers, nor things present nor things to come, nor powers, nor height nor depth, nor anything else in all creation, will be able to separate us from the love of God in Christ Jesus our Lord.* (Ro 8:37-39, ESV)

And the more the law, sin, and the devil fight against us, the more we will overthrow them (even if we must use *"unutterable groanings"*) by crying *"Abba! Father!"* In the face of that cry, conscience leaps free of its guilty burdens, the soul rejoices in Paradise to come, the law retreats in shame, and sin and the devil are crushed underfoot. No "son" of God, who recognises that "sonship" and rejoices in it, can ever again be enslaved, but must walk in liberty. And if the children of God stumble here and there, or find the cold hand of the law striving to drag them down again into the pit of bondage, let them but cry *"Abba Father!"* and their sliding feet will be steadied. They will be able to resume pursuing holiness and attaining heaven (He 12:14).

CONCLUSION

Alexander the Great was renowned for his generosity toward those who had served him well –

> (He) was naturally most munificent, and grew more so as his fortune increased, accompanying what he gave with that courtesy and freedom which, to speak truth, is necessary to make a benefit really obliging. I will give a few instances of this kind. Ariston, the captain of the Paeonians, having killed an enemy, brought his head to show him, and told him that in his country such a present was recompensed with a cup of gold. "With an empty one," said Alexander, smiling, "but I drink to you in this, which I give you full of wine." Another time, as one of the common soldiers was driving a mule laden with some of the king's treasure, the beast grew tired, and the soldier took it upon his own back, and began to march with it, till Alexander seeing the man so overcharged asked what was the matter; and when he was informed, just as he was ready to lay down his burden for weariness, "Do not faint

now," said he to him, "but finish the journey, and carry what you have there to your own tent for yourself." [86]

Like that mule-driver, we are all prone to fall into despair when it seems that hope is gone, when we feel too tired to carry on, or the burden is simply too heavy. But it is amazing what renewed hope can do! The thought of more wealth than he had ever dreamed possible put an irresistible surge of energy into the man's legs. His arms felt like the arms of Atlas. He jumped to his feet, caught up the sacks of gold (which the mule could not carry!), and got them to his tent, rejoicing every step of the way!

Let God open your eyes to the vistas of heaven by planting in you the revelation that you are not a slave but a son of God, a daughter of God, filling you with a sure hope of Paradise and riches beyond all telling. You too will find all the strength you need to "finish the journey" and reap his imperishable reward.

---

(86) From John Dryden's translation of Plutarch's *Life of Alexander*; from <u>The Lives of the Noble Greeks and Romans</u>; Modern Library, New York; pg. 801 ff.

Chapter Nineteen

ANGELS

> *If we, or even an **angel** from heaven, should preach a gospel to you other than what we preached to you, let him be accursed. ... The Law was brought to us by **angels** who used the hand of a mediator. ... Despite the trial that was in my flesh you did not despise me nor disdain me, but received me as if I were an **angel** of God, as if I were Christ Jesus himself.* (Ga 1:8; 3:19; 4;14)

> Matthew, Mark, Luke, and John,
> The bed be blest that I lie on.
> Four angels to my bed,
> Four angels round my head,
> One to watch, and one to pray,
> And two to bear my soul away.

There have been times in English history when more children were familiar with that old bed-time jingle than could recite the Lord's Prayer. Behind the poem lies the idea of angels appointed to be the personal guardians of people on earth.

We use the word "angel" today to describe what these spirits "are" more than what they "do". But in the Bible the word "angel" says almost nothing about the nature of these beings, but almost everything about their work. "Angel" means simply "messenger"; and in particular they are messengers who serve God by helping the church.

But are they real? It is fashionable in the modern world to scoff at the idea of angels. They are called relics of a long-gone age of superstition, useful now only for jokes and charming tales to delight children. Modern sophisticates insist that no intelligent person could believe in the actual existence of angels or that they could have any possible relevance to modern thought or influence on current affairs.

This is not the place to present a full angelology, but let me say that Paul's easy mention of angels [87] shows his acceptance of their existence and of their essential place in the economy of God. I am happy to share that view.

But supposing angels are real, what difference can it make? No one sees them or feels them, and the only tangible evidence we have for their existence is the Bible, although we might also add the testimony of contemporary witnesses. However, apart from the fact that some of those testimonies are inevitably suspect, doctrine cannot be safely built on personal experience. We are left then with the biblical account of angels, and the question remains: does it matter whether or not they are hovering around?

Yes, it does matter, for the veracity of the biblical record depends upon the presence and ministry of angels. If the Bible cannot be trusted here, then it cannot be trusted anywhere. I accept that record, therefore I also accept that angels have a powerful and ongoing influence upon our daily lives. We may not always be aware of what the angels are doing, or how often we are beneficiaries of their actions, but they are certainly working constantly on behalf of the church –

THEY SHARE OUR SALVATION

> *Christ appeared among us in human form, was approved by the Spirit, overseen by angels, proclaimed among the nations, believed on in the world, and taken up into glory.* (1 Ti 3:16)

Belief in angels is not unique to Christians. Far back into prehistory people of every culture and religion have embraced some sort of angelology –

> Many of the ancient Heathens had (probably from tradition) some notion of good and evil angels. They had some conception of a superior order of beings, between men and God, whom the Greeks generally termed demons (knowing ones), and the Romans, genii. Some of

---

(87) Three times in *Galatians*, and at least 30 times in all his letters (including *Hebrews*).

> these they supposed to be kind and benevolent, delighting in doing good; others, to be malicious and cruel, delighting in doing evil. But their conceptions both of one and the other were crude, imperfect, and confused; being only fragments of truth, partly delivered down by their forefathers, and partly borrowed from the inspired writings. ... An ancient poet, one who lived several ages before Socrates, speaks more determinately on this subject. Hesiod does not scruple to say, "Millions of spiritual creatures walk the earth unseen." [88]

Paul readily accepted that popular belief in angels, and asserted that everything about the incarnation, life, death, resurrection, and ascension of Jesus was closely watched by them. Why? Because the destiny of angels is inextricably linked with that of the church –

> *The angels of God rejoice when they see even one sinner who repents ... Through the church God reveals his infinite wisdom to the principalities and powers in the heavenlies ... The entire creation is eagerly waiting for the children of God to be revealed. ... The angels yearn to catch even a glimpse of the things that have been proclaimed to you through the gospel.* (Lu 15:10; Ep 3:9-11; Ro 8:19; 1 Pe 1:12; etc)

Precisely how much angels are intertwined with the church, and how much the destiny of the church will affect them, we are not told. A mystery lies at the heart of this conjunction of the visible with the invisible. But there is no doubt that your salvation and mine reaches beyond earth and into heaven.

Indeed, Paul makes the extraordinary claim that when God created the heavens and the earth they were incomplete (Ro 8:19-23). The universe was "good" but not perfect, and it cannot come to perfection without us. The whole cosmos, suggests the apostle,

---

[88] John Wesley, in a sermon preached August 29, 1782; The Wesley Centre Online – http://wesley.nnu.edu/john-wesley/the-sermons-of-john-wesley-1872-edition/sermon-71-of-good-angels/.

was designed simply so that the human race could come into existence and flourish, and then, out of that humanity, would arise the church, the people of God redeemed and set on a pathway to glory. We are that people. The universe groans in its imperfections while it waits eagerly for us, the sons of God, to be revealed.

Astonishingly, modern science, with its discovery of the exquisite balance required in nature to produce the universe, confirms that it does indeed seem to exist solely so that we can exist. Just a minute difference in even one of the forces at work during the Big Bang would have produced an altogether different world, one in which life could not have survived. Just a tiny change in the mass of the universe, in the number of galaxies, would have prevented our lovely planet from being formed.

So in some wonderful way the happiness of angels (indeed, of the universe) is dependent upon the triumph of the church. Hence they watch us with keen anticipation, probably sometimes mixed with anxiety, and sometimes overflowing with joy. But always the angels watch with the certain knowledge that without them our redemption will be incomplete, and without the church they will somehow be diminished.

THEY GUARD THE SAINTS

The idea of a guardian angel is first found in the promise Abraham made to his chief servant, when he sent him to find a wife for Isaac –

> *God will send his angel before you so that you may find a wife for my son in Nahor* (Ge 24:7).

Nonetheless, Hebrew thinking about the way in which angels provided personal guidance and protection remained largely undeveloped until after the people returned from their Exile (538 B.C.) Prior to that, Israel held mainly to a general idea of angels guiding and protecting the servants of God as a body, not as individuals (Ex 23:20-23; Nu 20:16). They thought more in terms of national rather than personal guardianship (cp. Da 12:1). That idea is still current. So there are people who would agree with the poet when he wrote the stirring lines –

> When Britain first, at Heaven's command,

> Arose from out the azure main,
> This was the charter of the land,
> And guardian angels sung this strain:
> "Rule, Britannia, rule the waves;
> Britons never, never, never shall be slaves." [89]

Daniel, too, hints that each nation may have its own divinely appointed guardian prince (Da 10:13); but since scripture offers no further explanation, the reference remains obscure. It does however confirm that the Jews accepted the reality of angels guarding or even ruling entire nations. That was until the fall of Jerusalem and the long subjection of the Jews by Babylon, Persia, and the Greeks. Israel's sufferings had a double effect upon their angelology –

- the pitiless ruin of their nation and their ongoing enslavement made God an object of terror to them (cp. the bewilderment and despair expressed in Jeremiah's *Lamentations*); so
- they found instead, mostly in Persian doctrine, a way to visualise many ranks of angels standing between them and the dread throne of the Almighty.

Those angels, they believed, acted both as protective barriers between a sinful people and their holy God, and as helpful intermediaries, carrying prayer up to God's throne, and fulfilling God's commissions on earth.

Even Moses was now said to have received the law from angels (Ac 7:38; Ga 3:19; He 2:2); which he may well have done, but there is no hint of it in the OT.

Once the angels were established as intermediaries between God and man, it was then easy to adopt the further Persian idea of every person having a patron spirit. The tradition was also accepted that God has assigned two angels to each person –

---

(89) The first stanza and refrain of Rule Britannia, which is the finale to the opera *Alfred*, by the Scottish Poet James Thomson (1700-1748). Set to music by Thomas Arne in 1740, it has become perhaps the best known of all British patriotic songs.

- the angel of the right hand; and
- the angel of the left hand (cp. the "two angels" mentioned in the nursery rhyme above).

DOPPELGÄNGERS

The concept of two angels was eventually expanded into the notion of one of the angels being evil, and the other good; the task of the evil angel being to entice its ward into sin, and the other to hold its ward to the path of righteousness. Those ideas have come all the way down into our own popular mythology, where the two spirits have taken the shape of a small red or black demon sitting on one shoulder, and a small white-haloed angel sitting on the other.

It was also believed that guardian angels would sometimes clone their ward's appearance (cp. Ac 12:14-15), [90] and were appointed to each person for life. Without accepting all those legendary accretions we may still allow that the Persians were correct in their general doctrine of angels. Those ideas were accepted by Christ and the apostles, along with the several scripture passages which show that angels are true helpers of the people of God –

- *see Genesis 22:11; Exodus 23:20-23; 2 Kings 6:16-17; Psalm 34:7; 91:11; Daniel 3:25; 6:22.*

The church too, from its beginning, has approved a belief in angels, and in particular that guardian angels are appointed to minister to the heirs of salvation (He 1:14) –

> How many times have we been strangely and unaccountably preserved, in sudden and dangerous falls! And it is well if we did not impute that preservation to chance, or to our own wisdom or strength. Not so: it was God who gave his angels charge over us, and in their hands they bore us up. Indeed, men of the world will always impute such deliverances to accident or second causes. To these, possibly, some of them might have imputed Daniel's preservation in the lion's den. But

---

(90) This gave rise to a belief in the legendary *doppelgänger* ("double-walker") – a ghostly apparition who is a double of and haunts a living person.

himself ascribes it to the true cause: "My God hath sent his angel, and shut the lions' mouths." (Dan. 6:22.) [91]

Of this angelic care I have myself (I believe) been the beneficiary on at least two occasions. The first occurred when I was about 8 years old. My mother had taken me to a beach where, unknown to us, there was a strong rip tide. I was caught in the flow, and would have been borne out to sea and to my death if a man had not suddenly appeared and carried me safely to the shore. I ran at once to tell my mother what had happened, and turned to point to my rescuer, who should easily have been visible on a near-deserted beach – but he was gone! There was no sight of him, and I have ever after assumed he was in fact an angel.

The second occasion, I was driving with my young wife (this was some 60 years ago), when we came to a sign that told drivers to beware of a steep incline just around the corner. Thinking "incline" meant a steep climb upward, I accelerated and swung around the corner, only to see the bitumen almost disappear in front of me. It was a steep *decline*! I found myself tearing down the hill in a 1938 car with mechanical brakes. I slammed my foot down with predictable results. The wheels locked, the car swung madly at a right angle, and headed straight for the side fence and a long drop to the valley below. I remember crying (whether in my mind or aloud I cannot say), "Jesus! Here we come!" – for it was inevitable that we would plunge over the edge and straight to glory. Instead, the car just came to a gentle stop. One moment we were rushing toward the fence. The next we were standing still, in the middle of the road. I have always believed that an angel of God protected us.

ROBERT BROWNING

Early in their marriage, Robert Browning and his wife Elizabeth visited an art gallery in Italy and found there a painting by Guercino, *The Guardian Angel*, which portrays a child kneeling in prayer on a flat tomb, hands clasped, and gazing heavenward. Overshadowing the child is an angel with outspread wings. The

---

(91) John Wesley, *op. cit.*

angel looks out upon the larger world, while holding the child's hands protectively. The Brownings were enthralled, and returned three times to the gallery simply to sit and gaze upon the painting. Later Browning wrote a poem to describe the experience –

> Dear and great Angel, wouldst thou only leave
> That child, when thou hast done with him, for me!
> Let me sit all the day here, that when eve
> Shall find performed thy special ministry,
> And time come for departure, thou, suspending
> Thy flight, mayst see another child for tending,
> Another still, to quiet and retrieve. (92)
>
> Then I shall feel thee step one step, no more,
> From where thou standest now, to where I gaze, –
> And suddenly my head is covered o'er
> With those wings, white above the child who prays
> Now on that tomb – and I shall feel thee guarding
> Me, out of all the world; for me, discarding
> Yon heaven thy home, that waits and opes its door. (93)

The words are lovely, the sentiment is charming, and angels certainly do care for us, just as scripture says, and as a multitude of people will testify. But does that mean we can claim an angel to serve us as

A PERMANENT GUARDIAN?

Every October the Roman Catholic Church celebrates the *Feast of the Holy Guardian Angel*. A prayer is associated with the festival, which begins –

> Dear Angel at my side,
> My good and loyal friend,

---

(92) When evening comes, and the angel no longer needs to care for the child, and is about to fly off to some larger duty, the poet asks him to stay instead, and to care for the poet. He is the "another" who is seeking rescue and quietness.

(93) He hopes the angel will heed his prayer, take one step from the child over to where he is sitting, and cover him with its snowy wings. He trusts that the angel will be willing to abandon the joys of heaven just to fulfil the duty of caring for the poet. (*The Guardian Angel*, by Robert Browning, 1812-1889; first two stanzas.)

> You have been with me since the moment I was born.
> You are my own personal guardian,
> Given me by God as my guide and protector,
> And you will stay with me till I die.

Catholic people are urged –

> frequently speak with your guardian angels, converse with them as true friends, and gratefully thank them for all they have done, for we cannot as of yet know of the many times they have rescued us from some calamity. Let us ask for their assistance as we live our daily lives in the Lord." [94]

I cannot say that such ideas are wrong, for there is in them much that is true. Yet despite common church teaching, and despite the times I have been rescued by an angel, [95] there seems no real warrant for supposing that we each have a personal, lifetime, angelic guardian, let alone one that shares our likeness. Jesus, for example, said that *"twelve legions"* of angels were available to him (Mt 26:53); and on one occasion a group of angels ministered to him (Mt 4:11; Mk 1:13); while on another occasion, just a single angel (Lu 22:43). But there is no suggestion in scripture that one particular angel was appointed to be his guardian. Note, too, how *Matthew 18:10* says that the angels of *"children"* (a term that probably also includes adult disciples) are in *"heaven"*, not on earth. The idea is that of having a high-born friend at court, which is always nice to know, but hardly endorses belief in a single, personal, permanent guardian angel.

Of course, we could, like Sir Thomas Browne, claim that both are true; that is, individual *nations* and *people* alike have a guardian angel –

---

(94) From the web site, *Catholic Online*.

(95) I have in mind the two anecdotes told just above, and also several other less dramatic, but no less real, occasions when I deeply believe angels protected me and sometimes my family as well. Sceptics will, of course, scorn all such claims as paltry superstition. But anyone who accepts the Bible as a true witness could hardly do other than believe in angels, and not just theoretically, but also practically.

> Therefore for Spirits I am so farre from denying their existence, that I could easily beleeve, that not onely whole Countries, but particular persons have their Tutelary, and Guardian Angels: It is not a new opinion of the Church of Rome, but an old one of *Pythagoras* and *Plato;* there is no heresie in it, and if not manifestly defin'd in Scripture, yet is it an opinion of a good and wholesome use in the course and actions of a man's life, and would serve as an *Hypothesis* to salve many doubts, whereof common Philosophy affordeth no solution. (96)

Sir Thomas admits that biblical evidence for a permanent guardian angel is sparse; but he also acknowledges the antiquity of the belief, and feels that its benefits are sufficient to justify holding to it. Personally, I am still inclined to doubt the proposition.

HOW DO ANGELS HELP US?

BY PHYSICAL ACTION

Angels cannot be restricted to spiritual actions alone, for they can and do influence, change, or control the material world. Hence we read in scripture about them touching, providing, igniting, destroying, making people sick, making them well, causing earthquakes, controlling the winds, moving great stones, opening prisons, breaking shackles, and so on. Any concordance will take you to scores of references.

There is no reason to suppose that their strength has weakened. Angels are just as capable of helping God's people today, and of effecting his judgments, as ever they were. Should we then ask for their help? Probably not. Jesus did not say that he could call legions of angels to help, but that he could ask the Father to send them (Mt 26:53). Prayer should always be addressed to the Father, through the Son, and by the power of the Holy Spirit. If God chooses, he may then either aid us personally or send an angel to do his bidding. There seems to be little point in addressing an

---

(96) *Religion Medici I.33*. From Sir Thomas Browne: The Major Works; Penguin Books, London, 1977; pg.101.

angel who may not even be near, when we can speak directly to the Father, who is never absent.

BY SPIRITUAL ACTION

Angels provide inner spiritual renewal; they fortify courage; they bring revelation; and so on (Lu 22:43; Da 10:17; Ez 8:1-4). However, they cannot gain access to your mind or spirit against your own will, for that level of irresistible penetration of your being belongs to God alone (1 Sa 16:7; 2 Sa 7:20; 1 Kg 8:39; 1 Ch 28:9; Je 17:10).

Angels also help in our worship (Ps 138:1; 1 Co 11:10; Re 8:3-4).

They are involved in our salvation: they convey good news (Lu 2:10-11); they rejoice when a soul is saved (Lu 15:10); they are linked with the church (Ep 3:9-11).

COMPANIONS AT DEATH

This, of course, was the idea behind the poem that opens this chapter. The underlying thought is this – if a child should die during the night, he or she would not die alone, but angels would be there to comfort the newly released soul and carry it safely to heaven. Jesus himself endorsed the consoling notion that angels are our companions at death, in his parable about *Dives and Lazarus* (Lu 16:22). He said –

> *The poor man died and was <u>carried by the angels</u>*
> *to Abraham's side.*

For anyone terrified of dying alone, a belief that the soul will be carried to heaven by angels must be deeply assuring.

ON THE LAST DAY

The last, the greatest, the most splendid service the angels will render the church on earth will be to call all the saints of all time together on the day of resurrection, and to present them glorious in Christ – see *Matthew 24:30-33; Mark 13:27; 1 Thessalonians 4:16-18*.

CONCLUSION

Three special benefits come to us from the doctrine of angels –

- Just as we learn other things by contrasting one against another, so we gain a better understanding of our own humanity and of our place in the scheme of things by measuring ourselves against the angels. Thus black has no meaning until it is contrasted with white; joy and sorrow gain deeper significance from each other; up and down, in and out, stillness and motion all derive meaning from the contrast between them; and even life cannot be fully known except by measuring it against death. So our measure is known by the measure of angels, and theirs, by ours.
- The glory of the cross is enhanced by recognising that even the mightiest of the angels have a vested interest in our salvation; without us, their full glory will remain unrealised.
- We gain a glimpse behind the veil, to perceive the spiritual realm that exists all around us, and with whose destiny ours is inextricably linked.

Chapter Twenty

FREEDOM

*For **freedom** Christ has set us **free**; stand firm therefore, and never again accept any yoke of slavery. ... Dear friends, you were called to **freedom**, but do not use that **freedom** as an excuse for succumbing to fleshly temptations. Rather, use it to serve each other in love* (Ga 5:1, 13).

In *Childe Harold's Pilgrimage* (Canto I.20), Lord Byron wrote –

> Deep in yon cave Honorius long did dwell,
> In hope to merit heaven by making life a hell.

Honorius was a 16th century monk, who lived in a Portuguese convent, and was reputedly 100 years old when he died in 1596. The last 30 years of his long life he spent immured in a tiny hole in a grotto close to the convent. There he gained renown for his piety and extreme asceticism. The grotto and cave still exist. But how well Byron summarises the futility of trying to gain righteousness by self-inflicted privations: "He hoped to merit heaven by making life a hell." Much the same idea was expressed by the poet Robert Southey, who was a contemporary of Byron. In his poem *Inscription for the Cell of Honorius, at the Cork Convent, near Cintra*, he wrote –

> Here, caverned like a beast, Honorius passed
> In self-affliction, solitude, and prayer,
> Long years of penance. He had rooted out
> All human feelings from his heart, and fled
> With fear and loathing from all human joys.

But then, with less sarcasm and more truth than Byron, Southey pointed out that no matter how sincere Honorius may have been, he was in error, for

> Not thus in making known his will divine
> Hath Christ enjoined.

Rather, says the poet, Christ is looking for his servants to serve others lovingly; not to disengage *from* the world, but to engage *with* it, to help the fatherless, to comfort the sick, to be a friend to one's neighbours. Those who do so, says he, will have "joy on earth ... precluding the eternal bliss of heaven." Yet he admires the anchorite's courage, and discipline, his constancy and zeal, and so admonishes his readers –

> Stranger! Do thou keep
> Thy better and thine easier rule as well.

We should be in agreement with all those sentiments. Thirty years in a narrow cell will not bring anyone any closer to God than will a simple, believing murmur of *"Jesus"*. Furthermore, any believer who escapes from the cell will be free to serve God and the church in the larger world. After all, Christ did not tell us to withdraw from the world, but to go out into it and proclaim the gospel (Mt 28:19-20; Mk 16:15-16). But let us also resolve, as the poet said, not to abuse the freedom we have in Christ, that "better and easier rule" the gospel puts before us. How gladly we can serve the King, for we serve him, not as slaves driven by a lash, but as his free-born children!

So Christ has set us free to serve God, the church, and our neighbour. But what is this *"freedom"*? Is he talking about the *manumission* of actual slaves, or about *political* liberties, or about freedom from physical or social *restraints*? No. They are all important freedoms, but Paul has in mind **spiritual** freedom. That is liberty from –

- the curse of the moral law (summarised in the Ten Commandments);
- any obligation to obey the rituals ordered by Moses (including the food laws, and rules about dress, and so on;
- an addiction to the love of this world and of sin;
- the powerful grip and guilt of sin;
- the dominion of the devil and all his works;
- any man-made rules about touching, eating, doing, going (Cl 2:20-22); and from
- all fear of death and the Day of Judgment.

That is freedom indeed! And it has been wrought for us by Christ. But it will not be effective unless we who have been set free learn to stand firm in that freedom, for we have been set free from sin to serve God in righteousness. Freedom *from* is the passive side of our deliverance; the active side is freedom *to* do and be all that the lord desires of us.

TWO WAYS OF LIFE

We find ourselves confronted by two different views of Christian life – one bound up by punctilious observance of certain rules and of struggles to be righteous; the other a scary liberty that is granted us in Christ. Why "scary"? Because the church has never been comfortable with the amazing level of freedom God has given us in the gospel. Always ecclesiastical authorities have been fearful of that freedom, worried that people will abuse it, anxious that they will take it too far. The only safe remedy, they say, is to create a body of rules and regulations to control the way people believe and live. The hermits and eremites were simply extreme examples of this principle. So even among Christian leaders who did not wish to lock themselves into caves, or squat on tall pillars, or tear their own flesh with bone-threaded whips, there were still many who wished to impose harsh restraints upon the people of God. Perhaps the best example of that ruinous law-keeping push is found in the writings of Clement of Alexandria (*circa 150 – 215*), in his work *The Instructor* –

- **<u>On Eating</u>**. "Some men, in truth, live that they may eat, as the irrational creatures, *'whose life is their belly, and nothing else.'* But the Instructor enjoins us to eat that we may live. For neither is food our business, nor is pleasure our aim; but both are on account of our life here, which the Word is training up to immortality. Wherefore also there is discrimination to be employed in reference to food. And it is to be simple, truly plain, suiting precisely simple and artless children – as ministering to life, not to luxury. And the life to which it conduces consists of two things – health and strength; to which plainness of fare is most suitable, being conducive both to digestion and lightness of body, from which come growth, and health, and right strength, not strength that is wrong or dangerous and wretched, as is that of athletes produced by compulsory feeding. We must therefore reject different varieties, which engender various mischiefs, such as a depraved habit of body and disorders of the stomach, the taste being vitiated by an unhappy art – that of cookery, and the useless art of making pastry. For people dare to call by the name of food their dabbling in luxuries, which glides into mischievous pleasures." (Book 2, ch. 1)

Clement continues by urging all Christians to desist from seeking pleasure in eating and to confine themselves to the plainest possible foods that need the least amount of preparation. And while he draws attention to the healthful benefits of eating wisely, still his motivation is to gain a higher status in heaven, a better right to approach the throne of God. He suggests that even our salvation may depend upon what foods we eat, or choose not to eat.

- **_On Drinking_**. "The natural, temperate, and necessary beverage ... for the thirsty is water. This was the simple drink of sobriety, which, flowing from the smitten rock, was supplied by the Lord to the ancient Hebrews. (Ex 17:1-16; Nu 20:1-29) ... I therefore admire those who have adopted an austere life, and who are fond of water, the medicine of temperance, and flee as far as possible from wine, shunning it as they would the danger of fire. It is proper, therefore, that boys and girls should keep as much as possible away from this medicine. For it is not right to pour into the burning season of life the hottest of all liquids – wine ... For hence wild impulses and burning lusts and fiery habits are kindled; and young men inflamed from within become prone to the indulgence of vicious propensities." (Book 2, ch. 2)

I too would enjoin temperance in all things, including wine. Nonetheless, Clement's vigorous admonitions practically make one's very salvation dependent upon a resolve to drink only water. One shudders to think what the good bishop might have said about tea, coffee, cocoa, fizzy soft drinks, and the like!

- **_On Costly Vessels_**. "The use of cups made of silver and gold, and of others inlaid with precious stones, is out of place, being only a deception of the vision. Away, then, with ... (fancy) cups ... and goblets, and ... the endless shapes of drinking vessels, and wine-coolers, and wine-pourers also. ... The elaborate vanity, too, of vessels in glass chased, more apt to break on account of the art, teaching us to fear while we drink, is to be banished from our well-ordered constitution. ... For my part, I (say) that a man is not to labour for wealth of gold or silver, nor to possess a useless vessel which is not for some necessary purpose, and moderate; so that the same thing may serve for many purposes, and the possession of a variety of things may be done away with." (Book 2, ch. 3)

And so he continues, insisting further that a truly holy life cannot be maintained apart self-denial, plain living, and abjuring anything costly and beautiful.

- **_On Laughing_**. "We ... must by no manner of means be allowed to stir up laughter. For it were absurd to be found imitators of things of which we are prohibited to be listeners. ... Laughter must be kept in check; for when given vent to in the right manner it indicates orderliness, but when it issues differently it shows a want of restraint. For, in a word, whatever things are natural to men we must not eradicate from them, but rather impose on them limits and suitable times. For man is not to laugh on all occasions because he is a laughing animal, any more than the horse neighs on all occasions because he is a neighing animal. But as rational beings, we are to regulate ourselves suitably, harmoniously relaxing the austerity and over-tension of our serious pursuits, not inharmoniously breaking them up altogether."

Clement, then, does allow some laughter in Christian life, but not much, and only when it is for proper cause and well-moderated, and does not disturb the proper austerity and sternness that should characterise our behaviour. He prefers that any response to humour should be limited to a smile, and presents a dour picture of Christian life. (Book 2, ch. 5)

- **_On Ointments_**. "The use of crowns and ointments is not necessary for us; for it impels to pleasures and indulgences ... For it is not right that ensnaring garments and unguents should be admitted into the city of truth; but it is highly requisite for the men who belong to us to give forth the odour not of ointments, but of nobleness and goodness. And let woman breathe the odour of the true royal ointment, that of Christ." (Book 2, ch. 8)

To those stern injunctions he adds many more paragraphs, indicting the use of any sort of fragrance or ornament, colourful garments and jewellery, both in men and women, all in the name of holiness, pleasing God, and attaining righteousness.

- ***On Sleeping***. "In remembrance of the precepts of temperance ... our talk must now be turned to sleep. Magnificence of bed-clothes, gold-embroidered carpets, and smooth carpets worked with gold, and long fine robes of purple, and costly fleecy cloaks, and manufactured rugs of purple, and mantles of thick pile, and couches softer than sleep, are to be banished. For, besides the reproach of voluptuousness, sleeping on downy feathers is injurious, when our bodies fall down as into a yawning hollow, on account of the softness of the bedding." (Book 2, ch. 9)

How severely the bishop would indict our modern soft beds, electric blankets, eiderdowns, doonas, and the like! He goes on to urge Christians to be content with a plain, firm bed, without any ornamentation, and with as few blankets as possible. All this is to display the life of Christ, and to plant one's feet safely on the highway to heaven.

Clement continues with admonitions on:– human ***coitus***, which he deems should never be used for pleasure, but only for procreation, and even then as seldom as possible; ***clothing***, which must always be plain, never ornamental, and only such as is necessary for good health; ***shoes***, which too he thinks should be banned and that Christians should go bare-foot, although he grudgingly allows the use of plain, simple sandals; and ***jewellery***, about which he says –

It is childish to admire excessively dark or green stones, and things cast out by the sea on foreign shores, particles of the earth. For to rush after stones that are pellucid and of peculiar colours, and stained glass, is only characteristic of silly people, who are attracted by things that have a striking show. Thus children, on seeing the fire, rush to it, attracted by its brightness ... Such is the case with the stones which silly women wear fastened to chains and set in necklaces, amethysts, ceraunites, [97] jaspers, topaz, and (emeralds). ... And the highly prized pearl has invaded the women's apartments to an extravagant extent. .... And the wretched creatures [98] are not ashamed at having bestowed the greatest pains about this little oyster, when they might adorn themselves with the sacred jewel, the Word of God. (Book 2, ch. 13)

He is just as furious in his denunciation of male ornamentation!

But, despite the good sense that underlies some of the counsel given by Clement, this is all "law". It is striving to become righteous by human effort. It is good works supplanting the grace of God. It has nothing to do with real holiness and is the antithesis of the liberty God has given us in Christ. Yes, that liberty is dangerous! Yes, it can be abused. Yes, it frightens some church leaders. But God entrusts us with it. Its potential benefits far outweigh its potential harm. And still Paul commands us: *"Stand fast in the freedom for which Christ has set you free, and never again become entangled in a yoke of bondage!"* (Ga 5:1)

WE HAVE BEEN FREED

Martin Luther begins his striking commentary on our text with these words –

Paul now drawing towards the end of his Epistle, disputeth very vehemently in defense of the doctrine of faith and Christian liberty, against the false apostles, the enemies and destroyers of the same; against whom he casteth out very thundering words to beat them down and

---

(97) I have been unable to identify this stone.
(98) That is, the pearl-adorned women, among whom I may number my wife. Not, I hasten to say, as a "wretched" woman, but simply as a devout and lovely lady, who also happens to wear a pearl necklace, which I gave her.

utterly to vanquish them. And therewithal he exhorteth the Galatians to fly their pernicious doctrine as a dangerous poison. In his exhortation he intermingleth threatenings and promises, trying every way that he may keep them in that liberty which Christ hath purchased for them.

We too should inveigh against every false apostle, every enemy of the gospel, every wrong doctrine, and indeed against anything and everything that tries to bring the people back under some legal yoke, some bondage to rule-keeping. No doubt some rules are useful, and good order may necessitate them, but not if the aim is to purchase God's favour or to build a quota of personal righteousness. God in Christ, for everyone who believes, has once and for all put an end to the law as a way of gaining *anything* from heaven (Ro 10:4). Believe it, then! Rejoice in the liberty you possess in Christ, and scorn any effort by man or devil to wrap chains of law around your soul.

In 1790, the Irish politician and orator John Curran made a speech in Dublin. In it he said –

> The condition upon which God hath given liberty to man is eternal vigilance; which condition if he break, servitude is at once the consequence of his crime and the punishment of his guilt.

That sentence has often been shortened into the aphorism, "Eternal vigilance is the price of liberty." If that is true in the political world it is even truer in the life of faith. An urge to enhance our claim upon God's bounty by performing some good work is endemic in our fallen nature. We are uneasy about trusting entirely and exclusively in the grace of God. Grace seems so ephemeral. We yearn to produce something tangible – a noble deed, a selfless sacrifice, a splendid gift, meticulous obedience to a set of rules, and so on. It is all a delusion. If we kept our eyes focussed upon Christ, we would in Calvary find all the solidity we could ever need! The cross is sufficient. Christ is enough. We should cry with Paul, *"I am determined to know nothing among you, nor to boast of anything except Christ and him crucified!"* (1 Co 2:1-2; Ep 2:9)

Every believer, then, must maintain an unwavering vigilance, watching and wary, so that we do not succumb to the enticements of the flesh, the law, the devil, but stick close to Jesus, confident only in the grace of God. By all means, let us do many noble deeds, make selfless sacrifices, offer splendid gifts, and set ourselves to live uprightly – but these things we do, not to secure safety, but because we *know* that by grace we are already safe! We behave godly not to gain some benefit from God, but because we are grateful for all the benefits grace has already bestowed upon us. Out of the bounty we have received – *"every spiritual blessing in the heavenlies"* (Ep 1:3) –we give back a little, and wish only to give back more and more. We cannot earn anything beyond what grace has already given us; we can only be thankful and strive to express that appreciation by the way we live. "It is indeed one thing to work so that we might earn love, but altogether another to work because we know that we are already loved." (99)

But since we have discovered the love of God in Christ, and perfect freedom in his service, how can we do other than joyfully serve him and each other? As Paul said in our text –

> *You were called to freedom, dear friends; but never think to use your freedom as an excuse for indulging your flesh. Rather, through love serve one another* (Ga 5:13).

Yet, to maintain our freedom, there is one thing we *can*, and *must* do, and that is never relax vigilance. For assuredly the law will never stop trying to ensnare your soul; the flesh will be ever pleading with you to build some personal righteousness; the devil will never cease hurling his fiery darts against you, tempting you to sin, waging war against your soul, and mocking your security in Christ. Block your ears to all those pernicious pleas. Wrap your arms around the cross. Stand firm in the knowledge that Christ has made you free, that every chain forged by the law, sin, flesh, death, and the devil has been broken, and that you are irrevocably set on victory in Christ. This is spiritual warfare. It is not easy. The

---

(99) Paraphrased from J. Vaughan in a sermon on *Galatians 5:1*.

battle can be fierce. The enemies of your soul are relentless. Small wonder, then, that the apostle elsewhere urges us to –

Remain watchful, stand firm in the faith, be brave, be strong. (1 Co 16:13)

THE YOKE OF SLAVERY

For freedom Christ has set us free. So stand firm, and never again become entangled by the yoke of slavery. (Ga 5:1)

Paul hath spoken most effectually and profoundly as concerning grace and Christian liberty, and with high and mighty words hath exhorted the Galatians to continue in the same; for it is easily lost. Therefore he biddeth them stand fast, lest that, through negligence ... they fall back again from grace and faith to the law and works. [100]

With deep scorn Paul abjures the idea that keeping religious laws and doing good works is the proper way to reach the throne of God. Rather, says he, all who succumb to it will find it a *"yoke of slavery"*, a manacle of bondage. It should be loathed by all who believe the gospel of Christ. Freedom or slavery? That is a choice we all have to make. But what madness is this? How could anyone who was once a slave but is now free, rationally choose to abandon that freedom and become again a slave? But that is just what a Christian does when he or she turns aside from grace, hoping instead to gain righteousness by doing some good work, keeping some rule, observing some rite or ceremony (Ga 4:9-10). Such people, says Paul with great vehemence, are renouncing Christ and embracing instead the rattling chains of servitude.

But this liberty of ours provides no licence to sin. Rather, since we are no longer slaves but have now become the sons of God, we are truly free to serve him with gladness. The bonds that held us in thrall are shattered, so that we are now free to fulfil all that the Father has purposed for our lives. No longer under the rule of Satan, we are free to serve the Saviour. No longer prisoners of the

---

[100] Martin Luther on *Galatians 5:1*; op. cit.

law we are free to proclaim the gospel. No longer restrained by ritual, we are free to worship God in spirit and in truth (Jn 4:23).

If you prize the freedom for which Christ has set you free, then you will surely take care never to be enticed away from it, but will rather stand fast, immovable, resolved to keep to it until the very end of your earthly pilgrimage. We should be like the cabin boy who without his father's permission would not shift from his place on the deck of a sinking ship –

> The boy stood on the burning deck
> Whence all but he had fled;
> The flame that lit the battle's wreck
> Shone round him o'er the dead.
>
> Yet beautiful and bright he stood,
> As born to rule the storm;
> A creature of heroic blood,
> A proud, though child-like form.
>
> The flames rolled on – he would not go
> Without his Father's word ... (101)

So too our resolve should be fixed – neither life, nor death, nor any other thing will ever shift us away from the gospel. How could I suppose that Christ, paying an awful price to set me free from one prison, would do so only to transfer me to another? Having been released from the gamut of Mosaic rules, regulations, and rituals, am I now to welcome another set of man-made prescriptions for life and holiness? It is absurd! For *freedom* Christ has set me *free*, (Ga 5:1) and in that liberty I will stand for ever!

---

(101) From the poem *Casabianca*, by Felicity Hemans (1793-1835); first three stanzas. The poem tells the true story of a young boy who was the son of Louis de Casabianca, the commander of the war ship *Orient*, during the Battle of the Nile in 1798. Because his father had commanded it, the boy remained at his post even after the ship had taken fire, and all the guns had been abandoned. He was unaware that his father had been killed, and he perished when the ship exploded after the flames reached its powder magazine.

ADDENDA

EARLY CHURCH LEGALISMS

Here are further examples of legalistic ideas from the early church, beginning with the African lawyer and Christian apologist and polemicist

TERTULLIAN

Tertullian (*circa* 155 – 240) has been called the Father of Western Theology, and his influence across the centuries has been enormous. But he was much prone to legalism. Admittedly, his rules, and those laid down by other church leaders were to some degree a reaction to the extreme decadence of the surrounding society, but there was usually also some shadow of attaining righteousness by law. I will also admit that I have ignored all the wonderful ideas promulgated by him and by other church fathers, and perhaps unfairly focussed only on their quainter legalities. Nonetheless, an enslaving law-based righteousness is present in their writings, and it put a poison into the church that still sickens many a sincere believer.

Let me summarise some of the ideas found in various writings by Tertullian –

"ON MONOGAMY"

Despite the clear mandate given by Paul, Tertullian opposed any second marriage, even after the death of a spouse. He deemed celibacy a better state, and thought that marriage gave too much scope for debauchery.

"TO MY WIFE"

In this book he grudgingly allows the propriety of a second marriage after the death of a spouse, yet he seems to regret his own marriage. This was not because of any lack in his wife, whom he tenderly describes as "my best beloved fellow servant in the Lord." His regret arose rather from his puritanical zeal. Hence he almost relishes the dissolution of the marriage at death, saying that in the world to come "(there will) be no resumption of voluptuous disgrace between us. No such frivolity, no such impurities, does God promise to his servants." (Book 1, ch. 1)

"ON CHASTITY"

In this work Tertullian views marriage, at best, as a kind of legalised fornication against Christ – "It is laws which seem to make the difference between marriage and fornication; through diversity of illicitness, not through the nature of the thing itself. Besides, what is the thing which takes place in all men and women to produce both marriage and fornication? Commixture of the flesh, of course; the concupiscence whereof the Lord put on the same footing with fornication. 'Then,' says someone, 'are you by this time destroying first – that is, single – marriage too?' And if so, not without reason; inasmuch as it, too, consists of that which is the essence of fornication." (Chapter 9). [102]

"ON THE PALLIUM"

This work contains six chapters devoted to denouncing the toga, with its elegant folds and fastenings, and its ornate footwear. Instead, Tertullian enjoins the wearing of the pallium, a loose, long robe, of which modern academic gowns are a direct descendant. He says of the pallium – "Nowhere is there a compulsory waste of time in dressing yourself in it, seeing that its whole art consists of loosely covering (the body)."

By contrast, a servant has to begin preparing a toga a full day before it is required by its owner (ch. 5). He also deplores the footwear associated with a toga – "they are implements of torture proper to the toga, most uncleanly protection to the feet, yes, and false too. For who would not find it expedient, in cold and heat, to stiffen with feet bare rather than in a shoe with feet bound? A mighty munition for the tread have the Venetian shoe factories provided in shape of effeminate boots!" He decides in the end to

---

(102) The chapter begins by saying that "second marriage will have to be termed no other than a species of fornication".

tolerate plain sandals, but still reckons that bare feet, if not more godly are certainly more manly.

He goes on to denounce many other sorts of extravagances and cruelties, all of which he associates with toga-wearing, and then concludes by saying –

> Remember that these ... were (all) men of the toga – (for) such as among the men of the pallium you would not easily find. These purulencies of a state who will eliminate and exsuppurate, save a bemantled speech? [103]

"ON THE APPAREL OF WOMEN"

> Female habit carries with it a twofold idea – dress and ornament. By "dress" we mean what they call "womanly gracing;" by "ornament," what it is suitable should be called "womanly disgracing." The former is accounted (to consist) in gold, and silver, and gems, and garments; the latter in care of the hair, and of the skin, and of those parts of the body which attract the eye. Against the one we lay the charge of ambition, against the other of prostitution. (Book 1, ch. 4)

Then, in a later chapter (8) he denounces the use of artificial colours –

> What legitimate honour can garments derive from adulteration with illegitimate colours? That which he himself has not produced is not pleasing to God, unless he was unable to order sheep to be born with purple and sky-blue fleeces! If he was able, then plainly he was unwilling: what God willed not, of course ought not to be fashioned. Those things, then, are not the best by nature which are not from God, the Author of nature. Thus they are understood to be from the devil, from the corrupter of

---

(103) That is, "Who can cleanse these pus-seeping wounds (in the church) and prevent them from breaking out again, except someone whose trustworthy speech is marked by wearing a pallium?"

nature: for there is no other whose they can be, if they are not God's.

A modern reader could hardly accord such weird ideas any sort of sense. They are simply ridiculous. But Tertullian, falling ever deeper into the mesh of law, is very serious about them. Then follow several chapters in which Tertullian excoriates women who dye or curl their hair, and who practice other forms of feminine adornment. In the middle of his fulminations he writes –

> There must be no overstepping of that line to which simple and sufficient refinements limit their desires – that line which is pleasing to God. For they who rub their skin with medicaments, stain their cheeks with rouge, make their eyes prominent with antimony, sin against him. To them, I suppose, the plastic skill of God is displeasing! In their own persons, I suppose, they convict, they censure, the Artificer of all things! For censure they, do when they amend, when they add to his work; taking these their additions, of course, from the adversary artificer. That adversary artificer is the devil. For who would show the way to change the body, but he who by wickedness transfigured man's spirit? (Book 2, ch. 5)

So the great lawyer urges Christian women to abhor all manner of cosmetics, adornments, jewellery, hair-dressing, fragrances, bangles, necklaces, rings, or anything at all that may serve to enhance a woman's beauty or disguise her plainness. Nor does he leave men unscathed. For, apart from insisting they should wear only a plain pallium, he adds –

> If it is true, (as it is,) that in men, for the sake of women (just as in women for the sake of men), there is implanted, by a defect of nature, the will to please; and if this sex of ours acknowledges to itself deceptive trickeries of form peculiarly its own, – (such as) to cut the beard too sharply; to pluck it out here and there; to shave round about (the mouth); to arrange the hair, and disguise its hoariness by dyes; to remove all the incipient down all over the body; to fix (each particular hair) in its place with (some) womanly pigment; to smooth all the rest of

the body by the aid of some rough powder or other: then, further, to take every opportunity for consulting the mirror; to gaze anxiously into it – even if all that were true, surely, once the knowledge of God has put an end to all wish to please by means of voluptuous attraction, all these things will be rejected as frivolous, as hostile to modesty. (Book 2, ch. 17, slightly paraphrased)

"ON THE VEILING OF VIRGINS"

This is a book of 17 chapters, in which Tertullian insists that all virgins should be veiled. Indeed, he prefers that married women, too, should wear a veil, and he admires the Arab custom of complete veiling –

Arabia's heathen females will be your judges, who cover not only the head, but the face also, so entirely, that they are content, with one eye free, to enjoy rather half the light than to prostitute the entire face. A female would rather see than be seen. And for this reason a certain Roman queen said that they were most unhappy, in that they could more easily fall in love than be fallen in love with; whereas they are rather happy, in their immunity from that second (and indeed more frequent) infelicity, that females are more apt to be fallen in love with than to fall in love. ... To us (charismatics) [104] the Lord has, even by prophecies, measured the space for the veil to extend over. For a certain sister of ours was thus addressed by an angel, stroking her neck, as if in applause: "Elegant neck, and deservedly bare! It is well for thee to unveil thyself" ... And of course, what you have said to one you have said to all. But how severe a chastisement will they likewise deserve, who, amid (the recital of) the Psalms, and at any mention of (the name of) God, continue uncovered; (who)

---

(104) Tertullian was a member of the Montanist movement, an early expression of what is today called the "Pentecostal" or "charismatic" movement. Montanism, named after its founder Montanus, began in the late 2nd century, flourished for two or three centuries, then gradually faded out until its remnants re-united with the main body of Christians.

even when about to spend time in prayer itself, with the utmost readiness place a fringe, or a tuft, or any thread whatever, on the crown of their heads, and suppose themselves to be covered? (Chapter 17)

Another example of pernicious legalism in the early church can be found in the writings of –

ATHENAGORAS

An Athenian philosopher and Christian convert, Athenagoras flourished during the second half of the second century. So his writings followed almost on the heels of the apostles, and they show how early legalism began to exert its invidious influence over Christians. Here are some of his stern views on marriage –

> Therefore, having the hope of eternal life, we despise the things of this life, even to the pleasures of the soul, each of us reckoning her his wife whom he has married according to the laws laid down by us, and that only for the purpose of having children. For as the husbandman throwing the seed into the ground awaits the harvest, not sowing more upon it, so to us the procreation of children is the measure of our indulgence in appetite. Nay, you would find many among us, both men and women, growing old unmarried, in hope of living in closer communion with God. But if the remaining in virginity and in the state of an eunuch brings nearer to God, while the indulgence of carnal thought and desire leads away from him, in those cases in which we shun the thoughts, much more do we reject the deeds. For we bestow our attention; not on the study of words, but on the exhibition and teaching of actions, – that a person should either remain as he was born, or be content with one marriage; for a second marriage is only a specious adultery. "For whosoever puts away his wife," says Jesus, "and marries another, commits adultery;" (Mt 19:9) not permitting a man to send her away whose virginity he has brought to an end, nor to marry again. For he who deprives himself of his first wife, even though she be dead, is a cloaked adulterer, resisting the hand of God,

because in the beginning God made one man and one woman, and dissolving the strictest union of flesh with flesh, formed for the intercourse of the race. (105)

Still further, consider the admonitions to men, presented in an anonymous document from about the year 200, known as

THE CONSTITUTIONS OF THE HOLY APOSTLES

That beauty which God and nature has bestowed on thee, do not further beautify; but modestly diminish it before men. Thus, do not thou permit the hair of thy head to grow too long, but rather cut it short; lest by a nice combing of thy hair, and wearing it long, and anointing thyself, thou draw upon thyself (an) ensnaring woman. Neither do thou wear over-fine garments to seduce any; neither do thou, with an evil subtilty, affect over-fine stockings or shoes for thy feet, but only such as suit the measures of decency and usefulness. Neither do thou put a gold ring upon thy fingers; for all these ornaments are the signs of lasciviousness ... It is not lawful for thee, a believer and a man of God, to permit the hair of thy head to grow long, and to brush it up together, nor to suffer it to spread abroad, nor to puff it up, nor by nice combing and platting to make it curl and shine; since that is contrary to the law ... Nor may men destroy the hair of their beards, and unnaturally change the form of a man. For the law says: "Ye shall not mar your beards." (Le 19:27) For God the Creator has made (a smooth cheek) decent for women, but has determined that it is unsuitable for men. But if thou do these things to please men, in contradiction to the law, thou wilt be abominable with God, who created thee after his own image. (Bk 1, ch. 2)

The instructions continue, dealing with women bathing –

---

(105) From A Plea for Christians (*circa 177*), ch. 33.

If the bath be appropriate for women, let her bathe orderly, modestly, and moderately. But let her not bathe without occasion, nor much, nor often, nor in the middle of the day. (Bk 1, ch 9)

Such rules seem to us today to be absurd, lacking any sensible reason, or biblical warrant. But in just such ways many early church leaders, bound up with rules, terrified of Christian liberty, tried to regulate the lives of the saints. Unhappily, much of that legalistic spirit still remains in the modern church.

Chapter Twenty-One

RIGHTEOUSNESS

> *By faith, and through the Spirit, we are eagerly waiting for the hope of **righteousness**. ... I do not annul the grace of God, for if **righteousness** were through the law, then Christ died for no purpose. ... Abraham believed God, and it was reckoned to him as **righteousness**"* (Ga 5:5; 2:21; 3:6).

The word ***righteousness*** occurs approximately 100 times in the NT. Paul described himself as a *"preacher of righteousness"*, and we should certainly be ***believers*** in it –

RIGHTEOUSNESS AND FAITH

No one can gain righteousness by personal achievement, no matter how noble, godly, sacrificial, pious, diligent, or admirable their efforts (Ro 10:2-3). Indeed, there is no obtaining of divine felicity until we abandon all claims of personal merit or wealth, and cast ourselves utterly upon divine mercy. We are like John Aubrey, who declared that he could find no happiness until he had lost everything –

> I was in as much affliction as a mortal could be, and never quiet till all (my property) was gone, (and I) wholly cast myself on God's providence ... Never quiet, nor anything of happiness, till divested of all – at what time providence raised me (unexpectedly) good friends. [106]

The attainment of a righteous state in the sight of God depends upon just two things (Ro 1:16-17) –

---

(106) John Aubrey (1626-97) was an English antiquary and author, most famous for his Brief Lives, a series of short biographies of famous people of the 16th and 17th centuries; ed. by Richard Barber; Folio Society, London, 1975; pg. 20, 21.

CLEAR TEACHING OF THE GOSPEL

It is *"in the gospel"*, says Paul, that *"the righteousness of God is revealed"*. How sorely we need teachers who understand righteousness, who know how to turn their backs once and for all upon any kind of works-based righteousness, who realise that if we are not made utterly righteous by the gift of God alone, we shall never attain any righteous standing before him.

CLEAR FAITH IN THE GOSPEL

The word is taught in vain if it is not believed, and it must be believed vigorously, and heartily, with complete trust in the righteous provision of God. There is no other way to be made righteous before God except by faith; hence the latter part of *Romans 1:17* can be translated: *"Those who are made righteous through faith shall live!"*

So we must become skilled in the **word** of righteousness, and strong in the **confession** of righteousness. Thus we are made righteous and able to approach the throne of God without shame or hindrance. It is an application of the dictum of Christ: *"You will know the truth, and the truth will set you free!"* (Jn 8:32) How can anyone ask then if there is any treasure or gift more to be desired than a thorough and dynamic knowledge of God's word? You wish to be free? Then simply *"know the truth!"* Nothing further is required, except to *believe* the truth once we have come to *know* it.

One of the most important influences in the life of Alexander the Great was the renowned philosopher Aristotle, who was the young prince's tutor for several years. Later, when Alexander was conducting his wars in Asia, he learned that Aristotle had gathered together many of those early lessons and had published them. He wrote the philosopher a curt note: "Alexander to Aristotle: may all be well with you. You did wrong to publish those private and divine doctrines. How shall I surpass others if those lessons you taught me now become common property? I would prefer to be different from other people in knowledge than in power. Farewell."

Thus the mightiest monarch on earth at that time valued *knowledge* above *power*. How much more should we value above anything and everything else in this world the peerless riches to be found in the word of righteousness God has spoken over us in Christ! But such an **affirmation** of righteousness must be followed by righteous **action.** A *profession* of faith that is not *practised* is **perjury.**

Hypocrisy is scorned more bitterly in scripture than almost any other fault (Ez 33:31-32; Is 9:17; 29:15; Je 42:20-22). Let us make sure then that what we know, and believe, and profess, we do indeed work out in daily life, not according to a set of rules or human traditions, but by faith and through the Spirit (Ga 5:5).

RIGHTEOUSNESS AND AUTHORITY

The righteous have instant authority over Satan. Only the presence of sin ever gave the devil the right to afflict human beings; once the sin problem is dealt with, human mastery over Satan is fully restored. For that reason, Satan wages unrelenting warfare upon your acceptance of righteousness in Christ. He does this in three ways –

- he prevents people from ever hearing or believing the "word of righteousness"; or
- if they do accept the gospel promise of righteousness, he entices them to compromise it by trying to add to the merits of Christ some good work of their own; or
- if they happen to commit some sin, he tries to persuade them that they have now lost their righteousness, and can re-build it only by many tears, struggles, sacrifices, and performance of many good works.

But if you show yourself unshakeable in faith, refusing to be turned aside from an absolute trust in the righteousness imparted to you in Christ (2 Co 5:21), Satan must soon flee. However, his flight is based on the presumption that you will continue to exercise your rightful authority over him and all his works.

The parents of the Dutch painter Rembrandt (1606-69) became impatient at the many hours he devoted to art. Before he was 15 years of age they had taken away his paints, brushes, canvasses, and all his painter's tools, and had strictly forbidden him to continue his "daubings on bits of paper". But he refused to be deterred. He painted on any substance he could find, and when no other paints were available he used soot for black and his own blood for red! Such dogged persistence persuaded his parents to allow him to study under a master painter in Leyden, and he went on to become the greatest of the old Dutch masters.

Thus should we persist bravely in our warfare against Satan and in our efforts to portray the beauty of Christ. See *James 4:7 – "resist the devil and he will flee from you!"* Notice that *"resist"* conveys the idea of persistence; there is always a certain stubborn determination in the life of faith, a refusal to give up, a resolve to press on until the goal is reached. They may take away everything we possess, but they cannot rob us of our inner compulsion to fulfil all that the Father has designed us to be and to do!

RIGHTEOUSNESS AND THE THRONE

Only righteous men and women have access to the throne of God; no sinner can approach it. Therefore we **must** set ourselves to stand in faith, for only those who **believe** are reckoned righteous by God. Note also that faith has nothing to do with how long you have managed to stay "good", nor with how "good" you feel, but only with how well you believe the promise. And why would anyone not be content with the righteousness that faith alone brings? It is after all the righteousness of God himself (2 Co 5:21). Add a handful of dirt to a mountain; take a handful away – has the mountain been increased or diminished? Likewise, it is absurd to suppose that **anything** you and I can do can either add anything to or take anything away from the infinite righteousness of God. It is simply impossible to gain any better or nearer access to the throne of God than we can gain by receiving the gift of God's own righteousness by faith, and by faith alone.

CONCLUSION

Through the **first** Adam we were made **unrighteousness**; but now through the **last** Adam we are made **righteous** (Ro 5:15-17). Why then do so many Christians fail to enjoy this free gift and to reign in life? It is because -

SOME DON'T YET KNOW WHO THEY TRULY ARE IN CHRIST.

Mark this: no-one can **grow** into righteousness; we are **made** righteous in Christ; but it will do us no good until we **know** what God in Christ has done for us. That is why we need to hear the *"word of righteousness"* and continually grow in our understanding of that word. That growth in understanding may not come quickly, nor even easily, but we need to persevere in reading and meditation in the gospel –

> I wish that undertakers [107] may not be disheartened with their small encouragement. Such who are ashamed of contemptible beginnings will never arrive at considerable endings. Yea, the greatest giant was (though never a dwarf) once an infant, and the longest line commenced from a little point at the first. [108]

SOME REFUSE TO BELIEVE THE GOSPEL AND TO ACCEPT THE GIFT

Like the Jews of old, they prefer to cling to their own righteousness (Ro 10:1-4). But God has resolved that no one can approach him with any kind of personal righteousness, but only with his own righteousness, received as a gift by faith.

SOME DO BELIEVE, BUT STILL FAIL TO ACT

We are commanded to act out our faith by taking authority over Satan and by possessing all that belongs to us in Christ. Christian life is *active* not passive. We are expected both to *believe* and to *do*.

In the year 326 B.C. Alexander the Great marched his troops into north India, determined to expand his empire to what he thought was the boundary of the earth. Many of the Indian princes at once capitulated to him, but one by the name of Porus decided to resist. He amassed a great army of soldiers and elephants and waited for

---

(107) He means, people who are undertaking to fulfil the rôle of a Christian.

(108) Dr Thomas Fuller (1608-61), who was perhaps the first man ever to earn a full-time living as a writer, in "The Worthies of England"; Fuller's Worthies, ed. Richard Barber; The Folio Society, London, 1987; pg. 97.

the Greek invasion. When it came, a terrible battle raged, but although they were outnumbered, the Greeks prevailed. Porus was wounded, and knowing the battle was lost, he began to retreat. Alexander, however, impressed by his skill and bravery, sent a message to him, urging him to return and to negotiate a fair surrender.

When the two men finally met each other, Alexander asked Porus: "How do you think I should treat you?" Porus at once replied, "Like a king!" Astonished, Alexander promised that he would; but then he asked, "What boon do you seek for yourself?" Porus, again without hesitation, simply said, "Everything!"

Deeply affected by the young prince's fine stature, courage, and wisdom, Alexander gave him back the whole of his kingdom and added more territory to it.

That is the kind of boldness God likes to find in his own royal priesthood, and that is the kind of response he gives to those who confidently claim their rights!

Chapter Twenty-Two

RIGHTEOUSNESS – 2

> *By faith, and through the Spirit, we are eagerly waiting for the hope of **righteousness**. ... I do not annul the grace of God, for if **righteousness** were through the law, then Christ died for no purpose. ... Abraham believed God, and it was reckoned to him as **righteousness**."* (Ga 5:5; 2:21; 3:6)

The continuance of sin upon the planet created a set of problems – three for God, and two for us – that had to be solved before the plan of redemption could be inaugurated.

THREE PROBLEMS GOD FACED

See *Romans 3:21-26*. The key thought is in vs. 26 –

> *Christ came to show the righteousness of God in our time, so that he might be both just and the justifier of everyone who believes in Jesus.*

That verse sets out the three problems God faced –

GOD HAD TO ESTABLISH HIS OWN RIGHTEOUSNESS

A serious question was being raised in the heavenlies as to whether or not the righteousness of God had been compromised, if not destroyed, by the existence of iniquity. The problem arose from the following facts –

- There were 14 charges that could be laid against us, and against the entire human race (count them in vs. 9-14).
- God's forbearance of this state had made him seem to be as unrighteous as we were (vs. 25b).
- So he had to find a way to demonstrate his undiminished righteousness, yet at the same time not jeopardise his desire to "justify" his people.

Then the second problem God faced was this –

GOD HAD TO RESTORE OUR RIGHTEOUSNESS

Four choices were available to the Almighty to solve the problem of a sin-corrupted world –

- He could simply surrender the world to iniquity, and then when its wickedness had run its full course, bring it under terrible judgment and annihilate the earth and every creature on it.

But that would have meant condemning all to the same doom, even those who had struggled against sin, seeking a better way. So perhaps God would turn to another possible solution –

- He could find a way to expiate past sin, and then tell men and women to get it right from now on.

That, of course, was the essence of the way of life promulgated by Moses. But it failed. Not even the most godly person could truly keep all the rules, and in the end the law simply made sin more sinful (vs. 19-20). So then, God might have turned to another possible solution –

- He could start the work of creation all over again.

But that would create the same problem as the first alternative: the good would be annihilated with the evil. Was there then no way to start again without destroying what he had already created? Yes, there was one possible solution remaining; although it is one that carried with it its own massive problem –

GOD HAD TO BRING THE NEW OUT OF THE OLD

The Father decided that he could protect his own righteousness while rescuing us from the consequences of our unrighteousness only by keeping the old and bringing the new out of it. But how is it possible to bring holiness out of unholiness, good out of evil, light out of dark? The principles of nature and the laws of God all seemed to cry that such a thing is impossible (cp. Ja 3:11-12). But the Lord decided that he could do it, by planting his own nature in us, thus changing us, and imputing his own righteousness to us.

But how could God achieve that miracle? Only through the blood of Jesus (Ro 3:21-25a), who allowed himself to be made sin for us, and cut off from God himself, so that we might be brought near.

But an even larger work was achieved at Calvary. Because Jesus is the Son of God, and therefore his life has an infinite, inexhaustible value, there came a point in his sufferings on the cross when heaven's ***justice*** was satisfied. Every angel in heaven, every demon in hell, could see that full atonement had been made for every sin of every sinner. The thundering voice of the violated law was silenced. The penalty of the broken commandments had been fully paid. The accusation that God had unjustly tolerated sin was crushed.

But then came the resurrection. Jesus walked out of the tomb. He who had been made sin so that he could die, was now made righteous again, so that he could live. But this vindication of the righteousness of Christ also vindicated heaven's righteousness. God had found a way to preserve both his eternal justice and the lives of his own people. Consequently, we may now rejoice in -

TWO PROBLEMS SOLVED FOR US

Everyone who has a heart toward God faces two problems –

THE PROBLEM OF JUDICIAL GUILT

How can we cope with the problem of the sins we commit ***after*** we believe in Christ? Have they not destroyed our righteousness?

Jesus provides the answer. He lay dead in sin (having been *"made sin"* for us although he had done no wrong), just as we do; **but then the Father spoke a word of righteousness over him**, and at once he rose from the dead, both holy and victorious. Indeed, he gladly yielded himself to sin and death, knowing that that righteous sentence would be spoken over him, and trusting it implicitly! The sinless Son was pronounced sinful, and died, so that we sinful sons might be pronounced sinless, and live!

Observe how powerful is the Word of God. Jesus had done no sin and he could not die (for death is the wages of sin); but a word from the Father made him altogether a sinner and death quickly seized him. In the same way, and by the same powerful word, we who had not done any righteousness have been declared righteousness, and alive for ever. There was no need for Jesus to do any sin before he was pronounced a sinner; there is no need for us to do any righteousness before we are pronounced righteous. Both transformations are wrought solely by the word of God. But with this exception. Unless Jesus had embraced the word of sin, by faith, he could not have died (cp. Mt 26:39-44; Lu 22:41-45). Unless we by faith embrace the word of righteousness we cannot live.

So, even in the darkest moments of failure, the gospel calls us to turn back to Christ, to repent, confess our wrongdoing, and at once hear again the pronouncement that we are the righteousness of God in Christ (2 Co 5:21). We should heartily believe that word, declare ourselves righteous, and walk on with joy! In fact, until we have thus opened our eyes to see ourselves as God sees us, we labour in vain, and to our continual hurt –

> It is most true that eyes are form'd to serve
> The inward light, and that the heavenly part
> Ought to be King, from whose rules who do swerve,
> Rebels to nature, strive for their own smart. [109]

THE PROBLEM OF INADEQUATE STRENGTH

We cannot be content merely to have sin forgiven, and righteousness imputed to us; we want to *live* in the reality of that righteousness. And this we can do, because of who Jesus is. His righteousness becomes an inexhaustible deposit, into which we are invited by grace to tap daily, and to find there access to all the resources of heaven. But we need the kind of boldness Alcmaeon showed, when he took advantage of an offer made to him by the richest man in the world, King Croesus of Lydia (6th. cent. B.C.) –

> Alcmaeon, the son of Megacles, gave all the assistance in
> his power to the Lydians who came from Croesus at
> Sardis to consult the oracle at Delphi; and Croesus, when

---

[109] Sir Philip Sidney (1554-86), <u>Astrophel and Stella</u>, stanza five, first four lines. "Smart" here means pain, hurt, or loss.

the Lydians told him of the good service he had rendered, invited him to Sardis and offered him, as a reward, as much gold as he could carry on his person at one time. Alcmaeon thought of a fine way of taking advantage of this unusual offer: he put on a large tunic, very loose and baggy in front, and a pair of the widest top-boots that he could find, and, thus clad, entered the treasury to which the king's servants conducted him. Here he attacked a heap of gold dust; he crammed into his boots, all up his legs, as much as they would hold, filled the baggy front of his tunic full, sprinkled the dust all over his hair, stuffed some more into his mouth, and then staggered out, scarcely able to drag one foot after another and looking, with his bulging cheeks and swollen figure, like anything rather than a man. When Croesus saw him he burst out laughing, and gave him all the gold he was carrying, and as much again in addition. In this way Alcmaeon's family suddenly found itself rich, and Alcmaeon was able to keep race-horses, with which he won the chariot race at Olympia. [110]

Similarly, let us fully avail ourselves of the Father's glorious gift!

THREE PROBLEMS WE FACE

We have seen that God faced three problems –

- he had to establish his own righteousness in the face of human sin;
- he had to create a righteous world without destroying the old one;
- he had to find a way to make us legally and practically righteous.

---

(110) Herodotus: The Histories; tr. Aubrey de Selincourt; rev. A. R. Burn; Penguin Books, London; 1983; pg. 432 (Book Six, 124-126). The Alcmaeonidae were a prominent and wealthy Athenian family in the 6th cent. B.C. It is known that the family was enriched by Croesus for services rendered to him, and that Alcmaeon won a chariot race circa. 592 B.C. The family retained its wealth and influence for nearly another 200 years before it vanished from the pages of history.

The Father's solution to those problems was found in the legal justification he is able to give us because of the triumph of Christ at Calvary. But we too faced three crushing problems, before which we were helpless: the **guilt** of sin; the **root** of sin; and the **practice** of sin. All three placed us under a terrible indictment –

THE GUILT OF SIN

How well we know that we have sinned! Indeed, one of the most pointless exercises is to tell people they are sinners; they already know it, and either don't care or are crying out for an answer. Notice that the only people Jesus ever denounced as sinners were the hypocritical religious leaders of his day, who thought they were blameless. The ordinary people knew that they were cut off from God and were yearning for a way of salvation. Some evangelical preaching would do well to remember this fact – constant denunciation of sin and sinners just makes preachers sound ugly.

God's solution is found in the blood of Jesus (1 Jn 1:9). The importance of the blood is that it is a symbol of the full satisfaction Christ has provided for the offended law of God; the penalty is paid, the law can demand no further requiting; a Victim has died in our place, we cannot be summoned to appear before the Judge nor ever again threatened with eternal death. The gospel requires us to accept this rescue by faith, independent of any feelings of worthiness or unworthiness of our own.

How marvellously the Father is now able to describe us in Christ (1 Pe 2:9-10); what a marvellous place he has brought us to! (He 12:22-24) Yet all of that solves only the surface problem, for we still find ourselves confronted by the greater problem of -

THE ROOT OF SIN

The daily sins we commit are not our real problem, for as often as we commit them they are covered by the blood. But the godly heart yearns for more, to be rid of the very impulse toward sin, to be free to live righteously –

All heavy minds

> Do seek to ease their charge,
> And that that most them binds
> To let at large." [111]

So God had to strike deeper, at the real root of our trouble, which is the awful fact that it is our very **nature** to sin. How did he do this? In two ways –

- By **_reckoning_** upon us in Christ his own righteousness, apart from any good works of ours. Can he do that?

Let me say it again: the Father was able to reckon Christ a sinner (2 Co 5:21), though he had done no sin (He 7:26). That reckoning was powerful enough to drive Jesus to the cross and death, which otherwise was not possible for a sinless man (Ez 18:4,20; Ro 6:23). Likewise, though we have done no righteousness (Ro 3:10,11), the Father has but to **_declare_** us righteous, and behold we are at once made fully righteous. If he can declare his righteous Son unrighteousness, then he can declare this unrighteous son righteous! The one, because he accepted it, caused the *death* of Jesus; the other, if I accept it, causes *life* to spring up in me. Then the whole was confirmed and guaranteed by the resurrection of Jesus from the dead, which showed him truly to be the Son of God with power (Ro 1:4).

The second way God deals with the root of sin is -

- By calling us to a **_revelation_** of the word of righteousness.

This revelation can come only by prayer focussed on the scripture (Ep 1:16-20; Cl 1:9-14). Nothing is more necessary for victorious Christian life. And the consequence of such an inner revelation is freedom from the devastating consciousness of sin; we no longer see ourselves as sinners struggling to become righteous, but rather as righteous people who sometimes are caught by sin!

Nothing is so unnerving as a sense of sin, and nothing so emboldens as a sense of righteousness (Pr 28:1). Those who know they are righteous are able to stand before the throne of God with

---

(111) Sir Thomas Wyatt (1503-42); Song #34, Stanza One.

boldness, with a sense of divine right; they gain a new sense of freedom in Christ –

- ***freedom from slavery***: to Satan, and to sin; and
- ***freedom from fear***: of man, and of judgment; along with
- ***freedom to*** enter bravely into God's presence, and to possess all his bountiful promises.

What could be more desired than such true freedom?

> If chance assign'd
> Were to my mind
> By very kind
> Of destiny,
> Yet would I crave
> *Nought else to have*
> *But life and liberty.*
>
> And if not so,
> Then let all go
> To wretched woe,
> And let me die:
> For the one or the other,
> There is none other:
> *My death, or life with liberty.* (112)

THE PRACTICE OF SIN

This is our third problem. For even when all the above has become true of us we must still find a way to sustain our new righteousness and new freedom. There are two ways to accomplish this –

RETAIN THE REVELATION OF RIGHTEOUSNESS

I mean, the kind of inner revelation Paul was talking about when he sternly rebuked the Galatians –

> *You foolish Galatians! Who has cast a spell on you? Before your eyes Jesus Christ was vividly portrayed as crucified! The only thing I want to learn from you is this: Did you*

---

(112) Sir Thomas Wyatt, Song #41, first and last of six stanzas.

> *receive the Spirit by doing the works of the law or by believing what you heard? Are you so stupid? Although you began with the Spirit, are you now trying to finish by human effort? Have you suffered so many things for nothing? — if indeed it was for nothing. Does God then give you the Spirit and work miracles among you by your doing the works of the law or by your believing what you heard?* (Ga 3:1-5, NET)

Indeed, elsewhere Paul craved the same kind of revelation for the churches at Ephesus, and Colossae, and for all churches everywhere, which means every true believer. He prayed most fervently that we might all possess an inner illumination, banishing darkness from our souls and filling us with light, wisdom, and spiritual knowledge, making us wise, strong, and powerful in God! (Ep 1:17-20; Cl 1:9-11).

Then the second way to sustain a righteous life is to

MAINTAIN THE MEANS OF GRACE

The Father does not oblige faith to stand by itself, unaided, for if so, it would soon weary and fail. We have been given many means of grace, by which spiritual life can be and must be constantly replenished – **Holy Spirit baptism; fellowship with the saints; regular prayer; the eucharist; scripture; and so on** – Christians who fail to use these resources have none to blame but themselves if they fail also of the grace of God –

> It is a law of fate
> That all things tend to slip back and grow worse;
> As when a man, who hardly rows a skiff
> Against the current, if he once relax,
> Is carried headlong down the stream again. [113]

Likewise, the apostle warns –

---

(113) Publius Vergilius Maro, The Georgics – Book One; tr. K. R. McKenzie; The Folio Society, London, 1969; pg. 19.

> *Therefore we must pay closer attention to what we have heard, so that we do not drift away. For ... how will we escape if we neglect such a great salvation?* (He 2:1-3)

Those who keep alive their **revelation** in the word of righteousness, and make daily use of the **means of grace** will be irresistibly drawn into an ever more righteous practice. Small wonder then that Paul made gaining a deeper insight into the promises of God the main focus of his prayer for the churches (see again Ep 1:16-19; Cl 1:9-12). In his prayer he says nothing about a big crowd, a splendid building, or even a harvest of souls. Rather he yearns that God would give them *"spiritual wisdom and revelation and ever increasing knowledge of him"*. He wants the *"eyes of their hearts to be enlightened, so that they might know the hope that lies in their calling, the riches of God's glorious inheritance in the saints, and the immeasurable greatness of the power available to them"*. If only such spiritual illumination would catch fire in their souls, and remain there, he knew that every other blessing would naturally follow.

Such people will also be invincible against the enemy. The word of God, the sharp *"Sword of the Holy Spirit"* will be in their hands as *Excalibur* was to King Arthur – so long as he wielded it with a pure heart; none could do him harm –

> King Arthur on horseback laid about with a sword and did marvellous deeds of arms, so that many of the knights had great joy in his deeds and hardiness ... and ever King Arthur was in the foremost press till his horse was slain underneath him. Therewith King Lot smote down King Arthur. With that, his four knights rescued him and set him on horseback; **then he drew his sword Excalibur**, and it was so bright in his enemies' eyes that it gave light like thirty torches. Therewith he put them back and slew many people. [114]

---

(114) Sir Thomas Malory, Le Morte D'Arthur, Book One, Chapter One, Section Nine; ed. R. M. Lumiansky; Collier Books, New York, 1982; pg. 13.

Our "Excalibur", the sharp two-edged sword of the Holy Spirit, is the Word of God, especially when it is taken up and wielded boldly by the hand of faith. (He 4:12; Ep 6:17)

Chapter Twenty-Three

BUTTERFLIES

For through the Spirit, by faith, we ourselves eagerly wait for the hope of righteousness (Ga 5:5).

Christians are like caterpillars, waiting for a glorious body to be revealed when we finally break out of our present casing! We can dream about that delightful future, rejoicing because it is guaranteed in Christ, while also recognising that it has present ramifications.

We encounter here a principle that is common in the gospel – the tension between a promise that is both *realised* and yet *potential* – "already" but "not yet"!

I want to look at it under two headings –

A BEAUTIFUL DREAM

Said Paul – *"We groan inwardly as we wait eagerly for our adoption as children, the redemption of our bodies."* (Ro 8:23)

The Greek expression "groan inwardly" is very strong, and has in it the idea of a woman travailing in birth, but pressing on, despite her pain, in anticipation of the joy of holding her baby in her arms.

Likewise, we groan because our present condition is one of "frustration" (vs. 20), which arises from the fact that we already possess "the firstfruits of the Spirit", which are a foretaste of the splendour to come, yet their full possession eludes us. Therefore we groan, because although we are destined to soar high in beauty, to achieve grandeur, we cannot yet do so.

"Firstfruits" were the first portion of the harvest that was taken aside and offered as a sacrifice of thanksgiving to God. They were a sign of the greater portion to come, a promise of an eventual abundance. For us it means that Heaven is inside us already, and we can't quite understand why it isn't happening now!

We feel as if we should be able to walk on water, fly through the air, pass through walls, move mountains, shake nations, do the impossible – and sometimes the servants of God have done such things and more! But mostly we find ourselves circumscribed by the realities of ordinary daily life, and mighty exploits remain out of reach. One day galaxies will bend to our will! But until then, we must "wait eagerly for" –

OUR FULL ADOPTION

Here is a wonderful idea – already, in a legal sense, we do possess the status of children of God, who are both born *of* the Father and adopted *by* the Father –

> *God sent forth his Son, born of woman, born under the law, to redeem those who were under the law, so that we might receive adoption as sons.* (Ga 4:4-5)

Behold the kindness of God, who gives us a double safeguard. A natural born child has to accept his parents' word that he is their true offspring. But a child adopted has a plethora of legal documents to prove the matter beyond doubt!

This idea of "adoption" was a Roman one – the practice had no legal basis or status among the Greeks or the Jews. Furthermore, Roman adoption differed somewhat from ours. A boy was usually adopted in order to provide an heir, to take the place of a first-born son (as Caesar adopted his nephew Octavian, who became Augustus, the first Roman Emperor). This might happen either because there was no natural heir, or because the natural heir had fallen out of favour and been disinherited.

As a mere child we might have an inferior position. As an adopted child, we are indeed assured the highest status and the greatest inheritance! An adoption once formalised could not be cancelled by the new father. A son, however, could renounce his adoption, and refuse his inheritance. The Father binds himself by the same rule. He cannot renounce us or deny us our rights as both natural and adopted children. But we can scorn his heavenly gift, reject his grace, and refuse to accept the prize. Or, to put it differently, wilful and ongoing rebellion may eventually cut a backslider asunder from Christ, and thrust that person back into a state of being dead in sin, unfit for heaven, destined for hell.

So we are already doubly the children of God and fully heirs of the kingdom, but we cannot yet seize every benefit of that divine status. Rather, we are waiting eagerly for the return of Christ and the day of resurrection, when we will be able to take possession of all the glory of our "adoption". On that day, too, we will be able to take up all the benefits of -

OUR FULL REDEMPTION

In this life the ramifications of our salvation are mostly inward, and the body remains substantially unchanged. But on that great coming day our present mortal bodies will be -

- **<u>Raised</u>** from the grave and made immortal.

Note: unlike most religions, we do not focus on being rescued from our bodies, which are an essential part of our being, but on the salvation of the whole person, body, soul, and spirit. Every part of our being has found redemption in Christ. It is not my soul that has been saved, nor my spirit, nor my body, but <u>me</u> – my entire being, every part of me, has been lifted from death to life, and brought from darkness to light!

- **<u>Made</u>** whole and glorious – "All defects and imperfections will be corrected: the blind will see, the deaf will hear, the lame will run, the mentally handicapped will understand, and amputees will be made whole." [115] – see also *Isaiah 35:6*.
- **<u>Removed</u>** from any possibility of rebellion against God.
- **<u>Transformed</u>** inwardly and outwardly to desire only holiness.
- **<u>Fitted</u>** to sit upon the throne of Christ and rule the universe as his co-heirs (Ro 8:17).

But above all, our bodies will be <u>conformed</u> to the loveliness of Christ – *"Our citizenship is in heaven, and from it we await a*

---

[115] <u>College Press NIV Commentary</u> – *Romans Volume 1*; in loc; College Press Pub. Co., 1998.

Saviour, the Lord Jesus Christ, who will transform our menial bodies to be like his glorious body" (Ph 3:20-21).

What radiant beauty will then belong to each of us!

A PRESENT REALITY

Because you are sons, God has sent the Spirit of his Son into our hearts, crying, "Abba! Father!" (Ga 4:5-6) ... We are waiting eagerly for our adoption as sons (Ro 8:23).

Earlier, Paul declared that we are <u>already</u> God's adopted children! Yet now he is saying that we are still waiting for our adoption to occur. How can we be both adopted and not yet adopted at the same time? Notice how Paul talks about a "spirit of adoption" versus a "spirit of slavery" (Ro 8:15). The word "spirit" implies that we possess all the *legal* and dynamic reality of our new birth and of our adoption, but not yet the *visible* substance of it, just as the caterpillar possesses in itself all that will be in the butterfly.

In this life we still have a choice as to which "spirit" will dominate us – the one that enslaves, or the one that liberates. Here are two steps to take –

- Though we are still in these mortal and corruptible bodies, we must visualise the glory that lies within us – that "spirit of sonship"!
- Proclaim to yourself your identity as a supernaturally born child of God and one who is also adopted, who already possesses all the splendour that will be!

How do you see yourself – as a worm or a butterfly!

The more you capture and hold a vision of who you truly are in Christ, the more you will show it in daily life.

Paul says that we should so let the Spirit rise within us that we cry, *"Abba! Father!"* I talked about this expression in an earlier chapter. But notice these additional comments – *"Abba"* was an Aramaic diminutive, equivalent to *"Dad, Daddy, Papa"*. It was a mark of being part of the family, for a Jewish law said, "Men-servants and maid-servants shall not call to their master, 'Abba'."

Even more remarkably, Jesus was the first person ever to address God as *"Abba!"* (Mk 14:36) – something no contemporary Jew would ever have dared to do! But we who have the witness of the Spirit within, are drawn into just such an intimacy with the Father. We relate to him not as a cringing slave to a remote and terrible tyrant, but as a child nestling lovingly in its papa's bosom.

So *"Abba"* is a metaphor of someone who has perceived his or her "sonship" [116] and "adoption", and is beginning to live in the fulness of it. It is a consequence of faith responding to the witness of the Spirit. We are drawn into an ever closer relationship with the Father and become ever more aware of our adoption and sonship.

The consequence of this adoption and sonship is that we should never again fall back into cowering, fettered slavery nor become paralysed by fear. That is, slavery to the law, to sin, to any bondage; fear of death and judgment.

We are brought into the Father's house, not as slaves but as children – children who are both born and adopted into the Father's family.

Let us then live in the joyful freedom and bold confidence of true children of God!

Are you born again? Do you hold your adoption papers? Then be the child of God you are!

An Ant nimbly running about in the sunshine in search of food came across a Chrysalis that was very near its time of change. The Chrysalis moved its tail, and thus attracted the attention of the Ant, who then saw for the first time that it was alive. "Poor, pitiable animal!" cried the Ant disdainfully. "What a sad fate is yours! While I can run hither and thither, at my pleasure, and, if I wish, ascend the tallest tree, you lie imprisoned here in your shell, with power only to move a joint or two of your scaly tail." The Chrysalis heard all this, but did not try to make any reply. A few

---

[116] Paul's application of the word "son" to both male and female believers is not a mark of ancient chauvinism. Rather, it is a way of conveying the idea that both sexes equally share the inheritance of a first-born son, with primogeniture.

days after, when the Ant passed that way again, nothing but the shell remained. Wondering what had become of its contents, he felt himself suddenly shaded and fanned by the gorgeous wings of a beautiful Butterfly. "Behold in me," said the Butterfly, "your much-pitied friend! Boast now of your powers to run and climb as long as you can get me to listen." So saying, the Butterfly rose in the air, and, borne along and aloft on the summer breeze, was soon lost to the sight of the Ant forever." *Moral:* Appearances are deceptive.

You may be more chrysalis than butterfly at present; but never forget that all the beauty and soaring splendour that will be is fully in you already!

Chapter Twenty-Four

LOVE

> *In Christ Jesus nothing has any value except <u>faith</u> that works by <u>love</u>.* (Ga 5:6)

We know that only by *faith* can we please God (cp. He 11:6). And see how powerful faith is: *"it <u>works</u>!"* The same Greek verb (*energeo*) is used in *Galatians 2:8; 3:5; Ephesians 1:20;* and *Colossians 1:29.* Therefore faith can be described as the one thing in the world for which all things are possible; it knows no barrier except the purpose and promise of God; it allows no boundary except the zeal of God's people in believing. It means that *your* faith has limitless power!

Yet many people complain that *their* faith does *not* work –

- they *believe,* but do not experience the power of God.
- they *pray,* but their prayers are not answered.
- they *trust,* but their confidence remains unrequited.

That is because faith <u>cannot stand alone</u>. Faith exists only in conjunction with two other things –

- **<u>First</u>** – faith is a response to a promise of God, and cannot <u>exist</u> independent of such a promise; and
- **<u>Second</u>** – *faith* is an expression of the character of God, and cannot <u>function</u> outside of that character; and above all, *"God is love."* (1 Jn 4:8)

Therefore, wherever true faith is found, it will rest upon a divine promise, and it will be motivated by divine love. Thus, in the end, *"faith <u>works</u> by love",* and has no real energy outside of love.

But at once we face a problem: *what does the text actually say?* The Greek verb is *energeo,* and there has been a great controversy over the Catholic and early Protestant readings of the word. The first says: *"faith is <u>energised</u> by love";* the second says: *"faith is <u>demonstrated</u> by love";* thus –

- "love gives life *to* faith," vs "faith shows its life *by* love".
- "faith is *made* alive by love," vs "faith shows it *is* alive by love".
- in the first love is the *cause*; in the second, the *result*.

Martin Luther (16th century) stormed against the Catholic position, and reduced the text to *"faith does loving works."* Rome retorted that *"love is the motivating principle of faith"*. In this case, I agree with Rome – love is indeed the energising power behind faith, without which faith is void. How does love do this? In three ways –

LOVE MAKES FAITH POWERFUL IN THE WORD

Faith comes from what is heard, and what is heard comes through the preached word of Christ. (Ro 10:17; NET)

So faith arises from the word of God, especially when it is *preached* – which cannot be restricted to an actual public address, but applies to any situation where the Word of God is being presented to a willing hearer (or reader). So the preacher may be a living person; but he may also be the Holy Spirit illuminating a passage of scripture to someone who is eager to discover truth; or the voice may speak from the pages of a book; or it may be heard in any other source that effectively conveys the Word of God.

But who will turn to scripture unless they love it? People learn scripture because we tell them to; but faith is not quickened because there is no love. The Bible yields its treasures to those who love it, as a chaste wife fully and gladly yields herself only to the husband she adores.

Further, one who loves the Word cannot doubt it; nor can he tolerate any failure of its promise. Love <u>compels</u> faith, for who can love, yet not trust? See how the psalmist (Ps 119) equates freedom and strength (verses 45-46) with love for the word of God (verses 47-48).

LOVE MAKES FAITH POWERFUL IN GOD

There is a difference between believing in God and believing God. Millions know there is a God and worship him; few have absolute trust in his providence and promise. Why? Because there can be no lasting faith without constant love. Love holds one firm in dark times, when God seems to be absent.

> Continents and oceans may separate a husband from his young wife, but she loves him, and because she knows he loves her, she will never once doubt him nor fear that his constancy might fail. (117)

Love gives infinite value to the words of love God has spoken. Thus, a young man's love letters may be awful, but his wife will not part with them for any price, not even when he begs her out of her love for him to do so! Nor will a true believer allow anything to part him or her from scripture. It is sweeter than honey, more precious than gold or silver, to be admired above the finest jewellery. Those who love the promise search it out and believe it, trusting to it their hopes and their very lives.

LOVE MAKES FAITH POWERFUL IN MINISTRY

Love was the invincible might of the early church. "How these Christians love one another!" was the cry of the pagans. But they loved, not by giving *things* so much as by giving *themselves* –

> You give but little when you give of your possessions.
> It is when you give of yourself that you truly give.
> For what are your possessions but things you keep and guard for fear that you may need them tomorrow? ...
> Is not dread of thirst when your well is full, the thirst that is unquenchable? ...
> Is there aught you would withhold?
> All you have shall someday be given;
> Therefore give now, that the season of giving may be yours and not your inheritors'.
> You often say, "I would give, but only to the deserving."
> The trees in your orchard say not so, nor the flocks in your pasture.
> They give that they may live, for to withhold is to perish.

---

(117) By a young man, who often had to travel far away, and for weeks at a time, written at the end of the first decade of their marriage.

> Surely he who is worthy to receive his days and his nights, is worthy of all else from you.
> And he who has deserved to drink from the ocean of life deserves to fill his cup at your little stream. [118]

We may preach brilliant sermons and gather huge crowds, but we will still fail to be truly the *"salt of the earth"* if we lack love! (Jn 13:35) Sadly, that quality of love has not always been maintained in the church –

Samuel Champlain in the early 17th century led three exploratory voyages to Canada from France, and on one of them founded Quebec in 1608. He eventually became Lt Governor of Canada, but during the French wars with the British was taken prisoner. He was later released, and returned to Canada, where he remained until his death.

On one of his early voyages "he brought with him two chaplains, one Catholic and one Protestant. Both of them died of scurvy. But not before they had so disgusted the sailors with their wrangles that the men gleefully buried them in a common grave, 'that they might continue their dispute throughout eternity!'"

A century later, still in Canada, it was not unknown for both Catholic and Protestant clergymen to gather their congregations, disguise themselves as Indians, and go out looking for people from the other side to scalp!

To a lesser degree, this is still true: we pray for people, go through the motions of faith, but often with little result. We must learn to love not just in words but also in actions. Further, if it is truly impossible to please God without faith, then it is impossible to please him without love, for love alone can energise faith. Further still, anyone who desires to have faith that can move mountains, do the impossible, and call up wonderful miracles of answered prayer, must thoroughly learn this: *without love there will be no power in faith.* And if by some chance the loveless do manage by faith to move a mountain, they will still be *"nothing"* (1 Co 13:2).

---

(118) Kahlil Gibran, The Prophet; Alfred A. Knopf, New York, 1968; pg. 19-21

Their miracles, their sacrifices, their glossolalia, their preaching, their knowledge may all be useful to others, but as for themselves, God hears only noisy gongs, sees only rowdy cymbals, and casts them aside as trash (vs. 1-3).

Christ himself provides the perfect example of faith working by love. What was the secret of his ministry? Surely his **_faith_**! But what was the secret of his faith? Surely his **_love_**! Likewise, our *faith* on behalf of others can be no more alive than our *love* for them. Love will drive you to pray, to believe, to have no rest until they are free!

You may say, "But how can I gain such a loving heart?" Paul has a more than adequate answer (Ro 5:5) –

> *These things will all happen because God has given us his Holy Spirit,* **who fills our hearts with divine love** (Ro 5:5).

So hear it again, my friend, and measure yourself by it –

> *In Christ Jesus nothing has any value, except faith that works by love!* (Ga 5:6)

Chapter Twenty-Five

CALLED

God set me apart before I was born, and **called** *me by his grace (Ga 1:15) ... This persuasion is not from him who* **calls** *you. (5:8) ... You were* **called** *to freedom. (vs. 13)*

Sei Shonagon was a lady-in-waiting to Queen Teishi in the 11th century Japanese court. Early in the century she published a delightful *Pillow Book,* which is still renowned today, and contains many charming lists of everyday objects and events. Here is one of them, called *Rare Things* –

> A son-in-law who is praised by his adoptive father; a young bride who is loved by her mother-in-law.
>
> A pair of silver tweezers that are actually good at plucking out hairs.
>
> A servant who does not speak badly about his master.
>
> A person who is in no way eccentric or imperfect, who is superior in both mind and body, and who remains flawless all his life.
>
> Two people who live together and remain awed by each other's excellence, so that they always treat each other with scrupulous care and respect. However much these people may try to hide their weaknesses, they usually fail.
>
> To avoid getting stains on the notebook into which one is copying stories, poems, or the like. If it is a very fine notebook, one takes the greatest care not to make a blot; yet somehow one never seems to succeed.
>
> When people, whether they be men or women or priests, have promised each other eternal friendship, it is rare for them to stay on good terms until the end.
>
> A servant who is pleasant to his master.

> One has given some silk to the fuller and, when he sends it back, it is so beautiful that one cries out in admiration. [119]

To Shonagon's diverse list we might add –

> Someone who truly understands and can explain what scripture means when it talks about *predestination* and *election*.

There is certainly no shortage of attempts to do so, for a multitude of books on the subject have been composed over the centuries. But unanimity is just as evasive now as it was in the beginning. A man has to be either very brave or very foolish even to attempt another explanation. Which am I? I will leave you to decide the answer to that question! [120]

ARMINIUS OR CALVIN?

"Are you an Arminian or a Calvinist?"

That is likely to be the first question some people will ask when you mention the word *"predestination"*. What would your answer be? Or perhaps you would rather ask what *my* answer would be! Actually, I am reluctant to be billeted in either of those camps; and I am fairly confident that the apostle Paul (if he were able to join in the debate) would also refuse to enlist on either side.

However, because of its importance in the history of Christian doctrine, the question really deserves a straighter answer than that. So let us see what better sense we can make of it.

Arminius and Calvin were two great scholars who chose two different ways to explain the method God uses to gather his church

---

(119) The Pillow Book of Sei Shonagon, tr. Ivan Morris, Penguin Classics, 1967; pg 83. I have merged the Morris translation with a later one by Meredith McKinney, Penguin Books, London, 2006.

(120) A handful of the paragraphs immediately following this introduction are identical to the opening paragraphs of the chapter on the same subject in my book Great Words of the Gospel (Vision Publishing, Ramona). In that chapter you will find a fair discussion of the biblical evidence. The remainder of this chapter, however, attacks the subject from a different perspective.

together. Both of them claimed to be Bible-based and to represent fairly the teaching of the NT. Both claimed Paul as an ally! Each insisted that in the end his view was the only true one. And across the centuries masses of Christians have been polarised around the one doctrine or the other –

- **John Calvin** (1509-1564) was a French theologian who based his doctrines on two key ideas: *the utter depravity of man;* and *the absolute sovereignty of God.*
- **Jacob Arminius** (1560-1609) was a Dutch theologian who emphasised *human freedom of choice.*

According to Calvin, we are saved by *God's* choice. According to Arminius we are saved by our *own* choice.

The issue is important, because it raises the questions: "Is salvation conditional, or unconditional? Once saved, is a person eternally saved? Or is it possible to fall away from Christ?"

Calvin would answer those four questions, *"No, yes, yes, no!"*

But *Arminius* would reply, *"Yes, no, no, yes!"*

The problem for us is, how would *Paul* answer them? That is what we will try to find out!

CROMWELL

In a letter in 1650 to the General Assembly of the Church of Scotland, Oliver Cromwell wrote, "I beseech you, in the bowels of Christ, think it possible you may be mistaken." [121] The Scottish divines were adamant that their doctrines alone were true (especially in their Calvinistic aspects), and their Church alone was wholly faithful to the gospel. Cromwell saw that their arrogance and stubbornness must lead eventually to their downfall. They remained stubborn, refused to yield, suffered a savage military defeat, and had to endure religious oppression for several generations – which might have been admirable if it had been based upon irrefragable truth. But since the subject of the debate

---

[121] England Under the Stuarts, G. M. Trevelyan; The Folio Society, London, 1996, pg. 266.

was indeed debatable, there was more folly than sense in such obduracy. Some ideas are worth dying for, some are not.

I beg you, then, to be flexible yourself, and to acknowledge that no one has any monopoly on the truth. At best we have opinions, some of which may be truer than others, but all of which fall short of a perfect understanding of all that scripture says. In some places and on some matters we have to be content with a measure of ignorance, which includes all attempts to formulate a dogma on *pre-destination*.

FREE WILL

Everything we have in our salvation is in Christ, through Christ, by Christ, and for Christ. That is the great bedrock of the gospel; in it every true Christian is anchored, and we cannot be moved away from it. However, that has not prevented a great debate from raging over the centuries on the conflict between human *free will* and *divine election*. Do we choose Christ, or does the Father choose us? Scripture gives ample support to both positions. That unsettling ambiguity can be avoided only by heinously elevating some texts over others, and (often) by ignoring some passages altogether. I cannot so misuse scripture. I try to be impartial in my interpretation of the Bible and to give equal weight to every text that deserves it (allowing, of course, that some passages are plainly more important than others).

In my opinion, there is a time to focus on divine election and a time to focus on human choice. Both are taught in the Bible. It is also often unclear whether scripture is describing the election of an individual or the election of the church. Mostly I think the biblical references to the elect are to the church as a corporate entity. If so, then individual Christians are "elect" only so long as they maintain a place in the church (that is, a local church; except that an exception must be made for people who are physically unable to be part of any congregation).

Predestination, then, can be understood, not in a *personal* but in a *generic* sense. That is, God has predestined everyone who calls upon the name of the Saviour to receive eternal life, sanctification, and a heavenly inheritance in Christ. Or, to put it differently, predestination belongs to the *church*, not to the *individual*. It is the *church* of which the apostles are speaking when they call us *predestined*. As a consequence, it is also of the church that we can affirm the *perseverance of the saints*. Individual Christians can (and do) backslide, and tear Christ out of their lives; but the true *church*, as the *Body of Christ*, cannot possibly fail.

However, I see no compelling reason to opt for one side of the argument or the other. I refuse to be bullied into any of the "schools", or to be committed to any systematic theology. I cannot see any reason for people to become angry over the matter, or to accuse each other of heresy, which has happened all too often over the centuries. Too many scholars have been like a man I once read about, who saw someone about to jump off the Sydney Harbour Bridge. He tried to talk the jumper out of taking his own life. He asked, "Well, are you a Christian?" To which the man replied, "Yes." He exclaimed, "Great; me too. What kind of Christian are you? Orthodox, Catholic, Protestant?" The answer came: "Protestant." "Me too. What kind of Protestant? Anglican, Baptist, Presbyterian, Methodist, Pentecostal?" The jumper, stepping back a little from edge, answered, "Pentecostal." The man got excited: "Me too. Are you an initial evidence or a third wave Pentecostal?" "Initial evidence." Now, the man got really excited: "Me too! Are you Premillenial, Post Millenial or Amillenial?" Stepping back still further, the jumper replied, "Premillenial". "Oh! This is wonderful," said the man. "Are you Arminian or Calvinist?" The jumper, who was now nearly safe from falling, declared, "Calvinist." At which the passer-by, becoming very angry, screamed: "Die, heretic!" and pushed him off the bridge.

It really has been that bad in the past, and in some places may still be!

A SYSTEMATIC BIBLE?

The Bible is not systematic. Indeed, the urge in the western mind to be rid of all ambiguity, contradiction, uncertainty, and the like, has been a curse on the church for centuries, and sits very uncomfortably with scripture. I am happy to live with a flexible theology that takes into account (I hope) everything the Bible teaches. Like any good chef, I pull out of the biblical pantry whatever is most needed for each time, place, and person, knowing that what is good for one meal may be wrong for another.

I like the response given by Charles Finney. He said that when he was speaking to a timid, fearful soul, he stressed divine sovereignty and the absolute security in Christ of every believer, even the most anxious. But when he faced arrogant self-righteousness, he quoted biblical warnings against placing any dependence upon self, and reminded them of the penalties that awaited backsliders.

And I am also very willing to allow the limitations of my own understanding of scripture, and to accept that the other person's viewpoint, if not better than mine, may at least be equally valid. So I have no urge to persecute or destroy anyone who differs from me in their interpretation of scripture.

LUTHER AND SPURGEON

On the Calvinist side Martin Luther (who was not a Calvinist) waged ferocious war against what he called the "idol of the human will". He denied that our willpower has anything whatsoever to do with salvation. Charles Spurgeon agreed, and stated –

> I will go as far as Martin Luther, in that strong assertion of his, where he says, "If any man doth ascribe of salvation, even the very least, to the free will of man, he knoweth nothing of grace, and he hath not learnt Jesus Christ aright." [122] It may seem a harsh sentiment; but he who in his soul believes that man does of his own free will turn to God, cannot have been taught of God, for that is one of the first principles taught us when God begins with us, that we have neither will nor power, but that he gives both; that he is 'Alpha and Omega' in the salvation of men. [123]

---

(122) From Luther's work, <u>On the Bondage of the Will</u>, of which book he was most proud and wished it to be preserved above all his other writings.

(123) I have no knowledge of the original source of this quote. Spurgeon was a highly successful Baptist preacher in London during the late 19th century.

Others have argued that several important doctrines – such as the call to repentance, the command to be baptised in water, the requirement to gather together in worship, the charge to give generously, the necessity of faith, even conversion itself – surely depend upon the existence of free will. Indeed, how can anyone say with any sense that human will has *no* part in our salvation? Almost the last words in the Bible are *"whoever WILL may come"*. (Re 22:17) Think, too, of the several other places where we are told to *"choose"* between obeying God or some other master. Indeed, every command in the NT, and there are dozens of them, presupposes that people have a choice about whether they respond with a "yes" or a "no". If their own will has no say in the matter, the supposed choices are made illusory, and the gospel becomes a farce of futility.

DIVINE SOVEREIGNTY

Against those "free will" arguments, of course, we must set the many passages where great emphasis is placed upon human depravity, and which stress divine sovereignty. Then there is the conflict between texts that seem to assure the everlasting safety of every born-again believer versus those that describe awful penalties for anyone who backslides.

So there are a profusion of ideas, and heated debate surrounds many of them. Then the matter is further complicated by the idea that we are -

ELECTED IN CHRIST

Someone has written –

> Get ready for a mindbender here. It is time we put Jesus Christ right back in the centre of our understanding of election! It is Christ himself who was the Decree of the Father at the dawn of creation. He is the Word. He is the Chosen One! He is the Predestined One ! He is both the Elector and the Elected. All our ideas of election must be changed and re-grounded in the Father's election of Jesus Christ. Jesus is God's elected choice for humanity. He is both the electing God and the elected man. In reading, say, *Ephesians*, we often forget to notice that our own

> personal election is always tied first and foremost to God's election of Christ. We are chosen *"in him"*, predestined *"in him"*, elect *"in him"*. For some reason, the *"in him"* part is often left off in this theological duel. He does not choose us independently of Christ. No, it is Christ who was chosen, therefore all of humanity was chosen in him. Just as all died in the first Adam, so all are represented in the Last Adam. (124)

There is much to commend in that passage. Its fault lies in its evasion of the issue. Certainly everything in Christian life must begin with Christ, continue with Christ, and end in Christ. It is all of him, by him, and for him (Cl 1:16-17). But we have not been stripped of all responsibility. God wants children not automatons. He calls us to become adults in our understanding and in our relationship with him (Ro 8:17; 1 Co 14:20; Ep 4:13, 14; He 5:12; 1 Pe 2:2; etc). He leaves space around us, room to move, to make choices of our own, even to go so far as rejecting Christ and the gospel (He 10:29; 2 Pe 2:20-22).

Then there is the interesting passage in James, which urges people to ask God for *"wisdom"* (Ja 1:5-6). He uses the word *sophia*, which means an insight into the true nature of things, as distinct from merely practical decisions about conduct. *Sophia* is the wisdom that enables one to make right choices. Those who possess *sophia* will naturally choose the things God approves; *sophia* is not a momentary acquisition, but a wisdom that is born within by prayer, study, and growth in grace. It marks the difference between, say, a trained motor engineer with a beginner who needs a driver's manual, or between the boy who at first needs the pattern book for his construction set, but then designs his own models. That is what the Father is seeking for his children. That they will grow up and be able to make their own wise choices, ones that will instinctively reflect his nature and his will.

---

(124) I have no knowledge of the original source of this quote.

CONCLUSION

How to reconcile those seeming contradictions? No one has yet managed to do so, even after 20 centuries of furious debate! Large libraries have been filled with countless tomes arguing for either the Calvinistic or Arminian viewpoints, or some place in the middle. But in the end, the matter can be resolved only by each side giving too much weight to some passages and too little to others. In my opinion, any fair reading of scripture will leave the matter unresolved and unresolvable. We are people looking through a dark glass (1 Co 13:12). Many things remain, and must remain, a mystery.

Chapter Twenty-Six

WALKING

> *But I say,* **walk** *in the Spirit, and you will not gratify the desires of the flesh. ... If we live by the Spirit, let us also* **walk** *in the Spirit.* (Ga 5:16, 25)

Sarcasm, insult, wit, insight, truth – they are all part of Martin Luther's commentary on our text –

> When I exhort you to walk in the Spirit, that ye fulfil not the concupiscence of the flesh, I do not require of you that ye should utterly put off the flesh, or kill it, but that ye should bridle and subdue it. For God will have mankind to endure even to the last day; and this cannot be done without parents, which do beget and bring up children. These means continuing, it must needs be that flesh also must continue, and consequently sin, for flesh will not be without sin. Therefore, in respect of the flesh we are sinners; but in respect of the Spirit, we are righteous. ...

> Which thing Jerome ... who was a marvellous lover and defender of chastity, doth plainly confess. "O (saith he) how often have I thought myself to be in the midst of the vain delights and pleasures of Rome, even when I was in the wild wilderness, which, being burnt up with the heat of the sun, yieldeth an ouglesome [125] habitation to the monks!" &c.

> Again, "I, who for fear of hell had condemned myself to such a prison, thought myself oftentimes to be dancing among young women, when I had no other

---

(125) The same as ugglesome, meaning fearful, gruesome, horrible, ugly, and the like.

company but scorpions and wild beasts. My face was pale with fasting, but my mind was en-flamed with desires in my cold body; and although my flesh was half dead already, yet the flames of fleshly lust boiled within me," &c.

If Jerome felt in himself such flames of fleshly lust, who lived in the barren wilderness with bread and water, what do our holy belly-gods, the clergymen, feel, think ye, who so stuff and stretch themselves with all kinds of dainty fare, that it is a marvel their bellies burst not? Wherefore these things are written ... to the universal church of Christ, and to all the faithful; whom Paul exhorteth to walk in the Spirit, that they fulfil not the lusts of the flesh ...

Paul (as I have said) doth not require of the godly, that they should utterly put off or destroy the flesh, but that they should so bridle it, that it might be subject to the Spirit. ...

If it will not be, marry a wife, for it is better to marry than to burn. Thus doing, thou walkest in the Spirit; that is, thou followest God's word, and doest his will. (126)

Martin Luther rightly allows that the divine command to procreate requires people to continue living in mortal and corruptible bodies. These bodies, says he, provoke us to sin, yet we are still deemed righteous by God, because of the gospel. And he is also very practical. He does not limit *"walking in the Spirit"* to ethereal realms, but also applies it to earthy matters, insisting that getting married, just as much, say, as prayer, can be part of what it means to *"walk in the Spirit"*. Many pietists of the day would have been horrified at such a statement, thinking, as they did, that lifelong celibacy was by far the more desirable state. There are still people today who reckon that married couples have made a lower choice, pandering to the flesh instead of yearning for heavenly blessing.

---

(126) Op. cit., in loc.

But Luther would have none of it. Nor would Paul. Nor would Christ. Nor would Sirach, who said that -

> *Three things are pleasant to see, for they delight the eyes of God and of other people: children playing happily together; friendship among neighbours; and a husband and wife who love each other.* (25:1)

WARFARE

Luther also acknowledges that between "flesh" (that is, our fallen nature) and the human spirit there is ongoing conflict. But he calls us to brave endeavour, to bold warfare, to press toward victory in Christ. He echoes Paul, who insists that if we *"walk in the Spirit we will not fulfil the desires of the flesh"!* (Ga 5:16).

But we cannot avoid the paradox – that is, the contrast between the pleasant serenity of *walking*, and the furious action of *fighting*. But both aspects are true – *"walking in the Spirit"* is both a calm *walk* in faith and a good *fight* of faith (1 Ti 6:12). Indeed, there are several places in scripture where Christian men and women are called to rise up in the empowering strength of the Holy Spirit and do great exploits in the name of the Lord. Here is one example –

> *On that day the Lord will pour out upon the House of David and the inhabitants of Jerusalem a spirit of grace .... Even the weakest person there will be as strong as David, and as for the strong, they will be like the Angel of the Lord!* (Zc 12:10, 8)

There is a challenge! Even the weakest among us should be as strong as David; and as for the strong – they should possess the might of an archangel! The prophet declares that we of *"that day"* should be bolder, braver, better even than the men of Gad –

> *Men from the tribe of Gad went over to join David at his stronghold in the wilderness. They were tough and experienced warriors, expert with shield and spear, whose faces were like the faces of lions and who were swift as gazelles upon the mountains ... These Gadites were officers of the army; the least could crush a hundred enemy*

soldiers, and the greatest could overpower a thousand. (1 Ch 12:8, 14)

That claim is so extraordinary that many translations soften it to, *"Some were high-ranking officers over a thousand troops, and others were officers over a hundred troops."* But that can't stand, because David had only 600 men in his fortress! (1 Sa 23:13) So he could hardly have had several officers each commanding a thousand! In any case, the translation given just above is the most natural reading of the passage.

How can we become like those mighty men of old? How can we be *"like the Angel of the Lord"*? (127) Surely the key is to -

BE FILLED WITH THE SPIRIT

Many years ago a chorus was popular in some churches –

> It's the Holy Ghost!
> It's the Holy Ghost!
> If anybody asks, asks, asks,
> What's the matter with you, you, you,
> Just tell them you're filled, filled, filled
> With the Holy Ghost!

That infilling comes to us through prayer and laying-on of hands –

> *The church in Jerusalem heard that Samaria had received the word of God, so they sent Peter and John to pray for them that they might receive the Holy Spirit, for he had not yet fallen on any of them, but they had only been baptised in the name of the Lord Jesus. Then <u>they laid their hands on them and they received the Holy Spirit</u>.* (Ac 8:14-17)

Pentecostals expect that the usual initial sign of that infilling will be golossolalia (Ac 2:4; 10:46-47; etc). They love this heavenly gift of speaking in tongues because it has a power to *"edify"* = *oikodomeo* (1 Co 14:4). The word means "to build up, to

---

(127) I don't mean, of course, that we may or should become fierce soldiers and fighters in a physical sense, but rather in our warfare against the principalities and powers of darkness we should be bold and supremely confident.

strengthen – as a house-builder lays a strong foundation, then a sturdy framework, then sundry courses of bricks, and a roof, until the house stands complete and firm. In the same way, nothing surpasses Holy Spirit baptism for imparting life, strength, vitality to the Spirit-filled believer!

Here is access to the supernatural; here is power to overcome every foe; here is revelation of the Word; here is the eternal glory of God!

STIR UP THE GIFT

How easy it is to allow the force of the Holy Spirit to drift away! Paul specifically warns against such folly –

> *How shall we escape judgment if we neglect the great salvation we have received? . . . God himself has borne witness to it by signs and wonders and various miracles and by gifts of the Holy Spirit. . . . So beware of drifting away!"* (He 2:3-4, 1)

Mark the two words, *"neglect"* and *"drift"*. The one means to become careless, no longer giving the matter any attention. The other means to drift, like a ship with no one at the rudder, or like a ring falling off a careless finger. Beware! Pay attention! Don't become so careless that you become a sieve out of which the glory of God drains away and leaves you hollow and strengthless. On the contrary, says Paul, we must continually *"stir up the gift of God that is within us by the laying-on of hands"* (2 Ti 1:6).

"Stir up" means to re-kindle, to fan the embers, as one would a dying fire. We do that by setting ourselves to use each God-given gift as often as possible – *"since God in his kindness has given each of us certain gifts, let us use them!"* (Ro 12:6) [128]

---

(128) Have you ever had the experience of some relative giving you a gift you don't want, and you hide it away until you hear that the relative plans to visit you? That is how many people treat the gifts of God. They trot them out only for display. How can that please the Lord?

WALK IN THE SPIRIT

Holy Spirit baptism begins as a supernatural event, an explosive force, an infusion of spectacular gifts, all of which recur from time to time. But there is another, more serene dimension of life in the Spirit, which Paul calls *"walking in the Spirit"*. (Ga 5:16, 25)However, he does not mean an aimless wandering, but a firm walk with purpose, which requires –

DECISION

We can drift *away* from salvation, but not *into* it. The currents of life may bring us near, but then the time of choice must come. Everything in Christian life begins with a decision – indeed, *"choose!"* is one of the key words in the Bible. It applies to the ministry of the Spirit and to the charismata just as much as to anything else. Without a decision, there will always be drift! Every journey begins with a choice. The only thing worse than no choice is a wrong choice, but they both result in a wrong end.

DIRECTION

There is an old saying, "All roads lead to Rome!" It was based on the idea that in the ancient empire, roads radiated out from Rome to every part of the empire, and therefore, if you traced any road to its source you would find yourself in Rome. Yet there were and have always been many roads that will never take you to Rome, but far away from it. So one needs to choose not only a destination, but how to get there reliably. Even in a modern car with a navigational system, it is possible to get lost. My navigator has several times misled me, taking me to a dead end, or an impossible dirt track, or, on one occasion to the edge of a wharf. I've learned to check a map as well!

All travellers need to be sure that the sign posts are reliable, and for us, in our spiritual pilgrimage, that means measuring everything by scripture.

DESTINATION

You should have a goal for today; and one for tomorrow; and one for the unfolding years; and one for eternity. Never succumb to the enticement of just drifting along, blown here and there like a piece of tumbleweed. Find out what God wants you to do, then do it in the power of the Holy Spirit. For each of us the Lord has a short-term plan, a long-term one, and a plan for eternity. Set yourself to discover the part of the plan that belongs to your present life, or at least, as much of it as you can. He will show you what he wants you to do and help you do it. My prayer is that when your earthly pilgrimage comes to its end you will be able to declare with Paul –

I have fought a good fight, I have finished the course, I have kept the faith. Now a crown of righteousness is waiting for me, which the Lord, the righteous judge, will give me when that day comes; and not to me only, but also to everyone who loves his appearing (2 Ti 4:7-8).

You will then indeed be shown as a person who in this life learned how to *"walk in the Spirit!"* (Ga 5:16, 25)

Chapter Twenty-Seven

BROTHER

You must all bear each other's burdens, and so fulfil the law of Christ. (Ga 6:2)

In 1917 a Roman Catholic priest, Father Edward Flanagan, founded "Boys Town" in Omaha, Nebraska, where troubled or homeless boys could go for help. He acted on the principle, "There are no bad boys. There is only bad environment, bad training, bad example, bad thinking." The principle is probably naïve and somewhat unbiblical, but it is certainly admirable.

Twenty-four years later, in 1941, Father Flanagan was looking at a magazine called *The Messenger* when he came across a drawing of a boy carrying a younger boy on his back, with the caption, *"He ain't heavy mister, he's my brother."* Father Flanagan thought the image and phrase captured the spirit of Boys Town, so he commissioned a statue of the drawing with the slightly altered inscription – "He's not heavy, Father; he's my brother!" That statue and phrase became the logo for Boys Town.

In 1979, girls too were welcomed into the home, its name was changed to "Girls and Boys Town", and the logo was updated with an added drawing of a girl carrying a younger girl.

Today (2015) the organisation has 12 sites across the USA and cares each year for many thousands of children and young people.

AN OLD STORY

The first known literary mention of its motto actually occurred much earlier than Father Flanagan's use of it. In 1924 the editor of Kiwanis Magazine, Roe Fulkerson, published a column carrying the title, *He's Not Heavy, He's My Brother*. In it Mr. Fulkerson writes of his encounter with "a spindly and physically weak lad" carrying a baby and "staggering towards a neighboring park." "Pretty big load for such a small kid," I said as I met him. "Why, mister," he smiled, "he ain't heavy; he's my brother."

Mr Fulkerson used this to illustrate his plea for a more compassionate lifestyle. But his story about the boy, the baby, and the park may be a little fictional. There are other earlier variations of the saying, attached to an old folk-story about some refugees fleeing from a war zone. The first version I personally encountered told about a family having to flee their homeland, along with many other citizens. Taking only what they could carry on their backs, they headed out. In the confusion of the escape, two children got separated from the rest. As they hurried along over rough terrain, the younger child, a girl, fell and injured her leg too badly to walk. Her elder brother removed his back pack, which held all that he had left in the world, replaced it with his little sister, and struggled on.

The hills were steep and the rocks were sharp, but he kept going, one painful step after another. As he was desperately straining to catch up with the rest of the group, an enemy soldier, high on a horse, came along and shouted, "Put that girl down, she's too heavy for you to carry."

"No sir, you don't understand," the lad responded; "she's not heavy, she's my sister."

And there are other versions of the story, with variations in the punch line; but all with the same idea, of heroic self-sacrifice.

What is the purpose of all this?

Simply to introduce the theme of this chapter, *"bear each other's burdens"* –

THINGS THAT ARE _NOT_ BURDENS

Some of the things we call "burdens" scarcely merit the label. They are niggling nuisances, annoyances, irritations indeed – but we exaggerate if we call them burdensome. Things like –

- a couple of arthritic knuckles
- a teen in greasy pants who sits on your white sofa
- a husband who leaves dishwater in the sink
- a wife who is never on time
- a daughter who hogs the phone for two hours every day
- a neighbour whose yard is a disgrace

- a neighbour who borrows things and never returns them
- a neighbour's dog that barks early every morning
- a spouse who tosses clothes everywhere
- a person who insists upon telling you every detail of every family ill
- neighbours who shout at and foully abuse each other
- teens who love very loud music
- noisy motor mowers, leaf blowers and motor bikes
- people who are never satisfied and keep on grizzling or nagging
- and the like! [129]

All those are irksome matters, and may provoke you into grinding your teeth, but they can hardly be called <u>burdens</u>! What then shall we describe as *"burdens"*?

TWO DIFFERENT KINDS OF BURDEN

Notice the strange contrast between verses 2 and 5, which say, *"You must all bear each other's burdens ... You must each bear your own burden!"* But in fact there is no contradiction, for Paul uses two different Greek words –

"PHORTION" (vs. 5)

"Phortion", in its most literal meaning, was used to describe a ship's cargo (Ac 27:10), which the owner of the ship had to see safely carried to its destination port. It also had a military use. It described the pack that each Roman soldier, and he alone, must carry. His commander would neither allow him to hand it over to another, nor allow another equally burdened soldier to offer to carry it for him. Therefore ...

- We cannot avoid assuming responsibility for those tasks that are peculiarly ours. There is a "cargo" that we are each called to carry, and cannot unship onto another; there is a pack that belongs to me alone, and I alone must carry it.

---

(129) Some of those items are my own invention; others I copied from a list whose source I have long-since forgotten.

- We cannot shirk this duty, nor allow anyone to deprive us of the service we are each called to render personally to God and to our neighbour.

In colloquial use *phortion* also meant that each person would gain his or her proper reward, much as a ship's owner in olden times would be recompensed, or penalised, according to the cargo he finally delivered. Or, as a soldier might be well-rewarded if he fought well or severely punished if he deserted his post.

> In the great day every man shall be properly rewarded. Knowing this, we should be little anxious about the sentiments of others, and should seek to maintain a good conscience toward God and man. (Barnes)

"BAROS" (vs. 2)

"Baros" means a "weight", especially one that is too heavy for an individual to carry, one that is "weighing him down". That burden can be shared, and we must be willing both to share it with another, and to share another's burden.

But that raises the question –

HOW CAN WE CARRY THEM?

The 17th century French fabulist Jean de la Fontaine tells this delightful story –

> One day mighty Jupiter said "Let all living things come before me to compare themselves, one with the other. Let no one be afraid to speak honestly even if they find fault. I shall ensure that no harm comes of it. Come Monkey, you are the one that should begin. Let all the others compare themselves to your beauty. Tell me, are you satisfied with yourself?" "Me?" he said. "Why Not! Is my body not as good as any of the others? And as for my face, there's nothing to reproach myself for on that score. But as for my brother the bear, I have to say that I find his features rather coarse. And no artist would ever pick him as a subject for a painting."

> Everyone expected the bear to reply angrily, but he didn't. Instead he praised his own physique quite loudly. Then

he went on to speak of the Elephant. He pointed out that the Elephant could use a longer tail and smaller ears. In short, he declared that the Elephant was quite misshapen and ugly.

The Elephant (wise beast that he was) did not retaliate. Instead, he opined as to how Madame Whale was really too fat. Madame Ant then said that she found the Mite a bit too small. It made her feel that she was a giant.

At this point Jupiter, hearing all these criticisms, angrily told them to stop. This didn't scare the other animals who were still self-satisfied. And among the most self-satisfied were the humans because that is how we are: fierce animals when it comes to criticizing others, and meek when it comes to speaking of our own faults. We forgive ourselves everything, and forgive others nothing.

We are all like someone with two bags suspended from his neck. We have a small bag in front full of our neighbours' faults, and a large bag behind filled with our own faults. Hence it is that we are quick to see the faults of others, and yet are often blind to our own failings. [130]

Let us cast aside that hardness of heart, and become less prone to judge the faults of others, and more eager to help them. Let us become the kind of people that others turn to in their distress or failure, knowing that we will not condemn them, but rather offer *"restoration"* (Ga 6:1). Paul there uses a Greek word that described a tradesman repairing a broken object, or a surgeon repairing a broken limb, or removing a perilous bodily growth. Thus we should assist each other with love, helping to repair what is broken and to heal what is sick.

---

[130] From the 17th century collection, <u>The Fables of</u> Jean de La Fontaine; *La Besace*, tr. by Michael Star; from the website http://www.aesopfables.com/fontaine.html. A "besace" is a bag with two pouches, carried over the shoulder by beggars.

JOHN BRADFORD

Paul says also that we should do these things while all the time reminding ourselves that we too will someday need the same help (vs. 1b). Remember the famous words of John Bradford, "There but for the grace of God, go I." They came out of the following incident –

> In 1553, the vehemently Roman Catholic queen, Mary Tudor, known to many as "Bloody Mary", ascended to the throne. During her short reign, as many as three hundred so-called "heretics" were put to death.
>
> In the first month of her reign, Bradford, who had become somewhat well known for his devotion to his religion, was arrested and imprisoned on a trivial charge. Confined to the Tower of London, he would never be a free man again. During his time in prison, he continued to write religious works and preach to all who would listen.
>
> At one point, he was put in a cell with three other reformers, Thomas Cranmer, Bishop Nicholas Ridley (the same Bishop who had ordained him), and Hugh Latimer. Their time was spent in careful study of the New Testament. All four were to become martyrs.
>
> At last, on January 31st, 1555, Bradford was brought to Newgate Prison to be burned at the stake. Though scheduled for 4:00 a.m., the burning was delayed due to the large crowd of gathered admirers. He was chained to the stake with a young man, John Leaf. Before the fire was lit, he begged forgiveness of any he had wronged, and offered forgiveness to those who had wronged him. He subsequently turned to his fellow and said, "Be of good comfort brother; for we shall have a merry supper with the Lord this night!"

And so Bradford and his companions died bravely. But before those events, on seeing a group of criminals being dragged to the scaffold, Bradford remarked, "There but for the grace of God, goes John Bradford." His words, without his name, are still very common ones today for expressing one's blessings compared to the fate of another. [131] Only, let us never speak them smugly or with self-righteous complacence.

An extension of these ideas is that we must be willing to allow others to help <u>us</u> with our own loads –

- It is not fortitude but folly to insist upon "going it alone".
- It is not more spiritual to *"cast your burdens* (only) *upon the Lord"* (Ps 55:22; Mt 11:28), for he usually chooses to help us through human agency.
- You should certainly trust God, but do not be too proud to accept help that the Lord sends through his people, and perhaps even through the ungodly.

Let us note also that scripture demands much more than just tolerating or "putting up with" each other's faults and foibles. Rather, we are to show active sympathy and compassion, and as far as possible help each other either to be rid of each encumbrance, or to alleviate it, or to endure patiently what cannot be changed.

But let us note at once that we cannot bear our brother's burdens and faults by —

- making <u>satisfaction</u> for them (for that is the work of Christ alone, Jn 19:17, where the gospel uses the verb form of *baros* for Jesus bearing the cross.
- <u>suffering</u> them to continue unrebuked (yet each reproof, as we have seen, should be seasoned with gentle grace (Ga 6:1).

Rather, we should bear each other's guilty burdens by —

- <u>consoling</u> the penitent;
- <u>forgiving</u> personal injury; and by
- <u>praying</u> for overcoming grace.

---

(131) From the <u>Encyclopedia of Word and Phrase Origins</u>, by Robert Hendrickson, *Facts on File*, New York, 1997.

CARRY EACH OTHER'S HURTS

We dare not emulate Cain, but must rather care for one another by —

BEARING WITH THOSE WHO ARE WEAK

It's easy to love God. It's easy to love Jesus. It's easy to pray for the heathen African ten thousand miles from the house where you live. It's hard to call a lousy tramp your brother and set him down at your table." *(Melvin Tolson [1900 – 1966], US poet and teacher.)*

MINISTERING TO THOSE WHO ARE HURT

Rabbi Hillel (c. 50 BC) was famous for inventing the sandwich, which was later re-invented in the late 18th cent by the Earl of Sandwich as a snack to eat at the gambling tables in London. Hillel's earlier effort came about by his zeal to observe literally a biblical command, which says that the food in the Passover meal must be eaten together. So he combined the meat, the bitter herbs, and the matzah wafers into what we now call (after the earl) a "sandwich".

But Hillel is still more famous for his response to a non-Jew, who approached him and asked him to explain the complex Jewish law while standing on one foot. The great sage and rabbi lifted one foot off the ground and answered: "Whatever you would find hateful if done to you, refrain from doing it to your neighbour. The rest is commentary – now go and learn!"

That is what Paul meant by *"fulfil the law of Christ"* (Ga 6:2b), which, among other things embraces the "Golden Rule" (Lu 6:31) – *"Do to others as you would have them do to you"* – or, as an English variant has it, "Do as you would be done by!"

Notice that we are not permitted merely to wait passively until some appeal for help is made to us. Rather, we must take the initiative, and *act*. *"Do it!"* said Jesus. So we are precluded from ignoring a brother or sister who is labouring under some affliction or struggling with a problem, whether physical, mental, spiritual, personal, or social. Love will urge us to action, to volunteer help, to hasten with all assistance, to mend, to heal, to comfort, to *"carry each others' burdens"*.

But that does not warrant us to be busy-bodies, meddlers, always prying, poking in our noses where they are not wanted (cp. James 5:9, 13-14). "Nosey Parkers" are disliked and unwanted. The expression comes from Matthew Parker, who was appointed archbishop of Canterbury by Queen Elizabeth I. He became renowned for demanding to know every detail about the lives and affairs of the bishops, clergy, and churches under his authority. And so the phrase has come down to us to describe anyone who insists on prying into matters that should not be their concern. [132]

Conclusion

In 1938, Spencer Tracey portrayed Father Flanagan in the movie *Boys Town*, which also starred Mickey Rooney. Then in 1969 Bobby Russell wrote the lyrics for a song based on the film — *He Ain't Heavy, He's My Brother!* It spent eleven weeks on the music charts, including two weeks in the top spot –

> The road is long, with many a winding turn
> That leads us to who knows where;
> But I'm strong,
> Strong enough to carry him;
> He ain't heavy, he's my brother!

Paul : ***"You must all bear each other's burdens."*** (Ga 6:2)

Jesus : ***"In everything, do to others what you would have them do to you, for this sums up the Law and the Prophets."*** (Mt 7:12)

---

[132] Most serious scholars deny the authenticity of attaching the saying to Matthew Parker, who was also famous for his scholarship, piety, and spotless character. But it is one of those saying, which if not true, one feels ought to be!

Chapter Twenty-Eight

GIVING

Remember the poor, which is something I have always been eager to do ... Bear each other's burdens, and so fulfil the law of Christ. ... If you are being taught by the word of God, then you should share your good things with the one who is teaching you. Don't be deceived! God cannot be mocked; what you sow is what you will surely reap. Sow to your own flesh and from the flesh you will reap corruption; but sow to the Spirit, and from the Spirit you will reap eternal life. (Ga 2:10; 6:2, 6-8)

Devout Christians hope to build great local churches. But a great church will be composed of great people, for you cannot build greatness on "little" people. Those great people, says Paul, will have a willingness to care for and uphold each other. They will also be generous in supporting their pastors and teachers, and in giving to the poor. They are far more eager to "sow" into the work of the kingdom of God than to gratify their own pleasures. Too much pandering to the flesh must bring a harvest of destruction; but sowing to the Spirit brings an enhanced quality of life that will carry into eternity.

We might sum it up by saying that these great people in a great [133] local church have two special attributes –

THEY ARE GREAT GIVERS

There should be a greatness about the *giving* of God's people. That "greatness" does, of course, include greatness of **quantity**, but even more it means greatness of **quality**, for **motive** is always

---

(133) By "great" I do not necessarily mean large numerically nor do I exclude it. But mostly, I mean a church great in all the things that truly matter, whether it is big or small, such as love, fellowship, care, heartfelt worship, faith, hope, sound doctrine, worthy practice, generosity, and readiness to meet the King when he comes.

more important than **money.** Only by such great giving can a church be built that is fit to contain the glory of God.

That principle is well illustrated in ancient Israel. I once read that when the people gave only out of their **surplus** (that is, their jewellery) the result was a **golden idol** (Ex 32:2-4), and the **wrath** of God fell upon them. But when they gave out of their **need** (that is, their household stuff) the result was a beautiful **tabernacle**, and the **glory** of the Lord fell on them. (Ex 35:20-29).

The rules have not changed. Whenever the people of God are mean or misdirected in their giving, the result is still idolatry; but generous and God-directed giving is an excellent key both to personal prosperity and church renewal.

How can you tell whether or not you are giving properly? It is necessary to understand the difference between –

RIGHT AND WRONG MOTIVES

FIVE WRONG MOTIVES

SELF-RIGHTEOUS

- these people think money can buy the favour of God, never realising that all effort to purchase a righteous standing by good works has been utterly condemned by the Cross.

IDOLATROUS

- these people find in money a chief goal in life and the source of all happiness, so they give as little as possible, for who will willingly abandon his or her god?

CARNAL

- these people find in money their true security; they have never learned to trust God, and they are afraid to give, for they fear that they might be left destitute.

DUTIFUL

- these people use money as part of their religious ritual; they give well, and regularly, but mainly out of habit and duty; their giving lacks any true spiritual dynamic.

PUNITIVE

- these people fear money; for them, prosperity would be an embarrassment; they are certain that they do not deserve any good thing; they give only to punish themselves, or to make amends for sin.

In contrast with those spurious motives for giving, or for parsimony, we should instead hold these -

TWO CORRECT MOTIVES

GIVING MUST BE AN ACT OF OBEDIENCE

Ask God what *he* wants you to give. Many people are afraid to do this, because they are sure God will ask them for more than they are willing to let go of! But note –

- it is foolish to give **less** than God demands, because he will in any case eventually get what he wants, plus a penalty! (Cp. Le 27:14-30; etc.)
- it is unnecessary, and may be equally foolish, to give **more** than God wants, for no one can increase the blessing of God merely by throwing cash at him.

Can a farmer increase his harvest by jamming more seed into the same piece of land? On the contrary, too much seed may jeopardise his entire crop! The Lord's opinion on the matter is clear – *"I prefer obedience to sacrifice!"* (1 Sa 15:22). So discover what the Lord wants you to give, and sow it – no more, nor any less. People who give too much sometimes cause more harm to the church than those who give too little! Note, too, that -

GIVING MUST BE AN ACT OF FAITH

You should give with a positive expectation of a divine response to your gift. The promises of God usually do not work of their own accord. They must be made to work, by faith. True believers firmly insist that the promise will be fulfilled; they boldly appropriate all that the Lord has spoken.

But let us come back to the question –

HOW MUCH TO GIVE?

Every believer needs to learn how to hear from God from time to time (Ja 1:5-7). Two common ways in which the purpose of God concerning your giving can be discerned are –

- **<u>an inner "impression"</u>** of the amount you should give, or some other form of direct communication (Is 30:21); and
- **<u>a sense of "peace"</u>** surrounding your use of what you feel the Lord is allowing you to keep (Cl 3:15).

However, obtaining such guidance pre-supposes a bed-rock of Spirit-wrought inner honesty. That place of honesty may not be easy to reach, and until it is reached you may need to be wary of placing too much trust in your own "impressions" or even in a sense of "peace". Nonetheless, if you are uncertain what the Lord is saying, and you are faced with a risk of giving either too little or too much, I think you had better err on the side of generosity rather than parsimony!

Never forget that the Father is more concerned about *you* – your character, your faith, your righteousness, your growing maturity – than he is about your money, which he doesn't need. As the song has it –

God owns the cattle on a thousand hills,
The wealth in every mine;
He owns the rivers and the rocks and rills,
The sun and stars that shine. [134]

The Lord who governs billions of galaxies hardly stands in need of our paltry dollars. He demands that we give, not because he is poor, but because we are so spiritually bankrupt that the only

---

[134] *He Owns the Cattle on a Thousand Hills*; words and music by John Petersham; 1948. The song is based on the words of *Psalm 50:11*.

remedy is to stir us to *sacrificial* and *believing* giving. He is seeking our growth into maturity, and into a greater capacity to receive great things from him. That is why obedience is more important than merely giving money, or even more money.

However, the Holy Spirit cannot reach us until we are truly ready to surrender to God whatever he asks. So we need to give, in order to be released in spirit, to grow into full stature in Christ, to come to that place where we are reflecting all that God knows we can be, and are catching all that he has for us.

However, as a general guide, you may suppose that the Lord will direct you to give

- **<u>to the church</u>** in regular tithes and offerings (Ma 3:10-11; Ro 12:13; 1 Co 16:1-2; Ga 2:10).
- **<u>to world-wide missions</u>** in sacrificial offerings (Ac 11:29; 13:47; Ro 15:25.
- **<u>to the poor</u>** according to their need and circumstances (Le 25:35; Ps 41:1-3; Pr 19:17).

You may also suppose that all Christian giving will be characterised by warm and cheerful generosity (Lu 6:38; 2 Co 9:7). The Holy Spirit is not likely to bid you to give parsimoniously, or coldly, or indifferently. But temper your generosity with wisdom. Remember that you can give too much as well as too little. Nor should you allow your giving to be controlled by sentiment, nor by an emotional response to some appeal, nor even by the fear of giving too little – let it rather be planned and disciplined, an obedient response to what you perceive to be the will of God. Thus Paul admonishes the church –

> *Each one of you should give what you have <u>decided in your heart</u> to give, not reluctantly, <u>nor under compulsion</u>, for God loves a cheerful giver.* (2 Co 9:7)

Observe the three rules stated there –

- "<u>decided in your heart</u>" has the sense, not of a spontaneous impulse, but of a deep moral resolution to be obedient in giving, and to give in a rational, careful, and controlled fashion, not guided by mere whim, nor in response to

emotional manipulation by a hopeful recipient, but only after proper consideration.
- "*not under compulsion*" has the sense of resisting the imposition of pressure, of not allowing yourself to be bullied into giving, of knowing when to resist the force of public opinion or of superior authority, of knowing when persuasion is coming to you from God or merely from some human manipulative technique.
- "*not reluctantly ... for God loves a cheerful giver*" – that is, giving that is grudging, done out of duty alone, empty of joy, lacking faith, dreary and soulless, will hardly please God, nor attract his blessing. There should be laughter in your soul, joy in your spirit, and happiness in your heart as you give!

Alison and I have put those rules into practice. I have kept a spreadsheet for many years, which lists all our income and automatically deducts 12½% as a tithe. That column is then balanced by our actual giving. At the time of writing, we are several hundred dollars in front of what the tithe column demands. In this way, based on what we feel the Lord is asking us to do, our giving is planned, systematic, controlled, and practical. There is an element of sacrifice in it and also of generosity – our income remains modest – but there is no risk of us being ruined by what we give.

Added to that, we surround our giving with believing prayer, expecting a 30, 60, 100-fold increase, according to the promise of Christ (Lu 6:38; Mt 13:8, 23), which he honours.

Then, still talking about great givers in a great church, let me say that as well as being great givers, -

THEY ARE GREAT GETTERS

To give generously without receiving largely is a pathway to poverty. "Giving" and "getting" belong together and cannot be separated. Always in scripture they are joined, and always those who give in obedience and faith are enjoined to expect an abundant return from the Lord.

Many years ago a couple came to the church I was pastoring. After a few weeks they requested an interview, but gave no explanation until we had begun to talk. Then they told me how offended they were because my family and I lived in a pleasant home, drove a relatively new car, dressed well, and looked too prosperous for a Christian pastor. They had come out of a city mission background, surrounded by poverty, and were scandalised by our seeming affluence. As it happens, my family was far from rich, but we did maintain a comfortable middle-class lifestyle on a modest salary enhanced by the grace and goodness of God.

As gently as possible, I tried to show the couple that they had a poverty mentality, that they should shake themselves out of it and start to expect greater and better things from God. I failed to console them. They remained offended and eventually left the church.

One of the concepts I put to them was the power of prayer to create miracles, and that if my family was doing well it was a testimony to how well prayer worked. "If I were to come home one day," I said, "and find that my house had burnt to the ground, and all our possessions turned to ashes, I would simply pray it all back again. Within months, I would expect to have a better house than we had lost, and better possessions. But they rejected the idea of such incredibly effective prayer. They were unable to believe that the Lord could and would behave so magnanimously.

Little did I know then that I would soon have a chance to put those ideas into practice! The Lord spoke to me and Alison, giving us a clear word that we had to give away all our possessions, and move interstate to set up a Bible College. We did so, and prospered. Then a second time God spoke, telling us now to give everything away again and move to the USA, where we would be able to expand the college into a worldwide outreach. We obeyed again, and again we prospered. Then a third time, the process was repeated when, after nearly ten years, we returned to Sydney, all but penniless, to take over another Bible College. We had a promise, too, that when we settled in Sydney, we would find ourselves living in a pleasant two-story home. That happened. We were able to purchase the house in which, at the time of writing, we are still living.

So what I had told that couple many years before came true. Whenever we gave away most of our stuff, so that we could move, the Lord quickly replaced it all with a better house and better possessions. Yet each time we had arrived at our new destination virtually penniless. God truly does answer prayer!

<u>Now I hasten to beg you not to emulate us</u>. Merely selling up and giving it all away won't achieve anything except your ruin, unless you do it in obedience to a plainly spoken word from God. Jesus told the rich ruler to give away all he possessed; but he did not give such a specific command to any other enquirer (Lu 18:22-23). The wealthy man walked away with regret; he could not surrender his riches. But suppose a bystander had observed this, and said to himself, "I will do what that man refused to do," would Jesus have been pleased? I doubt it. The Lord might have been pleased by the bystander's *willingness* to make such a sacrifice; but not by the *action*, unless perchance it was indeed the Father's will that he should do so.

Only in one thing should you copy our example – find out what God actually wants *you* to give, then give it gladly, and with faith, expecting his best blessing. The Lord may ask you to give more than you suppose, or less. That is not important. Just give what he asks, assured that in the end you cannot be diminished by it, but only enlarged.

But this does highlight the principle that those who give according to the will of God should then -

EXPECT A RETURN FROM GOD

If there is a greatness about the giving of the people to God, there should also be a greatness about their getting from God. When people say they want to give but don't want anything in return, they reveal, not piety, but either pride or unbelief. It is true that we should expect nothing back from the people we are helping, but we should certainly expect a return from God (see Mk 10:29-30; Lu 6:35). What is the measure of that divine return? The answer is found in –

TWO SPIRITUAL LAWS

THE LAW OF PROPORTIONATE RETURN

Several times in the references from the gospels quoted earlier in this chapter, Jesus in effect says, *"Give and you will get!"* The converse is true: if you want to get, then give; and, the measure of your getting will be the measure of your giving. Notice –

JESUS ENDORSES THE VALUE OF MONEY

Christ is not embarrassed by money; he knows you need it; he knows the church needs it; he understands, as you should, that your money and the way you handle it is a vital part of your relationship with God. If your spiritual life fails here, it will probably fail everywhere (Lu 16:10-11).

JESUS LEAVES NO ROOM FOR FEAR

His promise remains unchanged in both good times and bad. Refuse to allow your faith to be inhibited by the state of the national economy or by your personal need. On the universal scale, all such matters are trivial, and cannot possibly tax the resources of the Lord. So locate your supply in God, not in your employer, nor in your banker, nor in any human resource (cp. Ps 37:25; 34:10-11).

You are, of course, free to make use of whatever human resources are available; but never make them the repository of your faith, for that belongs to God alone. He is your true source (Mt 6:25-34; Ph 4:19).

Too often, when headlines are gloomy, people become afraid and tighten their purse strings. But when times are bad you need to be even more released in your spirit in the matter of giving than you are when times are good! If you **need** more, perhaps you should **give** more – not less! But in any case, give just what the Lord wants you to give. It is, after all, not more **money** you need, but more *faith*.

JESUS LEAVES NO ROOM TO AMASS TREASURE

We are not invited, but commanded in scripture to give freely and generously. Remember that God hates hoarders who gather goods solely for their own pleasure and their own enrichment (Mt 6:19-21).

JESUS PROMISES AN ABUNDANT RETURN

Beyond even a return that is proportionate to your giving, the Lord actually promises *"good measure, pressed down, shaken together, running over"* – and that is precisely what you should expect from him.

Then the second spiritual law that governs giving in the kingdom of God is -

THE LAW OF SOWING AND REAPING

See *2 Corinthians 9:6-10*, and notice that

- God wants you to have a surplus; he is able to provide for you abundantly (vs 8,9).
- He does this by using the law of sowing (vs 6) and of reaping (vs 10).
- In response to this law, you must *"make up your mind"* (RSV).

What is in your mind when, say, you drop your offering into the receptacle? If you can give perfunctorily, without concern, then perhaps you are not giving enough. You should at least give enough to hurt you enough to care about your gift! Then you will not be able to give without sincerely praying that God will use that gift to enhance both the prosperity of the church and your own prosperity!

You should view your gift as seed planted for a harvest. This removes any thought of greed or of selfishness. You become like a farmer, who cannot compel his land to yield a harvest, nor can he demand that it do so; but he can co-operate with it, according to the laws of the harvest, and so expect a rich return. Just so, you cannot buy the blessing of God, but you can sow seed for a harvest, with obedience and faith (cp. Pr 3:9-10; 11:24-25), confident of a good return.

REAPING THE HARVEST

No seed can be planted nor harvest reaped without two things –

LABOUR

- labour <u>diligently</u> (Ro 12:1)
- labour <u>resourcefully</u> (Pr 31:16,24)
- labour <u>prayerfully</u> (Mt 21:22)

I mean, God does not just hand out his bounty on golden plates. We are expect to work, using whatever skills and talents the Lord has given us. Even the animals and birds have to sally forth and gather what the Lord has provided (Ps 104:28). As Paul said, *"If any will not work, neither should they eat!"* (2 Th 3:10; and see also vs. 12, and 1 Th 4:11). So banish from your mind that you are like Danaë upon whom, though she was incarcerated in a bronze cell, Zeus poured himself in a shower of gold. The Lord is no myth. He is real, and expects his people to contribute zealously to their own prosperity by diligent toil.

MANAGEMENT

Learn to build **sales resistance**, avoiding the folly of the naïve trader in *Proverbs 20:14*, who allowed himself to be talked into selling his goods for less than their proper value. So you should resist both the smooth-talking buyer and seller.

Learn to get the **best buy**, being a wise steward of the resources God has put into your hands (Mt 13:44; Lu 16:8-9).

Learn to **pay bills** promptly, and as much as possible avoid unprofitable debt (Pr 3:28; Ro 13:7-8).

Learn to **be content** with enough (Pr 30:8; 1 Ti 6:8) for many have been destroyed by a hunger for wealth.

CONCLUSION

Bountiful giving and bountiful getting belong together in the church. You can hardly have one without the other! All giving and no getting = **poverty**. All getting and no giving = **parsimony**. You should expect to get more from God so that you can give more so that you can get more so that you can give more. The entire process can be summarised in three sentences:

- commit yourself to obey the command to give cheerfully and generously, as the Lord directs you.

- stir your heart to believe the promise of God, which says those who give will never lack any good thing.
- expect God to give you wisdom in how to earn and handle your money.

If you show yourself wise and faithful in managing money, the Father will not only give you more of that treasure, but even better, he will put into your hands a growing measure of those greater treasures that endure for eternity (Mt 6:19-20).

Sow to the Spirit, and from the Spirit you will reap eternal life! (Ga 6:8)

298

Chapter Twenty-Nine

GOLDEN

*Let us not grow weary of **doing good**, for in due season we will reap, if we do not give up. So then, as we have opportunity, let us **do good** to everyone, and especially to those who are of the household of faith* (Ga 6:9-10).

The demand of Jesus that we should do to other people as we would have them do to us, is commonly called "The Golden Rule" (Mt 7:12). In one form or another it occurs in nearly all major religions and cultures. Long before Jesus was born various sages, teachers, and religious leaders taught it to their followers –

- 700 BC, <u>Zoroaster</u> – "That nature alone is good that refuses to do to another whatever is not good for its own self;" and, "Whatever is disagreeable to yourself do not do unto others."
- 500 BC, <u>Buddhism</u> – "Do not hurt others in ways that you yourself would find hurtful."
- 500 BC, <u>Confucius</u> – "What you do not want done to yourself, do not do to others;" and, "One word that can serve as a principle of conduct for life is reciprocity. Do not impose on others what you yourself do not desire."
- 500 BC, <u>Jainism</u> – "A good man neither causes violence to others nor does he make others do so."
- 350 BC, <u>Isocrates</u> – "Do not do to others what would make you angry if done to you."
- 350 BC, <u>Aristotle</u> – "We should treat our friends as we would wish our friends to treat us."
- 300 BC, <u>Hinduism</u> – "One should not behave towards others in a way that is disagreeable to oneself. This is the essence of morality. All other activities are due to selfish desire."
- 300 BC, <u>Epicurus</u> – "It is impossible to live a pleasant life without living wisely and well and justly (agreeing 'neither to harm nor be harmed')."

- 250 BC, *Stoicism* – "What you do not want done to you, do not to another person."
- 180 BC, *Tobit* – "What you yourself hate, do not do to anyone else."
- 150 BC, *Mahabharata* – "This is the sum of duty: Do naught unto others that would cause you pain if done to you."
- 10 BC, *Hillel* – "What is hateful to you, do not do to your fellow man. This is the Law; all the rest is commentary."

As far as I know, that list is complete.

Did you notice that except perhaps for Aristotle (see below), the pagan and Jewish writers all presented the Rule negatively? That is, "Don't do to others what you don't want done to you."

Jesus alone expressed the *Rule* positively – that is, we must not merely refrain from doing harm, but rather must take a loving initiative –

> *In everything,* **do to others** *what you would have them do to you, for this sums up the Law and the Prophets.* (Mt 7:12)

It has been argued that those other philosophers, who expressed the Golden Rule negatively, were more pragmatic, more realistic, than Jesus; for to refrain from doing something is, for most people, much more achievable than to do something. That is, it is easier to make a decision to follow (say) Hillel's rule, [135] than to follow the rule given by Jesus; which is undoubtedly true. But Jesus ever aimed for the highest possible ideal in his teaching on ethics, faith, and worship; he was never interested in the easy road that the crowds prefer to follow (see the verses that immediately follow the Golden Rule, Mt 7:13-14).

---

(135) See the previous chapter. The questioner, of course, was hoping to embarrass Hillel into admitting that the Jewish legal and religious system, with its detailed rules and complex ritual, was impossible for anyone to understand, let alone observe, or even explain. Jesus, like Hillel, agrees that the Golden Rule is a summary of all the Law and the Prophets. But Hillel was passive in his application of the Rule, while Jesus was active.

The Greek philosopher Aristotle (350 B.C.) is the only ancient teacher who approached a positive statement, yet even he limits its application to a friend: "You should treat your friends as you want your friends to treat you." [136] In the end, all the others tended to echo the world's concept of "tit-for-tat" [137] – "What you do to me, I'll do to you!"

So the worldly philosophy is, "Do as you are done by!" But Christ says rather, "Do as you *would be* done by." He requires of us a quality that causes us to behave (as the Father does) with unconditional love toward every person, regardless of how they behave toward us.

IS THE GOLDEN RULE ALWAYS TRUE?

No! Because it truly works only within the framework of the gospel. Why? Because outside of Christ and the love of God it is open to several abuses –

- It can degenerate into a selfish desire to obtain personal benefit by doing good to others (cp. Lu 14:12).
- It can be turned into an excuse to do nothing – "I prefer to be left alone; so I will leave you alone."
- It can wrongly excuse crime, such as two thieves agreeing not to betray or hinder each other.
- Circumstances can distort it – for example –
- A person who yearns to die would be obliged to kill others.
- A masochist would be obliged to inflict pain on others.
- A member of a minority group would be obliged to agree with the majority opinion.
- It cannot be applied literally, say, to kings, judges, parents, or to other persons in authority, who must often do things they dislike intensely. Thus the Roman Emperor Septimius Severus (146-211), trying to mitigate the harshness of Roman law, had the negative form of the *Rule* inscribed on

---

(136) Lives of Philosophers 5.21.

(137) The expression is an alteration of an older phrase, "tip-for-tap"; that is, "If you dare even to *tap* me, I'll *tip* you right over!"

his palace walls – *"Whatever you do not want done to you, do not yourself to other people."* Yet he could not avoid imposing the death sentence on malefactors.

Only people who are governed by the laws of the Kingdom of God can discern in each case the true application of the *Rule*. This is because the children of the King truly do wish justice, truth, and righteousness to be done, not only by them but also to them, whatever the personal cost. That is why Christ alone gave the *Rule* its positive form, requiring us to take the initiative. We must "do" no matter how well or how badly we are "done by"!

To refrain from doing something is not difficult – indeed, life would be impossible if we could not generally trust people to behave properly, that is, to treat us fairly and kindly, with good manners and restraint. How then should we apply the Rule to ourselves day by day? –

- **Day by Day, show Christ to others as we wish others would show him to us.**

Thus the renowned bishop, St Richard of Chichester (1197-1253), prayed –

> Thanks be to Thee, my Lord Jesus Christ
> For all the benefits Thou hast given me,
> For all the pains and insults Thou hast borne for me.
> O most merciful Redeemer, friend and brother,
> May I know Thee more clearly,
> Love Thee more dearly,
> Follow Thee more nearly,
> Day by day.

For this, as for all applications of the *Rule,* we need to be full of the Word and the Spirit.

- **Day by Day, make the tough decisions that have to be made, and to accept graciously when they are made against us.**

This was the principle that enabled Jesus, governed by love, to drive the money changers out of the Temple with a thrashing whip. For indeed the Rule does not mean that we should ignore folly and vice, or even less, condone it. Always, the Rule remains subservient to the principles of the Kingdom.

- ***Day by Day, talk to others as we would have them talk to us.***

Not with angry shouts, abuse, violence, insult, and bitterness; but gently, kindly, patiently, compassionately, and with sympathy and love.

- ***Day by Day, give generously to others as we would have them give to us.***

Whether or not they are generous, and even if they are parsimonious.

- ***Day by Day, forgive those who injure us as we would wish to be forgiven.***

Remember the warning of Jesus – *"If you do not forgive, neither will you be forgiven!"* (Mt 6:15; Mk 11:25; Lu 6:36)

- ***Day by Day ascribe the best motives to other people, as we would have them do for us.***

Just as we think well of ourselves, so we should give others the benefit of the doubt.

- ***Day by Day, help other people as we would wish them to help us in our need.***

While we were still his enemies, God showed his love and kindness by visiting us in Christ. (Ep 2:4-5)

So here is the standard by which God will assess our character and our stewardship – "*The Golden Rule*".

How do you measure in God's sight?

We cannot hope to keep the Rule perfectly, but let us at least strive to make it the Golden Rule of our own daily lives. *As Jesus said ...*

> *Everyone will know that you are my disciples when they see how much you love one another* (Jn 13:35).

And in the words of our text –

Let us do good to everyone, especially to those who are of the household of faith. (Ga 6:10)

Chapter Thirty

CALVARY

But far be it from me to boast except in the **cross** *of our Lord Jesus Christ, by which the world has been* **crucified** *to me, and I to the world* (Ga 6:14).

Why is "Good Friday" called *Good*. Surely it is the wrong adjective for a day that is filled with such horror? In fact the name goes back a thousand years to when "good" did not mean "nice" but "holy"; and "holy" the day of our redemption certainly is.

But if this is a "holy" day, how then should we celebrate it?

Many churches, following a tradition that began several hundred years ago, hold a 3-hour service, from noon to 1500, to commemorate the final three hours that Jesus spent on the cross.

How do they occupy the time? Mostly by music, performed and sung. Hence the oratorio the *St Matthew Passion*, was composed in 1727 by JS Bach, for a Good Friday service in the Lutheran church of St Thomas, in Leipzig. It has been acclaimed as perhaps the most glorious music ever written, and of course it is still performed every year in thousands of churches and concert halls around the world.

When it was first presented, the *Passion* required two orchestras, two choirs and several soloists, and was interspersed with Bible readings, a homily, and congregational hymns. The entire service occupied rather more than three hours, and belittles some modern pentecostal claims that "we have the best worship the church has ever seen". I have little doubt that the *Lord* finds equal pleasure in any form of worship that arises from sincere and loving hearts; but the *angels* probably prefer the Bach variety! Or at least, when I reach Paradise myself, I hope the music in some part of it will be more akin to an oratorio than a collection of Top Forty pop songs.

In countries where Good Friday is not a public holiday, churches have to postpone the service until evening. Alison and I were shocked when we moved to the USA in 1981 and discovered, except for a handful of states, that Good Friday is an ordinary working day! [138] We felt it was quite sacrilegious!

In other places, some churches hold a special service at 3.00 pm on Good Friday, some have a dawn service, and some ignore the day altogether. In the end, whatever custom people follow, only one thing is truly important, that Christ is given pre-eminence, and that the day of his death is revered as truly "holy" – not by public observances, but in the hearts and minds of his people.

For Paul the cross of Christ was his only boast. Beside the cross, and what Christ accomplished there, all his own deeds were worthless, hardly warranting even a mention. But about the cross he boasted over and over again! Then he makes the remarkable statement that by the cross *"the world has been **crucified** to me, and I to the world"* (Ga 6:14). What does he mean?

First, he is not talking about the heavens and the earth wrought by the hand of God, in all their awesome beauty, majesty, and splendour. He means rather the organised and structured world of mankind, its pomp and circumstances, its enticements and illicit pleasures, its praise and honours, or indeed anything in human affairs that tends to draw the soul away from Christ and dim the vision of Paradise. It includes a greed for possessions, a hunger for sin, worship of material things, and scorn of spiritual reality.

That world, says Paul, is to him like a crucified victim, an object of horror and despair, something to be shunned and avoided at all costs. Conversely, the world in its turn, since he became a Christian, has viewed him with the same fearful hatred. He looks like an abhorred crucified victim to the world; and the world looks equally disgusting to him. Yet it is the world that God loves, and for which Christ died, and which can find hope only as it turns to Christ, no longer spurning the cross, but embracing it with joy.

---

(138) In 1990 we moved back to Sydney, and were pleased to discover that even in highly secularised Australia, Good Friday was still observed as a holy day. As I write, it is now 2015, and on Good Friday most businesses are closed, no major sporting events are scheduled, and the churches hold well-attended services.

THE CROSS HERALDED

In the ancient world all news was disseminated by heralds, who compelled attention by giving a loud blast on a trumpet, and then, in stentorian tones, shouted their message. They needed a powerful physique, strong lungs, and a very loud voice. Likewise, when God wanted a message proclaimed to all heaven, earth, and below the earth, he chose an angel whose voice could span the universe, reaching every creature, whether angels, demons, or humans! Then he bade the angel to get ready to make a loud proclamation.

But before the angel could speak, a man named John was called up into heaven by another angel of God. There John saw a glorious throne, upon which the Lord God was seated, holding in his hand a sealed scroll. He watched as the herald angel began to cry out across the span of all heaven and earth,

> *"Who is worthy to break these seals and to read this scroll?" But alas! – no one worthy could be found – whereupon John fell to weeping. (Re 5:1-4)*

He wept because he knew that the scroll contained the secrets of time, and of the coming judgment, and he yearned to know what the future held, but also and more importantly, *who held the future?* Would Satan prevail, or would God? Would John be saved or doomed? What did tomorrow hold for him? And what if no one could open the scroll?

One of the rulers of heaven told John not to weep, because indeed there was one who was worthy! And suddenly, says John,

> *I saw a Lamb looking as if it had just been slain, yet it was standing near the throne ... And the Lamb went and took the scroll from the right hand of God, who was seated on the throne. (vs. 6-7)*

Whereupon, the entire host of heaven broke into tumultuous song –

> *"Worthy is the Lamb!"* (vs. 12)

John kept on listening, and he heard more of their song –

> *"Worthy is the Lamb!" sang the angels, "to take the scroll and to open its seals, for you were slain, and by your blood you ransomed people for God from every tribe and language and people and nation, and you have made them kings and priests before our God, and they shall reign on the earth."* (Rev 5:9-10)

Thus the gospel of Christ, the slain and risen Lamb of God, has been and is still being heralded in heaven; and in that coming day it will resound across the earth in awful majesty and terrifying power.

THE CROSS A SCANDAL

"You were slain!" cried the angels to the Lamb, who was standing there before the throne of God, still bearing the wounds that had taken his life. He had died; but now he was alive again, and will be for ever. Can this be possible? You were slain – but now you are alive! Did he truly die? Is he truly alive?

The death of Christ has always been a scandal! So there have been several different views –

DOCETISM

Some have claimed that Jesus only seemed to die, but did not really do so. Thus, the 7th century Qur'an, [139] drawing on an ancient Christian heresy, says –

> The Jews boasted, "We have killed Christ Jesus, the son of Mary, the Apostle of God." But they did not kill him, nor even crucify him. It only seemed to be so.

That is, his body was an illusion; he had no true corporeality, and was actually a pure spirit, so could not physically die. People espoused this idea because the thought of God dying offended them. "It is not possible for God to die," they argued, "therefore Christ must only have *seemed* to die, but did not actually do so. This was because he did not have a real body." So the heresy

---

(139) Sura iv:157.

known as Docetism (from a Greek word meaning "to seem") became popular, and still has adherents.

ADOPTIONISM

Some have argued that Jesus died simply as a martyr, a good man, and became Son of God only after God raised him from the dead and "adopted" him. Hence, the heresy is known as "adoptionism". Others have been even more radical, arguing Jesus himself did not die, but someone else took his place, as a substitute, so the resurrection was actually a fraud, with the living man pretending to be the dead man raised.

But John is emphatic, *"You were slain!"* – and this death on a cross, and his victory over it, was the prime reason why he was found worthy to take the scroll from the hand of God. He was declared worthy also because he was the Lamb, the eternal King, and his death was an act of supreme love that culminated a life of perfect obedience to God.

One thing we can say incontestably – while people may choose to doubt the resurrection, there is no ancient fact more strongly attested than the life and death of Jesus of Nazareth. That he lived, that he died, are equally beyond doubt. They are simple facts of history.

THE CROSS A RANSOM

We Christians, of course, believe implicitly in the cross and in the empty tomb. But if this Lamb is also the Lion of the Tribe of Judah, and strong enough and worthy enough to seize the scroll from the hand of the Almighty, how could he die? Why did he die? The angels sang –

> *"Worthy is the Lamb! ... You were slain, and <u>by your blood you have ransomed people for God</u> from every tribe and language and people and nation."*

Here is the reason for his death – to <u>ransom</u> us, who were slaves.

Let me go back here to an idea mentioned earlier in this book. People have long been puzzled by the word *"ransom"*, which usually contains the idea of a price paid by someone to someone to release a captive. Hence some have suggested that the price was paid to Satan. Indeed, in the Middle Ages preachers talked with glee about how God tricked Satan into accepting Jesus as the price for releasing all his prisoners, but failed to warn the devil that Christ had power to raise himself from the dead.

But that is repulsive. God owed Satan nothing, and indeed his power was destroyed at the cross, and he himself was led out in chains! *"On the cross Christ stripped the spiritual powers of darkness of all their power, and publicly humiliated them."* (Cl 2:14-15)

It is better simply to see the word *"ransom"* as a metaphor of release. That is, the death of Christ was necessary to set us free from the guilt of sin, and also from its power. But who are these redeemed people? Are they many or few? Where are they found? Once again the song of the angels provides the answer –

> *"Worthy is the Lamb! ... By your blood you ransomed people for God from every tribe and language and people and nation!"*

Here is a powerful promise of worldwide outreach, and a guarantee that before Jesus comes the gospel will indeed be preached to every people group on earth! How strongly it is emphasised – *"every tribe and language and people and nation!"* That should stir two things in us –

- A vision of ourselves in that company; and
- A vision of an indestructible church.

If I would be safe, then, I need only ensure that I am part of that church! For if the church will be redeemed on that day, then so will I; and if the church rises to meet the Lord in the air when he comes, then so will I; and if the church will be crowned with acclamations, glory, splendour, and honour, then so will I!

But what does that mean? What benefit comes from belonging to the church?

THE CROSS AND A ROYAL PRIESTHOOD

Still the angels are singing, and they cry –

> *"Worthy is the Lamb! ... You ransomed people from every nation, and <u>you have made them kings and priests before our God</u>!"*

We who believe are all members of God's royal priesthood. We gained this status not by any worth or effort of our own, but simply because of the ransom that has come to us through the cross. And notice the past tense. The angels were talking about believers who were on earth during the time of John. They are today singing the same song about you. We do not have to wait until tomorrow. You are a royal priest <u>now</u>. This is perhaps the single greatest truth in the Bible – we are God's ROYAL PRIESTHOOD!

- <u>WE ARE PRIESTS</u> – therefore we have free and unfettered access to the throne of God.
- <u>WE ARE KINGS</u> – therefore we can speak with royal authority against, sin, sickness, Satan and all his dark works.
- <u>WE ARE KINGS AND PRIESTS</u> – therefore we rank second only to God himself in the whole universe – which should not be cause for arrogance, but rather of humble and eager service!

THE CROSS AND ETERNITY

Still singing about those who are redeemed by the blood of the Lamb, the angels affirm that *"they will reign on the earth"*. That authority in Christ begins NOW – not to make us masters of the universe, but rather, to make us able, as Jesus himself was, to fulfil the Father's purpose.

But here is the marvellous thing – successful use of that spiritual authority in this life will become the precursor to reigning with Christ for ever! We are training now to be princes in eternity!

CONCLUSION

The angels in heaven boast about the cross of Christ; and here on earth, we too, his church, should have no other boast. We cry with Paul, *"the world has been **crucified** to me, and I to the world."* (Ga 6:14) That is, if the world tries to intrude between me and the cross, then I consider it utterly dead. It has no appeal. It is loathsome. To me the world is like a crucified criminal, deserving only to be scorned and spurned. I will hold on to worldly things only insofar as I can hold them while I cling to the cross.

The world, too, says Paul, looks upon us as crucified. It despises us, and the Christ we serve, and, if it could, would gladly crucify him again. Lacking him as a victim, the world often attacks the church – not always overtly, but covertly, with subtle temptations and wily enticements, seeking to cut us away from our vision of Calvary. God forbid we should succumb! Let us rather the more loudly boast about the Cross, boldly declaring it to be the source of all our hope, life, love, joy, and salvation.

Notice that John was able to see all these things only when he had *"come up higher"*! (Re 4:1). If we too will climb to that higher perspective, then heaven's song will be joyously ours as well –

> *I looked (said John), and I saw the four living creatures and the twenty-four elders and the Lamb near the throne, and standing around them were millions upon millions of angels, who sang with a loud voice, "<u>Worthy is the Lamb</u> who was slain, to receive power and wealth and wisdom and might and honour and glory and blessing. And then I heard every creature in heaven and on earth and under the earth and in the sea – indeed, every living being – crying aloud, "To him who sits on the throne and to the Lamb be blessing and honour and glory and might forever and ever! Amen!"* (vs.11-13)

ADDENDUM
EDWARD GIBBON

The renowned historian was not favourably impressed by the antics of the ancient monks, hermits, anchorites, and their ilk. Nor should we be. Their disgraceful failure to understand the grace of God, their distortions of spiritual life, their all but insane self-mutilations, tortures, starvation, and other afflictions became a scandal in the church and to the secular world. Sadly, in some countries, not much has changed. Religious processions still occur, in which men and women tear their own flesh with bone-laced whips, or suffer themselves to be pinned to a cross, or in some way try by their agonies to atone for their sin, or perhaps to get closer to God. The true gospel is antagonistic to all such efforts.

Here is how Gibbon described some of the monks –

The monks ... indulged their unsocial, independent fanaticism. The most devout, or the most ambitious, of the spiritual brethren, renounced the convent, as they had renounced the world. The fervent monasteries of Egypt, Palestine, and Syria, were surrounded by a Laura, [140] a distant circle of solitary cells; and the extravagant penance of the Hermits was stimulated by applause and emulation. They sunk under the painful weight of crosses and chains; and their emaciated limbs were confined by collars, bracelets, gauntlets, and greaves of massy and rigid iron. All superfluous encumbrance of dress they contemptuously cast away; and some savage saints of both sexes have been admired, whose naked bodies were only covered by their long hair. They aspired to reduce themselves to the rude and miserable state in which the human brute is scarcely distinguishable above his kindred animals; and the numerous sect of Anachorets [141] derived their

---

(140) The word is defined in the next clause.

(141) Gibbon's definition here is somewhat quaint. The word has more the sense of "withdrawal", of abandoning society to retire to some lonely place, usually for some religious purpose.

name from their humble practice of grazing in the fields of Mesopotamia with the common herd.

They often usurped the den of some wild beast whom they affected to resemble; they buried themselves in some gloomy cavern, which art or nature had scooped out of the rock; and the marble quarries of Thebais are still inscribed with the monuments of their penance. The most perfect Hermits are supposed to have passed many days without food, many nights without sleep, and many years without speaking; and glorious was the man (I abuse that name) who contrived any cell, or seat, of a peculiar construction, which might expose him, in the most inconvenient posture, to the inclemency of the seasons.

Among these heroes of the monastic life, the name and genius of Simeon Stylites have been immortalized by the singular invention of an aerial penance. At the age of thirteen, the young Syrian deserted the profession of a shepherd, and threw himself into an austere monastery. After a long and painful novitiate, in which Simeon was repeatedly saved from pious suicide, he established his residence on a mountain, about thirty or forty miles to the east of Antioch. Within the space of a mandra, or circle of stones, to which he had attached himself by a ponderous chain, he ascended a column, which was successively raised from the height of nine, to that of sixty feet from the ground.

In this last and lofty station, the Syrian Anachoret resisted the heat of thirty summers, and the cold of as many winters. Habit and exercise instructed him to maintain his dangerous situation without fear or giddiness, and successively to assume the different postures of devotion. He sometimes prayed in an erect attitude, with his outstretched arms in the figure of a cross, but his most familiar practice was that of bending his meagre skeleton from the forehead to the feet; and a curious spectator, after numbering twelve hundred and forty-four repetitions, at length desisted from the endless account. The progress of an ulcer in his thigh might shorten, but it could not disturb, this celestial life; and the patient Hermit expired, without descending from his column.

A prince, who should capriciously inflict such tortures, would be deemed a tyrant; but it would surpass the power of a tyrant to impose a long and miserable existence on the reluctant victims of his cruelty.

This voluntary martyrdom must have gradually destroyed the sensibility both of the mind and body; nor can it be presumed that the fanatics, who torment themselves, are susceptible of any lively affection for the rest of mankind. [142] A cruel, unfeeling temper has distinguished the monks of every age and country: their stern indifference, which is seldom mollified by personal friendship, is inflamed by religious hatred; and their merciless zeal has strenuously administered the holy office of the Inquisition.

The monastic saints, who excite only the contempt and pity of a philosopher, were respected, and almost adored, by the prince and people. Successive crowds of pilgrims from Gaul and India saluted the divine pillar of Simeon: the tribes of Saracens disputed in arms the honor of his benediction; the queens of Arabia and Persia gratefully confessed his supernatural virtue; and the angelic Hermit was consulted by the younger Theodosius, in the most important concerns of the church and state. His remains were transported from the mountain of Telenissa, by a solemn procession of the patriarch, the master-general of the East, six bishops, twenty-one counts or tribunes, and six thousand soldiers; and Antioch revered his bones, as her glorious ornament and impregnable defense. [143]

---

(142) Gibbon is a little unkind here. Some of the hermits, or anchorites, were in fact quite joyful preachers and had enormous influence for good, except in their one madness of supposing that their heroic privations could bring them closer to God.

(143) Edward Gibbon (1737-1794), The History of the Decline and Fall of the Roman Empire, Chapter 37, Part One. I have omitted the numerous footnotes inserted by Gibbons.

INDEX OF TEXTS

1:01 .... 17, 19, 34	3:26 .... 147, 149, 153
1:01-02 16	3:29 .... 163, 168
1:01-10 13	4:01 .... 163, 168
1:02, 13, 22 35	4:04 .... 86, 171
1:03 58	4:04-05 .... 169, 171, 236
1:03, 06, 15 49	4:05 .... 157, 171
1:04 .... 25, 34	4:05-06 238
1:06 51	4:07 183
1:06-3:01 11	4:08 11
1:08 .... 11, 189	4:09-10 210
1:08-09 .... 59, 64	4:13, 19 11
1:11-19 13	4:14 189
1:15 247	4:4 174
2:01-10 11	5:01 ..... 67, 122, 146, 150, 160, 201, 207, 210, 211
2:01-14 13	
2:08 241	5:01-6:10 13
2:09 .... 65, 75	5:04 .... 49, 55, 56, 77
2:09, 21 49	5:05 ..... 151, 219, 221, 225, 235
2:10 .... 275, 279	5:06 .... 241, 245
2:15-16 108	5:08 247
2:16, 17 77	5:13 .... 151, 201, 209, 247
2:16-17 7	5:14 151
2:20 .... 89, 90, 95, 96, 131	5:16 .... 257, 259, 261, 263
2:21 .... 55, 219, 225	5:22 151
3:01 .... 97, 102, 104	5:25 .... 257, 261, 263
3:01-05 233	6:01 .... 269, 271
3:01-4:31 13	6:01b 269
3:02,03,05 105	6:02 .... 265, 267, 273, 275
3:05 .... 111, 115, 183, 241	6:02b 272
3:06 .... 219, 225	6:05 267
3:08-11 125	6:06-08 275
3:09 147	6:08 285
3:10-11 117	6:09-10 287
3:11, 24 77	6:10 291
3:13 .... 157, 159	6:11 13
3:19 189	6:11-18 13
3:22-23 147	6:14 .... 293, 294, 299
3:24 87	6:18 .... 49, 58

GLOSSARY

Abjure – to recant, reject, or retract.
Abrogate – to repeal, to annul, or formally revoke.
Amoral – neither moral nor immoral.
Anchorite – a hermit, a recluse, one who retires to a solitary place.
Antithesis – the exact opposite, extreme contrast.
Apologist – one who speaks or writes in defence of a doctrine, faith, or action.
Apotheosise – to raise or elevate to the place of a god, to deify.
Archaic – belonging to an earlier period, ancient.
Austere – morally strict, abstinent, ascetic.
Authenticate – to determine as genuine.
Braggadocio – vain boasting.
Bureaucracy – officials who are controlled by fixed rules and inflexible routines.
Burgeoning –putting forth buds, sprouting, growing rapidly.
Capricious – unsteady, changeable, fickle.
Cliché – an expression or idea that has become trite or obvious.
Conduce – to lead, bring together, or make something more likely.
Consanguinity – a blood relation, persons descended from the same ancestor.
Deleterious – baneful, destructive, hurtful.
Democracy – government by the people either directly or through elected representatives
Ecclesiastical –relating to a church, to the organisation of the church, or to the clergy.
Endemic – pervasive within a particular nation, region, locality or group.
Ephemeral – anything that has a brief existence.
Eponymous – bearing the same or similar name to another person or thing.
Eremite – a hermit, a religious recluse.
Esoteric – secret or hidden knowledge, private, confidential.
Eucharist – the sacrament of the Lord's supper or Communion
Excoriate – to flay, strip, or peel off the skin, literally or figuratively.

Exemplar – a person or thing regarded as worthy of imitation, a model or pattern.
Expiate – to make satisfaction, atonement, to pay the penalty of.
Featly – suitably, aptly.
Fiat – an order issued by legal authority, a decree.
Flagellant – one who whips himself or has himself whipped as a religious discipline.
Forensic – belonging to courts of law, used in courts or legal proceedings.
Gamut – the entire range or extent of anything.
Glossalistic – prayer or praise in a tongue given through Holy Spirit baptism.
Hermit – a person who retires from society and lives in solitude, often from religious motives.
Hesychastic – practising quietism, reclusive, a type of piety.
Illuministic – an illuminist is a person who professes to have extraordinary knowledge or enlightenment, especially in religion.
Immure – to enclose within walls, shut up, confine.
Incursion – a running in, an invasive act, coming in.
Inveigh – to make a violent verbal attack, to make strong denunciations.
Invidious – likely to incur ill will or hatred.
Irrefragable – unanswerable, incontestable, undeniable.
Judaisers – in the early church, a person who accepted Christianity but who also adhered to or advocated the Mosaic Law.
Laissez-faire – letting people do as they please.
Liturgy - liturgical – prescribed forms or ritual for public worship in Christian churches.
Meritorious - deserving reward or notice, worthy of fame, or happiness.
Meticulous – unusually careful, particularly in regard to small details.
Modality – relating to the form or shape of something, how it is done or made.
Monarchy – Rule by only one person.
Paradox – a statement that seems contradictory, unbelievable or absurd but that may be true in fact.
Parsimony – stinginess, miserliness, extreme frugality.

Paschal – connected with the Passover or the Eucharist.
Pellucid – transparent, admitting the passage of light.
Perjury – in law the wilful telling of a lie while under oath.
Pernicious – destructive, having the power of killing, destroying, injuring, fatal, deadly.
Piacular – an atrocious crime requiring a severe penalty, or major atonement.
Pious – having or showing religious devotion, zealous in the performance of religious obligations.
Poignant – sharply painful to the feelings, deeply distressing, evoking a keen sense of grief or sadness.
Polemicist – a skilled debater.
Preceptor – a teacher, instructor.
Primogeniture – in law, the right of the eldest son to inherit the estate of his father.
Prurience – lustful ideas or desires, an excessive interest in sex.
Pulpiteering – preaching constantly in an annoying manner or in inappropriate circumstances; a more or less contemptuous term for a preacher.
Punctilious – excessively careful in the observance of certain nice points of behaviour, ceremony etc.
Quantify – to determine or express the quantity of, to indicate the extent of.
Ramification – a result or development that (usually) complicates a matter, an unwelcome consequence, a result that must be taken into account.
Reciprocity – a relationship of mutual dependence or action, giving, sharing alike.
Redolent – suggestive of, sweet smelling, fragrant.
Resile – to go back and repeat.
Resuscitated – revived, to be brought back to life.
RIP – Rest in Peace.
Sacerdotal – pertaining to priests or the priesthood.
Sectarian – a member of any religious sect, narrow minded, bigoted.
Sodalist – a member of a sodality, people involved in a fellowship, a relationship rather than an organisation.
Stylites – a class of religious ascetics of the early Middle Ages, who by way of penance lived on the tops of high columns or pillars; also called pillar saints.

Subsidiary – acting in a supporting or secondary character, lower in rank or importance.
Supernal – celestial, ethereal, heavenly, divine.
Theocracy – a political entity ruled by a god, or by a priesthood representing the deity; for a Christian, acknowledging God alone as the true King.
Transcendental – existing outside of or beyond nature; excelling, surpassing normal experience..
Unguents – ointments.
Vernacular – the native speech of a country, a common language.
Vicarious – something performed or endured by one person in place of another.
Vigilance – a guard or watch.
Vindicate – to clear from criticism, censure or suspicion.
Vitiate – to make imperfect, faulty or impure; to spoil or corrupt.

BIBLIOGRAPHY

GENERAL WORKS

Ainsworth, WH; Rookwood; http://www.gutenberg.org/files/23564/23564-h/23564-h.htm.
Aristotle; Lives of Philosophers.
Aubrey, John; Brief Lives; by Richard Barber; Folio Society, London, 1975.
Australian Geographic magazine; July 25, 2012.
Bede, The Venerable; History of the English Speaking People; tr. by Leo Sherley-Price; Penguin Books, London, 1990.
Browne, Sir Thomas; Religion Medici; from Sir Thomas Browne: The Major Works; Penguin Books, London, 1977.
Browning, Robert; The Poems; The Heritage Press, Connecticut, 1971; and Dramatic Monologues; The Folio Society, London, 1991.
Carlyle, Thomas; Sartor Resartus; J. M. Dent & Sons Ltd, London; 1908; pg. xiii.
Chrysostom, John; Homilies on Second Corinthians, *Homily Seven*.
DeKoven, Stan; New Testament Survey; Vision Publishing, Ramona, CA.
Donne, John; The Complete English Poems; Penguin Books, New York, 1982.
Fuller, Thomas; The Worthies of England; ed. Richard Barber; The Folio Society, London, 1987.
Gibbons, Edward; Decline and Fall of the Roman Empire.
Gibran, Kahlin; The Prophet; Alfred A. Knopf, New York, 1968.
Hemans Felicity; *Casabianca*.
Hendrickson, Robert; Encyclopedia of Word and Phrase Origins; Facts on File, New York, 1997.
Herodotus: The Histories; tr. Aubrey de Selincourt; rev. A. R. Burn; Penguin Books, London; 1983.
International History Magazine, # 13, pg. 23.
International History Magazine; Editions Horizons, Lausanne.
Kayyam, Omar; the Ruba'iyat; tr. by Peter Avery & John Heath-Stubbs; Penguin Classics, 1983.

Livy; The History of Rome.
Luther, Martin; Commentary on Galatians, *in. loc.*
Luther, Martin; On the Bondage of the Will.
Luther, Martin; *The Distinction Between the Law and the* Gospel; tr. by Willard L. Burce; found on the web site of The Consortium for Classical and Lutheran Education (http://www.ccle.org/).
Malory, Sir Thomas; Le Morte D'Arthur; ed. RM Lumiansky; Collier MacMillan Publishers, London, 1986.
Petersham, John; *He Owns the Cattle on a Thousand Hills*; words and music, 1948.
Plutarch; The Lives of the Noble Greeks and Romans; tr. by John Dryden; Modern Library, New York; undated reprint of an 1864 edition.
Poe, Alexander; *The Raven*; Project Gutenberg; www.gutenberg.com; *in loc.*
Rule Britannia, from the opera *Alfred*, by the Scottish poet James Thomson (1700-1748), and set to music by Thomas Arne in 1740.
Schaff, Phillip; History of the Christian Church; New York, 1890.
Service, Robert; *Golden Days*; from Ballads of a Bohemian – Spring; T. Fisher Unwin, London, 1921; and The Best of Robert Service; Dodd, mead & Co., New York, 1953; and Rhymes of a Rolling Stone; Ernest Benn Ltd, London, 1929.
Silver Poets of the Sixteenth Century; ed. Gerald Bullett; JM Dent & sons Ltd, London, 1947.
Smith, William; A Smaller Classical Dictionary; John Murray, London, 1882.
Stoner, PW; Science Speaks; Moody Press, Chicago; 1976.
Tennyson, Alfred; Poetry; WW Norton & Co., London, 1971.
Tertullian; (c. 155-c. 240 AD), *Apology*.
Tertullian; A Plea for Christians (*circa 177*).
The Fables of Jean de La Fontaine; tr. by Michael Star; from the website http://www.aesopfables.com/fontaine.html.
The Gospel of Nicodemus; tr. by M.R. James; Clarendon Press, Oxford, 1924.
The Koran; tr. NJ Dawood; Penguin Books, London; 1999.
The Pillow Book of Sei Shonagon, tr. Ivan Morris, Penguin Classics, 1967; pg 83; and by Meredith McKinney, Penguin Books, London, 2006.

Theodoret, Religious History; *A History of the Monks of Syria*, Cistercian Publications, Kalamazoo, Michigan, 1985; tr. by RM Price. "Ecclesiastical History"; Bohn's Ecclesiastical Library; London, 1854.

Trevelyan, GM; England Under the Stuarts; The Folio Society, London, 1996.

Vasari, Georgio; Lives of the Artists; tr. by George Bull; The Folio Society, London, 1993; in three volumes.

Virgil (Publius Vergilius Maro), The Georgics – Book One; tr. K. R. McKenzie; The Folio Society, London, 1969.

Wesley, John; The Wesley Centre Online – *http://wesley.nnu.edu/john-wesley/the-sermons-of-john-wesley-1872-edition/sermon-71-of-good-angels*.

BIBLE COMMENTARIES

Anders, Max; editor, Holman New Testament Commentary; B & H Publishing Group; Nashville, Tennessee, 2004.
Baker Publishing House; The New Testament Commentary; Grand Rapids, Michigan, 1987.
Barnes, Albert (1798-1870); Notes on the Bible.
Bible Background Commentary; Nottingham, UK, 1993.
Bruce, F. F.; gen. ed. The New International Commentary on the New Testament; Wm. B. Eerdman's Pub. Co., Grand Rapids, Michigan; 1977.
Calvin, John (1509-1564); Calvin's Commentaries.
Clarke, Adam (1715-1832); Commentary on the Bible.
Excell, Joseph S. & Spence-Jones, HDM; editors, The Pulpit Commentary; 1881.
Gaebelein, Frank E; editor, The Expositor's Bible Commentary; Zondervan Publishers, Grand Rapids, Michigan.
Gill, John (1690-1771); Exposition of the Entire Bible.
Hawker, Robert; The Poor Man's Commentary On The Whole Bible; 1850.
Hendriksen, William; The New Testament Commentary; Baker Book House, Grand Rapids, Michigan; 1972.
Henry, Matthew; Commentary On The Whole Bible; Marshall, Morgan, and Scott; London, 1953.
Hodge, Charles (1797-1878); A Commentary on Ephesians; Intervarsity Press.
Hubbard, David A; gen. ed.; Word Biblical Commentary; Word Books, Waco, Texas; 1987.
Intervarsity Press; The IVP New Testament Commentary Series, Nottingham, UK.
Ironside, H. A; Expository Commentary (1876-1951).
Jamieson, Robert; Fausset, A. R.; & Brown, David; A Commentary on the Old and New Testaments, 1871.
Johnson B. W; The People's New Testament (1891).
Macdonald, William; Believer's Bible Commentary; Thomas Nelson Publishers; 1989.
Nelson's New Illustrated Bible Commentary; Thomas Nelson Inc, New York; 1999.
Poole, Matthew; Matthew Poole's Commentary; 1685

Robertson A. T.; Word Pictures in the New Testament; 1933.
Stern, David H.; Jewish New Testament Commentary; Jewish New Testament Publications, Inc., Clarksville, Maryland; 1982.
Tasker, R. V. G.; Tyndale New Testament Commentaries; Tyndale Press, London; 1964.
The Anchor Bible; Doubleday & Co., New York; 1966.
The College Press NIV Commentary; ed. Mark Mangano; College Press Pub. Co., Joplin, Missouri, 1996.
The Interpreter's Bible; Abingdon Press, New York, 1952.
Trapp, John; Commentary On The Old And New Testaments (1601-1669).
Vincent, Marvin R; Vincent's Word Studies; 1886
Walvoord, John & Zuck, Roy; The Bible Knowledge Commentary; Cook Communications; Colorado Springs, Colorado, 1989.
Wesley, John; Explanatory Notes on the Whole Bible (1703-1791).
Wiersbe, Warren W; Wiersbe's Expository Outlines; David C. Cook, Colorado Springs, Colorado.
Wiseman, D. J.; gen. ed., Tyndale Old Testament Commentaries; Intervarsity Press.
Word Inc.; The Preacher's Commentary; Nashville, Tennessee, 1992.
Word Search Corporation; Preacher's Outline and Sermon Bible; Nashville, Tennessee, 2010.

BIBLE VERSIONS

In addition to the *KJV* or *Authorised Version* of the Bible, the following versions or translations are cited, or were consulted by the author of this work.

CEV – *Contemporary English Version*; the American Bible Society, New York, NY; 1995.

ESV – *English Standard Version*; Crossway Bibles, a publishing ministry of Good News Publishers; Wheaton, Illinois; 2001.

GNB – *Good News Bible*; Second Edition, by the American Bible Society; New York, NY; 1992.

GW – *God's Word*; God's Word to the Nations Bible Society; Cleveland, Ohio; 1995.

JPS – *The JPS* Bible; the Jewish Publication Society; Philadelphia, PA; 1995.

ISV – *International Standard Version*, v. 1.2.2; The ISV Foundation, La Mirada, CA; 2001.

NET – *The New English Translation*; Biblical Studies Press; Richardson, Texas; 2006.

NIV – *New International Version*; Zondervan Bible Publishers, Grand Rapids, Michigan; 1978.

NJB – *New Jerusalem Bible*; Doubleday & Co. Inc; Garden City, New York; 1985

NRSV – *New Revised Standard Version*; the Division of Christian Education of the National Council of the Churches of Christ in the USA; 1989.

REB – *Revised English Bible with Apocrypha*; Oxford University Press; 1989.

RSV – *Revised Standard Version*, Thomas Nelson Inc., New York; 1959.

YLT – *Young's Literal Translation*; by NJ Young; 1898.

WEB – *World English Bible;* public domain.

Wuest – *The New Testament: An Expanded Translation;* by Kenneth S. Wuest; Wm. B. Eerdmans Publishing Co. Used by permission. All rights reserved.

www.ingramcontent.com/pod-product-compliance
Lightning Source LLC
Chambersburg PA
CBHW070720160426
43192CB00009B/1260